Projecting

Projecting America, 1958

Film and Cultural Diplomacy at the Brussels World's Fair

SARAH NILSEN

McFarland & Company, Inc., Publishers
Jefferson, North Carolina, and London

LIBRARY OF CONGRESS CATALOGUING-IN-PUBLICATION DATA

Nilsen, Sarah.
    Projecting America, 1958 : film and cultural diplomacy
at the Brussels World's Fair / Sarah Nilsen.
        p.   cm.
    Includes bibliographical references and index.

    ISBN 978-0-7864-6154-7
    softcover : 50# alkaline paper ∞

    1. Motion pictures in propaganda — United States — History.
2. Motion pictures — Political aspects — United States.   3. United
States — In motion pictures.   4. Documentary films — Political
aspects — United States.   5. Cold War — Motion pictures and
the war.   6. Motion pictures, American — Foreign countries —
Influence.   7. Exposition universelle et internationale (1958 :
Brussels, Belgium)   I. Title.
PN1995.9.P6N55   2011
791.43'658 — dc22   2011013607

BRITISH LIBRARY CATALOGUING DATA ARE AVAILABLE

On the cover: U.S. Pavilion at the Brussels World's Fair, 1958
(National Archives); inset image © 2011 Shutterstock

Manufactured in the United States of America

*McFarland & Company, Inc., Publishers
    Box 611, Jefferson, North Carolina 28640
    www.mcfarlandpub.com*

For Josh, Lena, and Samara

Contents

Acknowledgments

The years spent working on this project occurred during a time in which cultural and public diplomacy again became a topic of major social significance. Throughout my academic career, I have been very fortunate to have mentors and colleagues who have supported my research even when it was viewed by many as not being at the cutting edge of film studies scholarship; the study of propaganda film tends to be the purview of historians of foreign affairs and mass communication and not film historians. The genesis for this project began with Lynn Spigel at the University of Southern California, whose enthusiasm for historiography and cultural studies has sustained me during this project and the years since and whose work has been the model of excellence that I have attempted to emulate in my own work. She was the first person to point to world's fairs as events of major social and cultural significance. Studies of avant-garde cinema with David James, documentary film with Michael Renov, and modern art and architecture with Nancy Troy greatly enhanced my research and provided the foundational theoretical and methodological basis for the writing of this book.

The preliminary research and writing for this project was made possible by a USA–Canada Fulbright dissertation fellowship at the University of Toronto through the generous sponsorship of Charlie Keil. Further faculty development grants from the University of Wisconsin–Oshkosh and the University of Vermont provided additional funding for research trips to the National Archives in Maryland and the MIT Archives.

This project would not have been possible without the aid of many librarians and archivists who have helped tremendously in tracking now-obscure documents and who made historical research possible from Vermont and Wisconsin. At the Bailey-Howe Library at the University of Vermont, Martha Day, Lori Holiff, Scott Schaefer, and Barb Lamonda helped make this research a pleasure.

My colleagues in the English Department at the University of Vermont (UVM) have been exceptionally supportive. Special thanks to Tony Magistrale,

Dave Jenemann, Hyon Joo Murphree, Jinny Huh, and Liz Fenton, who provided useful criticism and support during the writing of the manuscript. I have been extremely fortunate to have my closest friends, Hilary Neroni and Todd McGowan, also be my most supportive and academically challenging colleagues at UVM. This book would not have been possible without their constant support, motivation, and inspiration. They have read every word, enhanced my arguments, helped choose and assemble the photos, and constantly challenged me to grow as a scholar.

The book is dedicated to my three children, Josh, Lena, and Samara, who were born during the writing of this book; each of their appearances marked a new iteration of the manuscript. They now eagerly await the final arrival of the book. My greatest thanks goes to my husband, Michael Ashooh, who has been here from the start of the project. Though pursuing his own academic interests in a completely different field, his comments and suggestions significantly shaped the entire project. His encouragement and love were crucial to allowing me to be able to balance my scholarly interests with the demands of raising a family.

Preface

Films may provide a high level of audience enjoyment and at the same time convey an equally high level of negative impressions about the United States. Because audiences like the extremities of storytelling is no reason to feed them that to the exclusion of all else. Children like candy. They will eat it to excess if fed only that. But no man in his right mind would prescribe a diet of chocolate bars and ice cream. Self restraint and control make a healthy child. I suggest that the image conveyed abroad of our land is not always a healthy one, and self restraint may nowadays be a good prescription. — Edward R. Murrow, speech to Hollywood filmmakers soon after becoming head of the United States Information Agency

Edward R. Murrow's comparison of Hollywood films to "chocolate bars and ice cream" that created negative impressions of the United States did not represent a new attitude. Throughout the late 1940s and the 1950s, government officials frequently and heatedly testified to the destructive impact of Hollywood films on audiences abroad. As the propaganda battles between the Soviets and the U.S. began to heat up during this period, United States propagandists maintained an ambivalent and contradictory stance toward Hollywood; they recognized and hoped to seize on the mass appeal of the movies to win over international audiences to the American way of life, while also being extremely concerned about the image of the nation that was being sent abroad through commercial films. When I first began researching and writing this book, I viewed public diplomacy and propaganda as though they were merely by-products of the Cold War. With the collapse of Communism and the triumphant expansion of corporate capitalism, it seemed that American soft power and in particular Hollywood films had successfully sold the American way of life globally. However, the events of 9/11 soon made clear that the image of America exported to other countries was once again a major concern for the U.S. government. Like during the height of the Cold War, Hollywood films became identified as one of the primary culprits for the rise of anti–American sentiments around the world. As a 2003 report by the House Advisory Group on Public Diplomacy for the Arab and Muslim World observed,

"Arabs and Muslims are ... bombarded with American sitcoms, violent films, and other entertainment, much of which distorts the perceptions of viewers" (Djerejian 21). The failure of American foreign policy abroad was linked to the dominance of American media globally, with U.S. movie production companies accounting for more than 70 percent of the total worldwide ticket sales of $12 billion by 2004. As researchers at Boston University discovered when studying teenagers' perceptions of American life from their exposure to U.S. entertainment media, "The majority of young people around the world ... learned that [Americans] are violent, criminally inclined, and that American women are sexually immoral" (DeFleur 72). President Bush appointed Charlotte Beers, the former CEO of the advertising agency Ogilvy & Mather, as Undersecretary of State for Public Diplomacy not, as Naomi Klein describes in her article about Brand America, to "improve relations with other countries but rather to perform an overhaul of the U.S.'s image abroad" (Klein). Hollywood was once again culpable for selling to global audiences an image of America that was antithetical to the foreign policy objectives and goals of the U.S. government.

Implicit in these arguments is the assumption that Hollywood films function as a national cinema that embodies the values and ideology of the American way of life. Audiences are presumed to understand implicit messages conveyed by these media texts and to correlate those messages and their values with the foreign policy objectives and actions of the U.S. government. But what actually constitutes the America that is portrayed by Hollywood films? And how do Hollywood films function as a national cinema? Several theorists have pointed out that Hollywood cinema is characterized by its international rather than national appeal and that its lack of national identity is expressly the cause for its popularity with global audiences. As the economist David Waterman's recent research on the dominance of American films abroad confirms, the "conventional wisdom that action-oriented genres 'travel well,' and that Hollywood dominates the world market for such films ... worldwide appeal of action or violence suggests that these may be the 'lowest common denominator' elements. Action and/or violence in themselves are not necessarily the most appealing elements to movie audiences — they are only the most *commonly* appealing" (Waterman 229).

The belief that Hollywood cinema is the national cinema of the United States and has constructed an image of America that is not only false but also dangerously distorted is consistent with the arguments made over 60 years ago and continues to support the same proposition that Hollywood cinema affects and shapes American foreign relations abroad in a way that is damaging to U.S. foreign relations. Throughout the Cold War, politicians attacked Hollywood filmmakers for producing films that exploited and sensationalized the most base aspects of American life: sex, violence, and excess materialism. The schism between government agencies and Hollywood has tended to be marginalized in histories of U.S. government relations with the film industry in order to emphasize the aggression of American hegemony and the impact of Hollywood films on the process of Americanization. Scholars such as Herbert Schiller in *Mass Communications and American Empire*, Thomas Guback in *The International Film Industry*, Kristin Thompson in *Exporting Entertainment*, Ian Jarvie in *Hollywood's Overseas Campaign*, and Kerry Segrave in *American Films Abroad* have extensively documented and generally denounced this aggressive behavior. And yet all of these studies fail to examine the manner in which these films were being received by specific audiences at specific times. Such a perspective would show how the image of America constructed for these audiences is often contradictory and rarely consistent with the foreign policy objectives of the U.S. government.

As many historians, including David Bordwell and Kristin Thompson, have shown, the classical Hollywood studio system developed a sophisticated and highly managed industrial model of production that relied heavily on generic forms of storytelling with set codes of visual iconography and narrative conventions. These films were produced in order to maintain a steady and massive audience base and, therefore, were created in order to have the broadest popular appeal. Concerns over the content and the possible illicit nature of the medium led to the creation of the industry-controlled Production Code Administration (PCA) in 1934, thus removing any government oversight over specific film content. The PCA, though, was never directly concerned with the national image of America that was being constructed through cinematic representation. National concerns focused on the manner in which other nations were being portrayed rather than the image of the United States itself. In the Production Code Administration Film Analysis Forms from 1949 and 1959, two sizeable sections of the questionnaire examine how "foreign countries [are] treated" and the "portrayal of Races and Nationals" with possible choices listed as "sympathetic," "unsympathetic," and/or "indifferent." As Jonathan Munby argues, "Evaluating the damage inflicted on the national self-image by Hollywood depended less on determining the degree to which public institutions were brought into disrepute, ... [than] on analyzing the way films portrayed the stability of home life and private desires" (Munby 179). Hollywood studios were more concerned about negative portrayals of foreign nationals than of the representation of American society.

The Hollywood studios were not invested in the production of films that would win global public support for the foreign policy objectives of the U.S.

government. And yet as a public relations strategy, the Hollywood studio executives clearly understood that it was to their advantage to develop strong ties with government representatives who could work to guarantee an ideal business environment for the freest circulation of their product abroad. So, studio executives in the postwar period would regularly appear before Congressional committees testifying to the patriotism of Hollywood films and arguing that they were amazingly successful in winning audiences over to the American way of life. Eric A. Johnston, who took over for Will Hays as the head of the Hollywood studios trade association, the Motion Picture Association of America (MPAA), in 1945 had spent many years previously as the head of the U.S. Chamber of Commerce and was extremely skilled in setting up an ideal market environment for the expansion of the film industry internationally. In a climate in which culture became linked to psychological warfare, Hollywood lobbyists were eager to claim that "American movies were doing too good a job of telling the story of freedom to people everywhere ... American movies have been called ambassadors for democracy — ambassadors the Kremlin would like recalled" ("Overseas Information Programs of the United States" 233).

The passage of the U.S. Information and Educational Exchange Act of 1948 (Smith–Mundt Act) established the programming mandate for U.S. overseas information and cultural programs and still serves as the foundation of U.S. public diplomacy. The act was specifically set up to help counter the damage to American prestige being caused by not only Soviet propaganda but also Hollywood films. The Congress, in recommending passage of the bill, declared that "truth can be a powerful weapon" and cited six principles required for the legislation to be successful in action: tell the truth; explain the motives of the United States; bolster morale and extend hope; give a true and convincing picture of American life, methods, and ideals; combat misrepresentation and distortion; and aggressively interpret and support American foreign policy. In the act, Congress put in three major "protections." The first was to protect the American media by requiring the State Department to maximize its use of private resources. The second was to ensure the State Department would not have a monopoly on broadcasting. The third, the prohibition on domestic dissemination by the State Department, was put in place because Congress feared the State Department — full of "loafers, incompetents" and "men of strong Soviet leaning"— could undermine the U.S. government ("Smith Mundt Act — Public Diplomacy"). With this act, Congress ceded most of the production of American propaganda to private resources whose primary objectives were far from the six principles of the legislation. Congress routinely underfunded the motion picture division of the U.S. information agencies, thereby giving tacit acceptance to the stated position of the MPAA that Hollywood films were in fact reliable instruments of public diplomacy. Additionally, the commissions for the production of specific documentaries on pressing political issues were granted to the lowest bidders, leading to the production of poorly funded documentaries frequently shot quickly by information agents with minimal film training. Many of these films were distributed to developing nations by means of mobile units that would travel into remote areas to screen pro–American films, while audiences in most industrialized nations were primarily watching commercial Hollywood films. This created a dissonance in the dominant images of America being circulated to audiences abroad. Westernized audiences were inundated with Hollywood films that had been originally targeted toward a domestic, U.S. audience, while illiterate audiences in developing nations were being introduced to America through sponsored documentaries that focused heavily on Americana themes and were never seen by American audiences.

Histories that characterize the postwar period as a time in which "the large studios formed a covert alliance with the Cold War state" (L. May 203) continue to mystify the relationship between Hollywood films and U.S. public diplomacy. Many film histories cite comments supposedly made by Johnston in a talk to movie writers in 1947 during the height of the House on Un-American Activities hearings and the blacklist as evidence of the collusion between the government and Hollywood studios in halting the production and distribution of films critical of the American way. The quote appears in Murray Schumach's book on movie and television censorship published in 1964 and is based on the memories of an unidentified writer, which Schumach admits "could have been at fault" (Schumach 139). Johnston's comments that "we'll have no more *Grapes of Wrath*, we'll have no more *Tobacco Roads*. We'll have no more films that show the seamy side of American life" are used as evidence that the "convergence of state interests, conservative populism, and the call of Eric Johnston to create a new era of labor-capital cooperation had borne fruit.... [T]he Cold Warriors aimed not just to eliminate subversive themes from the screen but to promote a positive vision of the virtues of the new American Way of unity and consumer democracy" (L. May 203). In fact, Johnston made no attempt to ban the circulation of *Grapes of Wrath* and was instead soon heralding the film in Congressional hearings as an example of the difficulty in judging which pictures may damage or help American propagandists abroad. Johnston testified that "many of the experts jumped on the picture, *Grapes of Wrath*. American critics said it shouldn't be shown because it depicted the seamy side of our country during the dark, depression days" ("Overseas Information Programs of the United States" 234). But according to Johnston, the Soviets had stolen the picture and showed it under the title "The Paradise That Is America." Unexpectedly, Johnston claimed "the audience didn't react according to Marx. The thing that impressed the audience was that the migrant workers in the picture drove away in their own cars when police chased them out of the tent-and-shanty towns. So the Red officials yanked the picture" (ibid. 235). In actuality, according to the Soviet film scholar Sergei Katperev, the exhibition permit for *Grapes of Wrath* reveals that the film was legally screened in the USSR from 1948 to 1955, the last year for unlicensed screenings of American films. The film that U.S. propagandists had been uniformly wary of was in fact freely circulating throughout the Soviet Union during a time when repeated demands were being made by Congress to control the image of America that were circulating abroad and were seen to be damaging to American prestige.

Johnston regularly fought any attempts by the U.S. government to ban the circulation of films that were found to present a damaging image of America abroad, claiming that critical judgment of film content was wholly subjective and therefore impossible. After years of complaints throughout the 1950s by government information agents abroad about the negative effects of Hollywood films on U.S. foreign policy objectives, the U.S. Information Agency (USIA) created their own list of blacklisted films that were seen as "painting a false picture abroad of the United States" ("U.S. Lists Movies It Limits Abroad"). The USIA was only permitted to outright deny distribution of these films because they were being released by film companies taking advantage of the government program, the Information Media Guaranty, which permitted the studios to convert blocked currencies into dollars by displaying their films abroad. The ban affected 12 countries and included 82 Hollywood films, including *All Quiet on the Western Front, House of Bamboo, The Sweet Smell of Success, The James Dean Story, All the King's Men, The Strange One, Blackboard Jungle, Salt of the Earth,* and *Somebody Up There Likes Me.* None of these films were banned in Western Europe, except for Spain, and indeed some of Hollywood's most memorable films, as historian Richard Pell notes, from the mid–1940s to the early 1960s—*Double Indemnity, The Big Sleep, Sunset Boulevard, All About Eve, High Noon, On the Waterfront, Rebel Without a Cause, East of Eden, Psycho, The Hustler, Splendor in the Grass*—"presented a far more disturbing portrait of life in the United States than a movie supposedly as 'negative' as *The Grapes of Wrath*" (Pells 215).

Throughout the 1950s and 1960s, the Hollywood studios were struggling to protect an industry experiencing radical upheaval due to the breakup of the studio system and the arrival of television. Johnston lobbied heavily and consistently for expansion into international markets as a way to guarantee the continued growth of the film industry. The MPAA under Johnston, though, was not going to jeopardize its market share by producing ideologically and politically loaded films that satisfied the demands of government officials. And yet as can be seen through the many congressional hearings held throughout the 1950s, Congress continued to view and evaluate Hollywood films as a legitimate aspect of American information programs. The specifications of the Smith-Mundt Act in the creation of an official U.S. information agency (the USIA) served only to further problematize the role of film in American public diplomacy. Resistant to creating a government-sponsored agency that created American propaganda films for distribution and that was mandated by law to rely on private entities that would not undercut the dominance of the Hollywood studios, the government simultaneously decried the damage of Hollywood films on foreign relations while de facto supporting their circulation as instruments of American soft power.

While the studios, under the leadership of Johnston, began to aggressively expand into international markets during the 1950s, the Eisenhower administration began to rely more heavily on culture to counter the rise of anti–American propaganda by the Soviets. Concerns about the nation's overseas image continued to mount from 1954 to 1956 with the victory of the revolutionary Vietminh over the French in Indochina, the Bandung Conference for "non-aligned" nations, and the Suez crisis. The Soviet launch of Sputnik on October 4, 1957, proved a propaganda coup for the Soviet Union, who, as John Foster Dulles, the U.S. Secretary of State, observed, played it "for all it was worth at home and abroad" (Hixson 123). Coupled with the Little Rock, Arkansas, school desegregation incident in the fall of 1957, which also received negative international coverage, U.S. propagandists faced a crisis in winning public support overseas for the American way of life. With USIA polls revealing rising anti–American sentiments among Western European allies, Eisenhower and his deputies "exploited print, film, trade fairs, exhibitions, and exchange programs to nurture a benevolent image of capitalism while reassuring foreign audiences that the United States was working diligently to ameliorate its own social problems" (Hixson 133). Increased governmental fears that Soviet propaganda had gained a distinct advantage over the United States through its participation in international trade fairs and exhibitions encouraged President Eisenhower to request "emergency" funding from Congress to expand U.S. participation at these events. The emergency trade fair program was put into effect in December 1954 at the Bangkok Constitution Fair, and participation in overseas cultural events broadened significantly. With the passage of the International Culture Exchange and Trade Fair Participation Act of 1956, Congress provided regular funding for cultural events that enhanced the image of America abroad. The Brussels World's Fair of 1958 presented by far the "most significant opportunity for the United States to use culture as an asset to the nation's foreign policy" (Hixson 141). Planning for the Brussels exhibition, the first world's fair of the postwar era, began under the Office of the U.S. Commissioner General for the Brussels Exposition (BRE), a division of the State Department. When several congressional representatives threatened to cut the original $15 million appropriation for the fair, Eisenhower committed his administration's prestige on maintaining appropriate funding for a cultural event that was seen as central to building an image of America as a nation that would effectively counter anti–American Soviet propaganda. The Brussels World's Fair represented the culmination of cultural diplomatic skills that had been hewn since the start of the Eisenhower administration. As the premiere nation-building event for the United States directed toward an ambivalent and increasingly hostile Western European audience, the U.S. propagandists along with the Soviets waged an all-out war on the cultural front. The fair provides an exceptional demonstration of the efficacy of the use of culture as a means of public diplomacy. The U.S. planners for the fair relied on both high and low cultural forms to construct a saleable image of America; films played a central role along with theatrical production, classical musical performances, and jazz concerts to construct in the minds of the millions of visitors to the fair a distinct and lasting image of the United States.

This book examines the efficacy of film as an element of political persuasion in a free and democratic society. Rather than attempt to clarify or reconstruct a coherent and stable message from these films, this work argues that the disparate and disconjugate efforts of the U.S. government to present an American image to a European audience had paradoxical effects, both undermining the intended nationalistic efforts and also presenting a viable image of American democracy as a vital and fecund cultural and economic force confronting Europe. By the late 1950s, America's foreign diplomacy depended on the soft power of film as one means to combat the crass propaganda of the Soviet Union, and also as a way to foster the support of neutral countries for the United States' foreign policy objectives.

Introduction: The Brussels World's Fair of 1958

On April 17, 1958, the Brussels World's Fair was opened by Belgium's young King Baudouin. Seven years of construction went into building this fair in Heysel Park, five miles from Brussels. With 160,000 visitors watching, and 50 Belgian Air Force jets flying overhead, the King lit the symbolic flame that marked the start of the world's first "Atomic Fair." With the Atomium as its symbol, the fair contained 50 national pavilions and 8 international exhibits in addition to the first world's fair exhibit by the Holy See. The ideological heart of the Brussels World's fair was the U.S. pavilion and the adjacent pavilion of the Soviet Union. The political and ideological struggles that defined the Cold War permeated the construction and management of the fair, often in quite subtle ways. As a children's book about world's fairs explained, "At the fair, our country was proud to give the world the feel and smell of America. Because we hoped to show the United States as a happy country in which people had real freedom, everything about our exhibit was made to be like life in America" (Roesch 72). The political and cultural context, together with the opportunity to reach a massive audience, ensured an unprecedented level of concern for the messages and images presented. By the time the fair closed on October 19, 1958, forty million people, the largest crowd ever to visit a world's fair, had come to see the first world's fair of the Cold War.

The Brussels World's Fair was the first major international exhibition since the New York World's Fair of 1939. As the *Canadian Geographical Journal* reported, "The results of nearly two decades of human effort and knowledge, painfully acquired in war and peace, are here set out as a measure of our material progress since the last exhibition was held" (Seeley 143). What does one pavilion made for a world's fair in the 1950s reveal about the society that created it? What forces were involved in the construction of the site, and do they correspond to larger trends beyond the ephemeral status of such an international event? An exploration of the development of the American pavilion at the Brussels World's Fair of 1958 reveals many of the social concerns of the times. The site was constructed and managed in direct dialogue with other contemporaneous institutions and events. World's fairs typically reinforced the status quo with their emphasis on portraying nations and industry in a positive light. Directed to an international audience, the displays in the various exhibits tended to be simplified for easy, unambiguous mass consumption. The first world's fair following World War II generated considerable debate concerning how the image of America might be presented to a European audience. A variety of politicians, artists, museum administrators, and academics were consulted to determine what it meant to be an American, and how to render our distinct national identity visually for an international audience. Examining the outcomes of these decisions, and their filmic representations, in terms of the social, political and cultural context in which they were made reveals much about conceptions of national identity and related efforts at cultural diplomacy. An analysis of the discursive interplay among cinema and contemporaneous institutions of spectacle explains how meanings were made and organized in a unified historical context.

By examining a variety of filmic images presented at the Brussels World's Fair, we see what they reveal about the interaction of culture and politics in America's Cold War strategy of nation building, and the central relationship between these efforts and economic forces. As Tom Gunning has noted, world's fairs "provided an image of the world wide power of capitalism; they transformed a market place into a symbolic landscape that not only celebrated but exemplified modernity; and they formed a spectacle in which commodity provided the entertainment, and the commodity form of entertainment itself was raised to a new technical perfection" (Gunning 423–424). The Cold War debates about the ideological differences between the United States and the Soviet Union hinged on the opposition between capitalism and communism, and, therefore, central to the discourse amongst American cultural strategists was the necessity of presenting capitalism as the key determinant in the American way of life. The difficulty created by this emphasis, though, was the widespread perception by many Europeans (as U.S. government surveys revealed) that Americans were materialistic and lacking in culture. The debate and discussion surrounding the Brussels World's Fair revealed a nation obsessed and dissatisfied with its image abroad. At a time when American power appeared and was, in fact, extremely secure internationally, our national identity was fragmented and incoherent. The major discursive cause for the failure by the U.S. government to provide and create a stable image that could be sold internationally was the perception that American cultural production was merely commercial culture and thus inadequate and embarrassing in the face of European high culture.

The Brussels World's Fair of 1958 has often been characterized as the site of a soft power battle of ideology between the United States and the Soviet Union at the height of the Cold War. The recent successful launching of Sputnik in 1957 had the United States scrambling to reclaim its image as the dominant technological and industrial leader of the world. The two nations received much of the press coverage and, for the first time, a world's fair became the site for covert operations. Another battle was being fought within the American pavilion itself over the most effective means of presenting the image of America to a European audience. The American pavilion was a model of 1950s affluent society in which the anxieties of the atomic age had been subsumed into a paradise of consumption. Created during a period of unprecedented interconnection between private and state entities in the development of the U.S. propaganda program, the pavilion was a product of a coalition of business leaders, government bureaucrats and academics. A crystalline building designed by the American modernist architect Edward Durell Stone, with forty entrances and exits, the pavilion was, according to the official U.S. guidebook, "expressive of the American spirit, with a feeling of openness and naturalness" (Rydell 202).

The pavilion was constructed under the guidance of America's tastemakers who moved between the highest levels of governmental, academic, and cultural institutions. Development and construction of the pavilion was overseen by the Office of the U.S. Commissioner General for the Brussels Exposition, which was set up as a temporary arm of the State Department. Chosen to head the commission was Howard Cullman, head of the New York Port Authority, director of the Metropolitan Opera, and a renowned Broadway angel. His deputies were James Plaut, director of the Boston Institute of Contemporary Art and, of particular note, Katherine Howard, a former assistant administrator of Civil Defense. This "high-brow" group created a pavilion noted for its fashion models, and its emphasis on a "soft sell" that left many visitors bewildered and confused.

Stone's two-story modern pavilion was considered by many the most beautiful at the fair. Inside the building grew 10 50-foot willow trees, while outside 130 apple trees were planted, and state flags flew over the main entrance. Stone himself exclaimed while examining the building, "God, isn't that the most beautiful damned thing you've ever seen in your whole life? ... I feel the need for richness, exuberance, and pure, unadulterated freshness" ("More Than Modern" 48). The building represented the good taste of a country that had gained the confidence of being a global leader. Located between the Vatican and the Soviets, between heaven and hell as some quipped, the American pavilion was literally a representation of America's international policy in so far as it presented to a specifically European audience

U.S. Air Force Command Band of Wiesbaden plays the National Anthem as 40 American pavilion guides form a color guard of honor to lower the 13 U.S. standards on the American site during closing day ceremonies. Approximately 10,000 persons watched the observance at 6 P.M. (National Archives).

a persuasive and recognizable image of American ideology. By the late 1950s, America's cultural diplomacy had been refined in order to combat the crass propaganda of the communist countries. By displaying to the foreign populations that America was a cultured nation, many of the fears about this new atomic superpower would be assuaged. By avoiding a propagandistic tone, the government could emphasize the common interests that America shared with the rest of the world. As George Allen, the head of USIA, stated in 1958, "Fortunately for ourselves and for others, our national interests coincide with the interests of a large proportion of mankind; the desire for liberty, peace and progress. I would not be so bold as to say that the real image of America can become a guide to all — but it most certainly should be an example to many" (Sandeen 116).

The displays within the American pavilion were designed to provide glimpses of American life through a showcase of consumer objects. The State Department and the USIA called on more than "thirty prominent Americans in all fields of activity" to determine what aspects of life in the United States should be emphasized in the American pavilion. Those who contributed included Thomas J. Watson, Jr., president of IBM, Walter Paepcke, chairman of Container Corporation of America, Erwin D. Canham, editor of the Christian Science Monitor, and Victor Reuther, president of the AFL-CIO. In addition, leading intellectuals such as David Reisman and Arthur Schlesinger, Jr., provided their own vision of what the American pavilion should look like. This initial survey lead to a three-day conference at MIT established for the "exchange of ideas among the exhibit staff, the designers, and the group of outstanding scholars and practical men selected by MIT itself" ("Progress Report" 134). At this stage much emphasis was placed on creating an image of America for the predominantly European visitors who would be attending the fair. The commission recognized that "the sheer mass of American wealth and the sheer power of American industry had been dinned into European ears ad nauseam. Another repetition of production statistics could be counted on to arouse boredom, perhaps irritation, certainly envy. What the conference set out to define were the facts and statistics the European does not know" ("Progress Report" 135). After synthesizing the conclusions of the MIT and other study groups, the Deputy Commissioner of the fair stated,

> We now believe that the dominant theme, simply stated, should be that the United States constitutes a society in ferment.... The American people are dynamic, energetic, impatient and restless for change; and that because of the vastness of our country, the diversity of our origins, and the free conditions pertaining to American enterprise, we are committed to a constant, unremitting search for an improved way of life ["Progress Report" 136].

The planning committee's concern with image building reflected the mass-mediated society of the postwar period, in which the construction of a saleable image was seen as central to effective information programs.

U.S. companies were not permitted to set up commercial displays within the pavilion because the USIA, consistent with its soft-sell strategies, wanted to downplay the country's industrial power, and focus instead on the rich diversity of individual Americans and their daily lives. This was much easier to convey in the sort of venue the pavilion made available. "The American continent can be tasted in a few precious samples, the way a wine taster feels the sun, the soil, and the air of his country with each sip" ("Progress Report" 139). The focus of the installation was on portraying an "American," but not the American most Europeans were familiar with as soldiers, tourists, or movie

United States Pavilion: On opening day of the Brussels World's Fair 162,000 people from many parts of the world visited the fairgrounds; of that number an estimated 60,000 crowded into the huge U.S. pavilion (National Archives).

stars. The committee felt it was necessary to show the average American existing in a world of idyllic consumption and material accumulation. As the designers explained,

> Much less known is the life he leads in his own country, except perhaps from literature and from the misrepresentations of motion pictures. Of undeniable interest ... will be his native environment, especially the man-made kind; his house and the objects he accumulates in the pursuit of happiness; his likes and dislikes as reflected in his surroundings ... his pet loves and pet hates; the things that make him laugh ... pictures and objects ... furnish the best means for understanding him ["Progress Report" 139].

While the panels of America's cultural elites were able to present a very broad and general conception of the spirit of the pavilion's exhibits, their advice had little concrete structure. This was an image of the average American distilled through the tastes of those in power; a political and cultural elite. The actual pavilion employed both high art museum exhibition techniques and low-brow objects and displays. The juxtaposing of high and low failed to present a cohesive image that transcended the materiality of mere objects; many spectators saw simply kitsch.

The pavilion was an open space that contained multiple levels and areas divided by displays and exhibits. With a large circular opening in the roof, rain and sun flowed into the fountain pool in the center of the building. A long ramp and walkway into the center of the pool served as a modeling runway throughout the summer. The pavilion was designed with no singular directional flow to the exhibit, thus encouraging visitors to wander at will. Many relaxed on the large wooden benches that encircled the live trees. Dividing walls were covered in various Saul Steinberg caricatures of American life. Exhibition areas were structured as fragments of images, glimpses of American life in areas such as the "Faces of America," and "Islands of Living." Unlike

Models pose during the daily fashion show at the U.S. Pavilion at the Brussels World's Fair (National Archive).

the Soviets' emphasis on military might and technological advances in their pavilion, America's identity was constructed through visual manifestations of life drawn primarily from the domestic sphere.

The significance of the domestic arena in an international exhibit at the height of the Cold War can be understood through the guidance of Katherine Graham Howard. Howard, heiress to the R. J. Reynolds tobacco fortune, was "more than an orchid-bearer." In an article in *Time* magazine, she was singled out as a potential female candidate for the new Eisenhower Administration. She was described as "the poised and pleasant G.O.P. national committee woman from Redding, Mass., secretary of the Republican National Committee and of the Chicago convention (whose most memorable appearance on television was the day she slipped off her shoes on the platform to ease her tired feet). A Republican worker for two decades, she came out for Ike before the convention, [and] was in his campaign retinue from beginning to end as the only woman member on the top strategy committee" ("More Than Orchid" 17). By the time of her appointment to the fair commission, Howard had been appointed the key spokesperson for the Federal Civil Defense Administration (FCDA), an organization at the forefront of preparing the public for possible nuclear annihilation. According to Howard, the main training ground for Civil Defense, and the main front for preparing for the Cold War "actually exist[ed] in our homes, right in our living rooms" (Oakes 107).

The decision to construct the American pavilion in Brussels around the home was an overtly political act representing the crucial role that the family played in the fight against communist insurgency. The focal displays in the pavilion were on the home and home life. A fully functioning kitchen, complete with several ovens, dishwashers, and stoves, formed a glassed-in exhibit in which a typical American housewife explained the pleasures and efficiencies of the new suburban home. A patio area with barbeque equipment formed another fragmented re-creation of American domestic life, along with an open two-story home containing children's toys and a scattering of furniture. The American home had been opened to the public eye. This house was peopled with random female mannequins and stray pieces of furniture. Mannequins proliferated in the display cases. Within one, a pair of bridal mannequins strode hand in hand into their suburban dream.

While the Cold War era has been marked as the period of the return of women into the privacy of the home, during this period the home had actually become very much a site open to public scrutiny. Television shows, such as *The Adventures of Ozzie and Harriet*, that focused on day-to-day activities of the family proliferated, providing a window into the supposedly private realm of the house. And in Brussels, the glassed-in kitchens and wall-less house of the pavilion transformed the American home into virtual television sound stages that starred representative American citizens playing their roles for a European audience already conditioned to see images of American domestic life through Hollywood movies. In fact, the pavilion did have its own running color television station where visitors could become part of the show. Were the predominantly European visitors capable of recognizing the political implications of these public displays of the home? Were adequate connections made between the domestic displays and the overriding implications of the atomic theme of the exhibition? In Civil Defense, the family was recast as an "agency of the state. When the state entered the home, patriotism, which now included nuclear housekeeping, would become a family value" ("United States Speaks" 113).

Howard was appointed assistant administrator of the FCDA by Eisenhower in 1953 and became deputy administrator in the same year. While driving in her specially equipped, anti-nuclear car in case of an enemy attack, she gave 63 speeches, appeared on 28 radio programs, 14 television shows, and held 12 press conferences in her first year in office. A very deft media pundit, Howard's position provided her with easy access to Congress, NATO and other national security agencies. In addition, she also became very skilled in her use of the press to achieve her political ends. Howard's active role within the Eisenhower administration was not something she publicly acknowledged. "Howard's own account of her life as a Washington bureaucrat [was] only superficially concerned with the philosophy, politics, and organization of civil defense. Her main interests seem[ed] to have been her domestic affairs and the social life of Washington officialdom, especially ceremonial matters such as the seating arrangement at state dinners, who wore what, who poured tea, and poured coffee at which ends of the table, who was ritually favored, and who was diminished by the unspoken rules of White House protocol" ("United States Speaks" 133).

Even while occupying a high-

Mrs. Katherine Howard of Boston, who was appointed by President Eisenhower as a Deputy United States Commissioner General to the Brussels World's Fair of 1958 (National Archives).

level position within the Eisenhower administration, Howard portrayed the job of the housewife as the most important role for women in American society because of her importance in the success of the civil defense program. The mother would be the stabilizing force in the 11 million new suburban homes that had been built between 1948 and 1958. Raising kids with the correct mores of the American way would be crucial in keeping the family intact even during a possible Soviet attack. One example that Howard provided of a model American was a housewife in Norfolk, Virginia, who, four hours after a huge meteor exploded, called her local newspaper to find out whether the light and explosion had been caused by an atomic bomb. She had been delayed in calling because she needed to finish doing her wash and putting it out to dry. For Howard, "The priorities of the Norfolk housewife were in order because if a nuclear attack had occurred there would be meals to cook, beds to make and clothes to wash" ("United States Speaks" 136). The smooth running of the nation, even under siege, would be dependent on the diligent American housewife.

The emphasis then within the American pavilion on the domestic sphere can be understood more clearly in the context of Howard's insistence on the primacy of the family as a political force. Representations of the life of the suburban family could be compared with the Soviet displays of military hardware. The war against atomic destruction was to be won by each and every family that survived the onslaught. In a speech before the Continental Congress of the Daughters of the American Revolution, Howard described the national qualities of Americans that separated them from the forces of Communism. Comparing the American Revolution to the Cold War, she offered as the main weapons of the American family "the love of family, loyalty to country, aid to others, faith in God, a fierce regard for freedom — and the willingness to work together in the traditional American ways.... If our morale was shattered, the forces of atheistic Communism would almost certainly engulf all of Free Europe, what remains of free Asia — and perhaps even this beloved Land as well" ("United States Speaks" 143–44).

The pavilion's emphasis on the family as a political entity was closely aligned with a consumerist ethos. The image of a robust, egalitarian capitalist system was crucial in fighting the battle against Communism, and women shoppers were at the forefront of that offensive. The Brussels setting provided a venue to showcase consumer products for Europe's recovering markets. The American fair commission did not officially allow commercial displays on the grounds because they did not want the fair to become a tradeshow. The State Department was making a distinction between international exhibitions, such as the Brussels World's Fair, and the various USIA "people's capitalism" displays that were presented at hundreds of international tradeshows throughout the Cold War. This distinction may have had more to do with diplomatic protocol and the more comprehensive and formal planning of this event than the actual differences in the content of the displays. Many of the exhibits at Brussels, including Disney's Circarama, had been and continued to be a regular part of the USIA tradeshow displays. Corporate sponsorship at the tradeshows, though, was much more direct than Ford's sponsorship of Disney's Circarama at the Brussels World's Fair. So, the emphasis on domestic abundance and prosperity also offered a means to highlight and promote American products, while abiding by the ban on corporate sponsorship within the pavilion.

World's fairs in Brussels were not a new phenomenon. Between 1851 and 1958, there had already been 30 international exhibitions. In a country the size of Maryland, the Belgian government perceived the event as a chance for a temporary economic boom. The cost for the event was "at least $120 million for everything from new roads to a new heliport. That's in addition to nearly $400 million budgeted directly to Baron Moens de Fernig who has been running a two hundred man staff plus a two thousand man exhibition company" ("Big Show Opens" 86). Belgium wanted the fair for a variety of reasons, the most obvious of which was "the prestige value. Many Belgians have long wanted to revive the country's reputation as a cultural center — typified by Flemish painters — which ha[d] lost out to a passion for business and trading during the past century. Besides this, the fair [would] place Brussels in the lead as the place for locating the capital of the new common market in Western Europe" ("Big Show Opens" 86).

But by the time the fair opened, Belgium was "slipping fast into an export recession" at the height of a "world trade slump" ("Big Show Opens" 85–86). The American economy was also feeling the impact of recession with domestic production dipping sharply in the final quarter of 1957. Even though the economies of Europe had borne up well in the face of U.S. recession, most of them were dependent on the maintenance of a high level of U.S. imports.

This project examines the films that were presented as part of the U.S. government's American pavilion at the Brussels World's Fair. It analyzes both the images that were chosen to "project America" and the ideological implications of those images. Constructing a stable and universally acceptable image of America was far from easy. American identity itself was being challenged by the end of the late 1950s in terms of both the civil rights protests in the South and transformations within the structure of the nuclear family. These emerging social movements served to challenge the hegemonic view of America that the USIA was attempting to present. Under the Eisenhower administration, many of the government-sponsored cultural productions assumed an institutionalized position that led to the unique intersection of artists, government officials and corporate entities. By positioning the films that were projected at the Brussels World's Fair as part of Eisenhower's psychological warfare program, I will explore the broader cultural forces that played a role in the construction of American national identity. Films produced and released under the auspices of the USIA are treated as one element within the culture of the Cold War, as they reflect the foreign policy goals of the Eisenhower administration.

The historical consideration of films produced as part of the American government's propaganda programs has been primarily a concern of historians and political scientists. Film historians have tended to view propaganda films as monolithic in structure and devoid of any scholarly or aesthetic appeal. Furthermore, the concept of American propaganda itself is anathema to our ideological perceptions of a free society. But during the Eisenhower years, the attainment of a free world was thought by many to be dependent on the use of propaganda abroad and on the domestic front. Films were an instrumental part of an effort by the U.S. government to promote the American way of life abroad. The neglect of these films by historians is unfortunate, as they reveal not only the official filmic construction of America as a nation but also the manner in which culture played a central role in the foreign policy of the United States. Furthermore, these films problematize our conceptions of film production and exhibition, and the divide between both mainstream Hollywood filmmaking and the avant-garde.

During the Eisenhower administration, the relationship between the American film industry and the U.S. government reached an unprecedented alignment as a result of the House Un-American Activities Committee (HUAC) hearings. Chapter 1 of the book charts out the history of the use of film by U.S. information agencies as a means of cultural diplomacy during the postwar period. Many film histories have documented the impact of HUAC on Hollywood production, but Senator McCarthy's hearings initially led to the purging of the State Department's propaganda programs, including the Voice of America, which he charged with being soft on communism. As a result of these hearings, Eisenhower removed the propaganda program from the State Department and created the USIA, which was more directly accountable to the president. The USIA assigned propaganda a more prominent and permanent place in the U.S. foreign policy apparatus. While the HUAC hearings led to a chill within both Hollywood and the USIA, they simultaneously encouraged the production of films that would uphold the American way of life and fight communist propaganda. The USIA considered film vital in its cultural diplomacy strategy, which included supporting the Free World, convincing neutral countries of the desirability of the American ideology, and subverting communist regimes. Hollywood and the USIA formed a mutually beneficial and cooperative relationship during the Eisenhower administration that supported both Hollywood profits and American propaganda goals. The USIA's Motion Picture Division produced hundreds of films by Hollywood directors on short-term contracts. These overtly sponsored media productions were central to Cold War cultural diplomacy. They were also part of the strategic framework of a national security state, designed to promote an image of America that would win a total campaign for the hearts and minds of the world. But as this book richly documents, even during a period when Hollywood would appear to represent the apotheosis of state business, in fact, the government propagandists under Eisenhower considered one of their primary goals the correction of the distorted image of America that Hollywood projected internationally.

Each subsequent chapter of the book undertakes a filmic analysis that focuses on the effects of social and political forces on the production, exhibition, and reception of these films. By reading these films within the context of American foreign policy objectives, a more nuanced and complex understanding of how film functioned as a part of American cultural diplomacy during the Cold War is revealed. In many theories of national cinemas, Hollywood is described as a hegemonic force against which other national cinemas struggle to identify themselves. Yet, the cinematic rendering of American national identity presented through Hollywood films was frequently inconsistent, fragmented, and incoherent. Even Walt Disney, one of America's foremost cultural diplomats during the Cold War, struggled during the development and production of *USA in Circarama* to create a cohesive, saleable and persuasive image of the American way of life.

Chapter 2 reveals that the original impetus for the Disney film arose from extensive discussions between the panel members contracted by the government to directly consider the question of what constitutes American national identity. This panel, consisting of academic elites who were members of the CIA–funded Center for International Studies at MIT turned to "Uncle Walt" to help sell the American way of life. With funding from the Ford Motor Company, Disney combined the panel's suggestions with the technology he had developed for his 360-degree Circarama attraction at Disneyland to produce *USA in Circarama*. The launch of Sputnik the year before the fair had caused a national panic about covert Soviet surveillance. In response, Eisenhower proposed his "Open Skies" initiative, which called for the opening of the skies over the United States and the Soviet Union for military reconnaissance. The policy generated considerable positive reception from European allies, though it was summarily rejected by the Soviets.

In *USA in Circarama*, Disney retrofitted a bomber plane to shoot footage of America's vast and exceptional terrain. Using 11 cameras and projected onto a 360-degree screen, Disney's widescreen technology and aerial footage emphasized American transparency and openness in opposition to the secrecy of the Soviet empire. Disney showed a nation amenable to international scrutiny. While moving across the nation, the film focuses on natural wonders such as the Grand Canyon and centers of industry including Ford's Rouge River plant. America is depicted as a singular, unified organism, pulsating with the heartbeat of a booming, capitalist economy. The film was the hit of the Brussels World's Fair and continued to tour years later with the USIA throughout the world. Disney, with his years of experience as America's entertainer, was much better prepared than the country's propagandists to teach the world the rightness of the American way of life. His combination of corporate skills and entertainment savvy moved the heartstrings of the European middle class, and his sentimental nationalism made his audiences literally weep in mutual understanding and identification. Disney's values were simple and straightforward; his message of a triumphant consumer culture was easily sold to the European market. As he explained, "You don't build it for yourself. You know what the people want and you build it for them." Disney's *USA in Circarama* clearly showed who was best equipped to sell America to the world; by the 1950s, Walt Disney had become America's best salesman.

A Hollywood film that was equally successful in capturing the image of America desired by the Eisenhower administration was *South Pacific*. Chapter 3 analyzes the film within the context of the American pavilion and argues that *South Pacific* articulates on a formal level a specifically American technological sublime that was a central element of Cold War national identity. One of Eisenhower's key policy strategies was his Atoms for Peace program, which attempted to create a positive image for nuclear power not only for a domestic audience but also abroad. Released during an international skirmish over leadership in the new atomic age, it is appropriate that the only film chosen by the Motion Picture Association for America for its European premiere at the fair was *South Pacific*. The film exemplifies how the tropes of atomic energy had become suffused with specific American cultural themes. By contextualizing the film within the propaganda milieu of the fair, this chapter shows how *South Pacific* was expressive of the emergence within the dominant culture of a utopian relationship with the atom based on a nationalistic imperative at a time when America's nuclear dominance was not assured. The widescreen technology of the Todd-AO lens and the expressive use of Technicolor were the ideal equipment for capturing the atomic sublime, a visual trope that had permeated the global culture of the 1950s. At the height of the Cold War, the image that was chosen to represent America's atomic power was not only optimistic, but also sublime. The Atoms for Peace program was a crucial aspect of Eisenhower's psychological campaign against the Soviets, and *South Pacific* worked to bolster this strategy by nullifying European fears of American dominance through its cinematic spectacle. When American dominance seemed to be challenged, Balai Hai beckoned those willing to recognize the "terrible beauty" of America's destiny. This was a terrible beauty premised on the maintenance of clearly delineated positions of power in terms of both race and gender, which was meant to guarantee America's continued position as the natural and divine leader of the global, nuclear community. This image of American supremacy proved extremely ineffectual with European audiences and critics at the fair who roundly criticized the film.

The one film that most effectively controverted Eisenhower's propaganda objectives was Orson Welles' *Touch of Evil*. Not an official American entry, the resounding applause and acclaim that greeted its European premiere was a radical departure from the reception the film had received from both American critics and audiences. Feted by the French film critics from the *Cahiers du Cinema*, the popular press provided extensive coverage of Welles' visit to the fair. Heralded as an auteur, his film garnered the ebullient praise and adulation that the official American entry, *South Pacific*, had not. Chapter 4 shows that the wide divergence in critical and popular opinion about the film can be traced to the state of French-American foreign relations. By analyzing the film within the political context of the fair, I argue that the *Cahiers du Cinéma*'s politiques des auteurs (Policy of Auteurs) needs to be examined as a political discourse directly arising out of, and shaped by, the political and cultural forces of the Cold War. Auteur theory reflected the position of economic and social power that Europe was experiencing in the 1950s, and its celebration of American films revealed a cultural elitism that stemmed from a renewed confidence in their international status. The B-film quality of *Touch of Evil*, with its reliance on gangsters, violence and hooliganism, were all–American filmic tropes that European critics and audiences expected and celebrated. This was their preferred image of America, and the image that the Eisenhower government was struggling to suppress. The America that Welles creates in the film, with its bullying, self-righteous, materialistic, and obscene presence, was consistent with the sentiments of many elite Europeans toward the United States throughout the Cold War.

The Eisenhower administration's eager appropriation of the arts as a central component of their cultural diplomacy strategies included the use of Abstract Expressionist art and jazz. Additionally, avant-garde film was brought on board in order to express the individualism and freedom offered under the American system. Both Shirley Clarke and D. A. Pennebaker were commissioned, at the start of their careers, to produce short loop films for the American pavilion. Projected on television monitors scattered throughout the pavilion, the films were meant to represent fragments of American life. Chapter 5 considers how racial tensions in the United States and, in particular, the international controversy and negative publicity generated by the desegregation crisis in Little Rock, Arkansas, created one of the major sources of anti–American sentiment at the fair. The "Unfinished Business" exhibit directly addressed racial inequality in America, but was removed following vociferous complaints from American visitors and politicians. The only remaining images of African Americans in the pavilion could be found in the short experimental loop films that included images of racial diversity and ethnicity. The films were silent and non-linear montages, thematically structured, and edited in Clarke's "visual jazz" style. Audience studies conducted at the fair revealed that the most popular loop films were those that articulated the dominant mainstream conceptions of a white, suburban, middle-class society with its emphasis on "melting pot" assimilation and gendered consumption. The more formally experimental and non-representational loop films left viewers mystified and resistant. The spontaneous individuality of the experimental and avant-garde films did not find an audience among European visitors, and themes of racial inequality and unrest were too difficult to assimilate into the soft-sell image of American consumerism.

American corporations were not allowed private exhibitions within the American pavilion, but those companies with European branches were afforded space on the fairgrounds. The central attraction of the IBM exhibit was the short film *The Information Machine*, by modern designers and filmmakers Ray and Charles Eames. The film uses drawn-animation and live-action footage to present a theoretical history of the evolution of information communication. For IBM, as chapter 6 reveals, the world's fair was an arena in which to establish brand recognition for a cosmopolitan, managerial class. National interests were secondary to plans for continued market dominance in the international marketplace. The United States had become synonymous with modernity, and IBM understood the necessity for creating a brand that would make its corporation immediately identifiable by the consumer. As the postwar consumer market boomed in the United States, industrial designers, like the Eameses, played a significant role in producing product styling that made product choices a crucial aspect of middle-class taste cultures. Like the mobilization of culture as part of America's foreign policy strategy, design was also seen as a necessary emblem of American taste and ideology. With their connections to the corporate, cultural, and governmental realms within American society, the Eameses embodied a specifically 1950s position as the "new intellectual class" or the "power elites." While utilizing avant-garde innovation and cutting-edge artistic experimentation in their films, the Eameses maintained extremely close ideological ties with their corporate and government sponsors. The Eameses' goal, along with that of IBM, was to popularize the computer for the average person by making the vernacular of tomorrow less intimidating and more user friendly. Their film, with its hand drawings and lettering in the apparently artless style then popular in American graphics, was used to lend childlike simplicity to the world of high technology. The Eameses' films produced for IBM signaled the globalization of American corporate capital and the beginning of the information revolution. Though produced outside the directives of the fair planners, the film realized the USIA's goal of selling the American way through the integration of global business interests with cultural objectives.

This book challenges the dominant conception of propaganda films as speaking in a cohesive and unitary voice. Even during a period of intense consensus culture, analysis of the production and reception of the canonical Hollywood films and ephemeral government-sponsored films screened at the Brussels World's Fair reveals the difficulties experienced by propagandists in constructing an image of America that was recognizable and persuasive for an international audience. These films problematize our conceptions of commercial film production and exhibition, and the relationships between Hollywood filmmaking, avant-garde film and American propaganda. The U.S. Information Agency drew together an eclectic group of filmmakers culled from both the mainstream and the independent filmmaking worlds. By reading these films through the context of foreign affairs, a more nuanced and complex understanding of how film functions as a tool of propaganda is achieved. Millions of people watched the USIA films throughout the world. They were set up in a dialectical relationship with Hollywood films in projecting an image of America. These government-backed films were seen as necessary correctives to the popular "distortions" continually put forward by Hollywood. This project then examines the social construction of national identity through film and its relationship to other forms of cultural expression, including fashion and music. What was the impact of the USIA films on shaping and changing people's perceptions of America and its role in the global community? As one USIA operator revealed, "If I was to write a book on this, I would have a chapter called 'The Grand Illusion'—that we control the image of America. We don't control it; as the greatest power of the world the impact that we have goes far beyond what we, as an agency, do. What we have is not an impact but an effect on the way in which they adjust the lenses through which they see us" (Bogart and Bogart 223).

CHAPTER 1

Film and Cultural Diplomacy in the Early Cold War

Telling America's Story to the World— Motto of the USIA, 1953–1999

In June and July of 1962, Gallup Poll, Ltd., conducted for the U.S. Information Agency a classified survey of 650 respondents in Great Britain, West Germany, France and Italy to determine the impact of American commercial movies in Western Europe. The purpose of the survey was to provide a quantitative analysis of ways in which Hollywood cinema was responsible for constructing a positive or negative image of America abroad. The survey questions and its results would have been no surprise to government information agents who had been in conflict with various executives of Hollywood studios since World War II regarding attempts to devise an effective overseas propaganda program that could successfully draw on the power of motion pictures to sell the American way of life in Europe. The study focused on the "impressions of American life communicated by U.S. films" and whether or not the picture of American life presented was accurate ("The Impact of American Commercial Movies in Western Europe" 5). The main reasons provided by respondents for their negative impressions of American life were crime, violence and brutality. Respondents specifically associated Hollywood films with the portrayal of "gangster, criminals, gambling. Far too much gangsterism and delinquency.... The cowboys; the hoodlums; the Far West; Lots of fights; too many holdups; too much shooting" (ibid. 12). Along with violence, all four nations surveyed agreed that Hollywood consistently left a bad impression in its "depiction of the treatment of Negroes in America" (ibid. 17). The primary reason for positive "good impressions" of American life was the "high standard of living and the material rewards of American society, as shown in U.S. movies" (ibid. 8). The study concluded that

> in the end, despite a considerable amount of unfavorable effects, the net
> impact of American commercial films on West European audiences appears to

be more gain than loss — though in Britain and France the results appear are rather evenly divided.... Among the clear "gains" for the image of America projected by the movies are those who receive a favorable impression of American life and belief that the facts are as presented or even better; among the "losses" are those who get a negative impression of America and feel that the picture is a true one, or even a whitewashing [ibid. 26].

The study's findings repeat Edward Bernays's own observations 12 years earlier during his independently conducted study of British hostility to America and Americans and the motivation for anti–American sentiments. The nephew of Sigmund Freud and the father of public relations, Bernays had argued that Hollywood films "exploit extremes in American society and give the impression that all America is ... either a world of luxurious penthouses, mink coats, motor yachts, expensive automobiles, where everyone has a swimming pool in his back garden or a world of dope addicts with monkeys on their backs, of gangsters, rackets and corruption." He concluded that American films were doing harm to international relationships (Bernays 19). This conflicted state of affairs between the private Hollywood film industry and the state would persist throughout the Cold War and had a significant effect on the oppositional stance that the U.S. information agencies took toward Hollywood productions.

The opposition between the state and private media industries at this time has been unnoticed in many film histories, which have tended to favor a cultural imperialist argument that draws heavily on Thomas Guback's early work on film and foreign affairs in the 1960s and 1970s. Guback, even while documenting the differences between the state and the industry during the postwar period, concluded that "the industry found the state to be an active and effective advocate that used diplomatic power to further the interests of the private sector." Drawing on postwar Germany to illustrate the use of film as part of the U.S. occupation forces strategy of denazification, he argued that "there is hardly an adversarial relationship between state and business, and that their partnership might best be described as a coalescence of interests" (Guback 272). Following this model, American hegemony is understood as a unified and cohesive force that fundamentally relies on films and other unbalanced and unidirectional mass media outlets. Such mass media outlets are then interpreted to reflect the dominance of American world power. Powerful multinational corporations, in league with the U.S. government, use the media as an instrument to maintain and expand the American empire.

This basic argument has been the most prevalent and enduring theme of a long history of treatises on American media dominance (Waterman 170). Central to these arguments is the conflation of Hollywood and the U.S. government as hegemonic forces articulating the same goals and agendas in the promotion and dissemination of the American way. The conflation of the state with Hollywood becomes particularly pronounced in histories of cinema of the 1950s in which both Hollywood productions and government-produced media are presumed to represent a clearly articulated, universally held, and simultaneously culturally transformative ideology. Lary May assumes such a view when he notes how the "convergence of state interests, conservative populism, and the call of Eric Johnston (head of the MPAA) to create a new era of labor-capital cooperation had borne fruit." This alliance had apparently sought to achieve mutually advantageous goals. "Yet along with the elimination of radical unions and the destruction of the careers of dissenting artists, the Cold Warriors aimed not just to eliminate subversive themes from the screen but to promote a positive vision of the virtues of the American Way of unity and consumer democracy" (L. May 203). Tony Shaw articulates these assumptions when he writes that

> the relationship between the U.S. government and filmmakers during the Cold War was far more consensual and, in creative terms, something of a two-way street. It was in this sense a real network, one in which the partners felt they had a genuine stake and room for maneuver. Thus, the state might doctor, assist, initiate and advise on certain projects. It might even wholly finance, produce and market others. Yet, on many other occasions it might simply hitch a ride on films made entirely privately, including some dating from before the start of the Cold War proper [Shaw 168].

In fact, however, the U.S. government was consistently and persistently critical of the damage that Hollywood films were thought to be inflicting on American prestige abroad. The primary drive of the MPAA was the expansion of the film market abroad as the domestic market began to shrink and the studios were under the threat of collapse. Hollywood producers, therefore, had the dual need to satisfy both domestic and foreign audiences and were adamant in their refusal to introduce any content that could be interpreted by audiences as propaganda and not entertainment. In response to the intransigence of the Hollywood executives, the U.S. information agencies chose to create their own productions directly and intentionally in opposition to Hollywood films in an attempt to create an image of America that was based on the premise of truth. The films produced by the U.S. government were overwhelming documentaries directed toward an audience that both was barely literate and had limited contact with any mass media. Never exhibited in the United States, these films were frequently distributed via mobile film units and screened in non-traditional venues and were often part of a much larger program that included books, discussions and other events. These films were not made for profit and were seen by an estimated one-half billion people by 1959 ("The Overseas Film Program" 2). Understanding the development of the political and industry infrastructure that made the dissemination of these films possible, as the well as the main figures and their motivations, shows a much more antagonistic and fraught relationship between Hollywood and the government regarding how to project the American image abroad. Yet while the goals and strategies were at times quite opposed, and while the trajectories of these institutions' ambitions were quite distinct, by the time of the Brussels World's Fair of 1958 there was a fascinating, unintended transference of objectives and interests — and failures — between these institutions.

Throughout much of its history, the American film industry has depended upon a mutually advantageous relationship with the U.S. government. The U.S. government exerted political influence on the motion picture industry through negative pressures, which resulted in self-regulation, or constructive engagement, which included the overt sponsorship of films or covert alliances between filmmakers and the government. During the early Cold War this relationship began to fray because of challenges faced by both Hollywood and the U.S. government. Engaged with the Soviet Union in a battle for the hearts and minds of the world, the U.S. government became directly involved in the creation of a public diplomacy strategy that was centered on the need for developing and transmitting an image of America that was both recognizable and persuasive to audiences abroad. While this official iconography of American national identity was negotiated in Congressional hearings and inquiries, it was nevertheless ultimately viewed by the state as damaged, distorted, and destructive because of the widespread distribution of Hollywood films abroad. Foreign policy debates throughout the 1950s concerning the impact of motion pictures on the American national image abroad continually reiterated the damaging effects of Hollywood films on international public opinion and the need to counter those images with a full, fair, and balanced rendering of America — its people, institutions, and traditions.

While the U.S. government was engaged in creating and sustaining an information agency that was capable of countering the onslaught of vituperative Soviet propaganda, the Hollywood studio system was experiencing a series of cataclysmic events that would permanently affect its own dominance within both the national and the global marketplace. The Paramount decree dismantling the studio system and, even more importantly, the arrival of television heralded a significant transformation in the structure of the motion picture business and disruption of Hollywood's global dominance.

A key figure who played a sizeable role in the discursive battles of the time and someone who moved easily between the government agencies and

Hollywood was Eric A. Johnston, head of the Motion Picture Association of America. "Capitalism's Pin-Up Boy," as the *New York Times* called him, Johnston would be a pivotal player in the key Congressional investigations and hearings, including the House of Un-American Activities hearings, at which the question of the visual rhetoric for American national identity would be hotly debated and contested. The selection of Johnston to run the postwar MPAA revealed how much the studios were concerned about maintaining economic dominance in the marketplace. Johnston was a Washington, D.C., player who had successfully served four times as president of the U.S. Chamber of Commerce. When he was hired to replace Will Hays as head of the MPAA in 1945, not only did he promise to continue Hays' policy of endorsing American business and the capitalist interests that supported and profited from that business, but he also publicly took the initiative in the evolving Cold War. During a well-publicized visit to the USSR as a member of the Economic Policy Subcommittee of the State Department, Johnston told his hosts that "in economic ideology and practice my country is not only different from yours ... it is more different from yours than any other country in the world.... We are determined to remain so — and even to become more so" (Lewis 37).

Concern over the power that Hollywood films had in shaping foreign policy became a major issue for American propagandists during World War II with the creation of a governmental agency responsible for international intelligence gathering: the Office of War Information (OWI) and the Office of Strategic Services (OSS), precursors to the postwar creation of the CIA. Set up in 1942 and headed by Elmer Davis, the war agency was designed to carry on information and propaganda activities and psychological warfare chiefly through the use of the mass media. The OWI's direction was to "formulate and carry out, through the use of press, radio, motion pictures and other facilities, information programs designed to facilitate the development of an intelligent understanding, at home and abroad, of the status and progress of the war effort and of the war facilities, activities and aims of the Government" (Executive Order 9182, Federal Register VII, p. 4468, 1942). The story of the OWI was primarily one of propaganda carried through mass media with the intention of shaping world opinion in favor of the American war effort. One of the agency's most important and controversial activities was its Hollywood office, the Bureau of Motion Pictures (BMP), which consisted of both domestic and overseas branches. Following President Roosevelt's belief that movies were among the most effective means of reaching the public, Davis argued that the motion picture "could be the most powerful instrument of propaganda in the world, whether it tries to be or not" (Koppes 89). The BMP believed that every film enhanced or diminished America's reputation abroad and hence affected the nation's power. The Domestic Branch of the BMP was headed by Lowell Mellett, a former Scripps-Howard newspaper editor who had been a Roosevelt aide since 1939. When the Hollywood studios offered to actively participate in the war effort in December of 1941, Roosevelt instructed Mellett to advise Hollywood on how it could further the war effort. By May 1943, the BMP released 98 subjects and 110 reels for domestic release that were mainly converted from films produced by other agencies and private companies. Additionally, the OWI had 27 films made for non-theatrical showings and 19 for commercial theaters. There was a running debate within the agency over the content of Hollywood-made films with Mellett, which concerned whether, when the government spoke to the people, there needed to be a sense of responsibility, dignity and propriety that was itself anathema to Hollywood productions (R. MacCann 131).

While there was congressional consensus that films could be a powerful weapon abroad, there was much disagreement about the use of government films at home. Therefore, appropriations for the overseas branch was $24 million while the domestic branch received only $7 million. With the German government flooding Europe with hourly newscasts and the Japanese government using 46 radio stations in Chinese, Indian and European languages, there was great need for, as Elmer Davis explained to Congress, the OWI to "keep continually before the public eye the power and strength of the United States, to keep the peoples informed of our great and increasing contribution to the United States war efforts on all fronts; and to assure them that the war aims of the United States ... will conduce to the eventual good of the entire world" (3–13 House Hearings 78th Congress 2nd Session, National War Agencies Appropriation Bill for 1945). Robert Riskin, Frank Capra's screenwriter, was chosen to head the overseas branch of the BMP. During hearings for the 1944 appropriations, Riskin argued that commercial Hollywood films were providing neutral and allied nations "only a partial and often not very serious idea of Americans and the American scene." The Bureau of Overseas Motion Pictures was therefore attempting to "spread the true facts about America without destroying the entertainment value of the media," and yet those types of truthful and factual films did not exist since there had been too much "emphasis on Hollywood luxury and swimming pools. Glamour is the right word.... And we, the greatest motion picture producing country in the world, were represented by films which indicated that we were taking no serious interest in the war and had no interest in anything but frivolity and luxury" (R. MacCann 140). Because of this, for the first time the government consciously set out to tell the world in a series of films what it was like to live in America.

In November 1944, OWI staff member David Wilson submitted a memorandum to the organization's think tank, the Washington Review Board, entitled "Draft Outline of a Directive on Projection of America." This was one of many reports generated by the OWI in its attempts at confronting the challenge of what image of America should be shown to the world following the end of the war. Wilson's memorandum was particularly noteworthy for the double meaning of its title: "projection" in the sense of forecast or prediction and "projection" as related to the most popular and presumably influential medium of communication about American culture during and after World War II, the motion picture (Wilson 83). Responding to Wilson's memorandum in early 1945, Norman Cousins, then-head of OWI's USA Division, argued that explicit guidance was needed for dealing with "controversial questions being asked about America — questions concerning minorities, races, injustices" (Wilson 95).

The OWI had made sincere efforts to remove or reduce manifestations of overt racism and racial stereotyping from Hollywood-produced films and to press for increased attention to the role of African Americans in the war. However, the blunt observation by Philleo Nash, a highly placed OWI official who later was an adviser to President Harry Truman — "It is not and should not be the responsibility of the Office of War Information to attempt to solve the problem of Negro-White relations" — represented the viewpoint of the Washington establishment (Wilson 98n45).

The OWI was not the only government agency charged with producing non-commercial, independent films for distribution abroad in order to sway public opinion in support of the United States and its allies' wartime objectives. The Office of the Coordinator of Inter-American Affairs was created by executive order of the Council of National Defense in the State Department on August 16, 1940, with Nelson Rockefeller as its head. The Motion Picture Division was set up in October under John Hay Whitney, vice president of the Museum of Modern Art and the president of their film library and one of Rockefeller's close friends. One of Rockefeller's first efforts was to see that Hollywood films did not present negative images of Latin America. Whitney, well liked in Hollywood and a financial backer of *Gone with the Wind*, persuaded the Production Code Administration to hire Addison Durland to join their staff as head of a special Latin American division. As part of Roosevelt's Good Neighbor Policy, Durland worked to prevent negative images of America to be exported to Latin America in order to "encourage the people of the hemisphere to adopt American ideas and values" (R. F. Smith 80). A production unit was created in late 1942 in order to use film to create friendship and understanding between the Americas. More than 300 projectors were sent out throughout South American during the war, and by the war's end some 70 sound trucks were in use for trips into surrounding towns and villages.

Not only did the BMP create films outside of the auspices of the mainstream Hollywood studios, but also as increasingly bad reports began to flood the offices of the OWI singling out Hollywood films as having negative effects on audiences abroad, Davis looked for a way to keep Hollywood from putting across "day in and day out, the most outrageous caricature of the American character" (Koppes 96). A liaison office was set up in Hollywood and headed by Nelson Poynter, a Scripps-Howard colleague of Mellett's. Additionally, a representative of the BMP's overseas branch joined its domestic office in Hollywood in order to be able to object to commercial films found to be harmful to foreign relations.

In 1942 the OWI produced the Government Information Manual for the Motion Picture Industry, which gave precise political directives to ensure that its feature films mobilized public opinion in favor of the American war effort. The Roosevelt Administration asked Hollywood to project an image of a strong America, while simultaneously depicting the heroism of Britain, the depravity of the Hitler dictatorship, and the brutality of the Japanese imperialists (C. S. Goldstein 45). In 1943, the Production Code Administration, the studio's in-house censors, followed the OWI's recommendations in almost all cases. The OWI had become the "censor's advance guard," even though the studios had initially proposed that an in-house censor be chosen. Hollywood could chose to make any film it wanted, but as the *Motion Picture Herald* reported, "No one would produce a picture known in advance to be doomed to domestic exhibition exclusively" (Koppes 101). By the fall of 1943, the OWI read all the studios' scripts except for Paramount, which agreed to discuss its scripts with OWI in general terms. The OWI focused its attack on films containing American lawlessness or corruption, racial problems, and distortions of military or political facts with particular sensitivity about the depiction of home-front race relations. As Koppes reports, from mid–1943 until the end of the war, OWI exerted an influence over an American mass medium never equaled before or since by a government agency (ibid. 103).

The OWI undertook polling as a means to determine the efficacy of U.S. cultural activities on its targeted audiences. Polls carried out in liberated and occupied territories provided feedback to guide propaganda services in radio, press, and film, thus providing a responsive mechanism in which audience response would determine future production in order to address the ideological and political gaps and failings of the propaganda campaigns. The OWI would use this polling in determine what government-sponsored documentary films to produce in order to counter the damaging effects of mainstream Hollywood entertainment films on audience opinion abroad. These productions would be produced by the same studios that were being censored by the BMP.

Even before the prospects for the cessation of hostilities became viable, the Hollywood studios began preparations for the resumption and expansion of business practices abroad. In the prewar period, the Motion Pictures Producers and Distributors of America (MPPDA) had an International Department that represented members in trade matters overseas. In 1944 the Chief of the Motion Picture Section of the government's War Production Board urged the film industry to set up a permanent organization for presenting to the government the industry's global trade needs and for drafting specific recommendations for unhindered access to world markets after the war. In response, the MPPDA established the Motion Picture Export Association, Inc. (MPEA), on June 5, 1945, which empowered Columbia, Loews, Paramount, RKO, 20 Century–Fox, United Artists, Universal, and Warner Brothers to divide markets among members, set rental prices on films, establish terms of trade, negotiate film import agreements abroad, represent members before foreign governments and trade associations, and collect and disseminate intelligence about overseas markets (Guback 255). In 1946 the MPAA also prepared a code under which problems of international relations involving motion pictures would be handled within the industry. The code was drawn up by a committee consisting of Col. Jason Joy of 20th Century–Fox, Luigi Luraschi of Paramount, and Robert Vogel of Metro-Goldwyn-Mayer. The recommendations of the committee included the establishment of an informal "foreign committee," made up of experts on international affairs from the association's 10 major studios, which would study problems in the field, advise on the selection of technical directors, and work in cooperation with Joseph I. Breen's Production Code Administration. According to Byron Price, chairman of the board of directors of the Association of Motion Picture Producers, "The film industry is fully aware of its vital responsibilities in helping to build a better and friendlier world. But we firmly believe that freedom of the screen can best be preserved and all problems most effectively handled if production and distribution matters connected with films destined for foreign countries remain a responsibility of the industry, not a Government agency" ("Film Code Drafted on Trading Abroad" 43).

The postwar goals of the film industry in securing markets abroad caused immediate problems in the postwar occupation of Germany in July 1945. The planners of the U.S. occupation strategy, like their Soviet counterparts, viewed film as a means of political reeducation, and not just a means of diversion. Acting in concert with the OWI and the Supreme Headquarters Allied Expeditionary Force, SHAEF's Psychological Warfare Division forces operating under Brigadier General Robert A. McClure, who became information chief of the U.S. Control Group Council for the U.S. Zone in Germany, developed a thorough and comprehensive plan of action for films. The first phase of the SHAEF plan was the complete shutting down of all German motion picture theaters, the impounding of all films made during the Third Reich, and test showings of official atrocity documentaries and newsreels. The second phase of the plan was to include the gradual reopening of selected theaters throughout the occupied area (Joseph, "Film Program for Germany" 16). Two and half years before the end of the war, a selection of American feature films was made after extensive surveys by qualified committees in Washington, D.C., New York, and London, operating under the Combined Chiefs of Staff, the State Department, and the Office of War Information for postwar distribution abroad. The criteria for the selection of the features was to insure, first, American filmmaking at its best, and second, a story approach that would coincide with the definition of Allied policy in the German area (ibid. 16). Additionally, the MPPDA mandated that the OWI select an equal number of titles from each of the eight major studios in order to maintain parity, thus closing down the distribution of independent productions to Germany.

Care was taken in the selection of the films in order to present a favorable image of the American policy and ideology while helping "re-orient the German mind after twelve years of Nazism." Films such as *Grapes of Wrath*, "which might be considered one of Hollywood's greatest films," were disqualified because of the "background it shows and the story it tells," while *Gone with the Wind* was also not allowed because "the Negro incidents in the picture were found objectionable" (Joseph, "Our Film Program in Germany I: How Far Was It a Success?" 126). *The Maltese Falcon* was rapidly withdrawn from exhibition because censors feared it would be read by the German public as a glorification of the criminal war and a critique of the American police. Robert Joseph, who served as OMGUS (Office of Military Government, United States) film officer for Berlin and as deputy film officer for Germany until 1947, explained that the German Committees had established a loose working principle, one that the ICD (Information Control Division, OMGUS) and the ICB followed, that "Information Control would not under any circumstances ever mean entertaining the vanquished people" (ibid. 124).

The Soviet military administration began screening Soviet and German films in early July 1945; they also had a large portion of Germany's movie resources under their control and had been taking the most aggressive steps in the field (Hill, "Whither Go German Films?" X3). *Variety* reported that "American film companies are being left at the post in Germany with Russia racing down a straightaway field in utilizing pictures as a propaganda medium for their political philosophy" (Ullman 1). The British also began to reopen movie theaters in their zone and sector by July 1945. The Americans were the last to react, but by the end of July, they had begun to reopen theaters, and by the end of 1945 the ICD had opened 350 movie theaters in the American zone and sector. Due to the limited availability of appropriate German films, the OMGUS made newsreels for the German public and brought in material from the United States. By September 1945 the 30 previously chosen Hollywood feature films, most between two and five years old, had been included in the reeducation program for postwar Germany. The Hollywood studios had much to gain in their partnership with the government in the postwar period. Prewar Europe had been an important market, and American films had been banned from Nazi Germany and Nazi-occupied Europe in 1940.

The Hollywood studios were eager to position themselves as strongly as possible in the European market, yet they wanted to dictate the terms of its business strategy in Europe. The view of OMGUS was that the German film industry needed to be started again as a business enterprise, not as an American one. "The view of our government was that there be no economic exclusiveness in our occupation of Germany" (Norman 62). The American film industry responded by limiting the number of films released to the Military Government, and, therefore, even with theaters open there were not enough films available to show in them. Therefore, between July 1945 and May 1947 only 50 American feature films had been released in Germany. Because of the tensions between Hollywood and the Military Government, General McClure held a number of conferences with film industry leaders in the United States. He gained little concessions from the American film industry except for its desire to "utilize the military occupation to establish the exclusive position for American films and American distribution machinery" (ibid. 64).

The motion picture trade press began to wage a steady public relations campaign of adverse criticism against the War and State Departments' film programs in response to the Military Government's decision to oppose the demands of the film industry. According to Joseph, the "MPEA's function is the distribution of film for profit.... Denazification is not a part of the MPEA's function. However, denazification is the basis of ICD operations" (Joseph, "Our Film Program in Germany I: How Far Was It a Success?" 127). The disinterest of the film industry in assisting the Military Government for ideological and political interests was widely understood and supported by the industry trade journals. As Gladwin Hill, an American war correspondent and film critic, reported when he returned to Hollywood in 1947, it was "widely taken for granted that the motion picture industry refrained from wholeheartedly assisting the occupation film program lest it jeopardize commercial distribution" (Hill, "Our Film Program in Germany II: How Far Was It a Failure?" 135).

The film industry had hoped to receive concessions from the Military Government, which would provide them with a dominant position in the German market. The American film industry, through its European representatives in Paris and its members on the staff of the Military Government as distribution experts, attempted to establish a monopoly of not only motion picture distribution but also production and the ownership of theaters. The MPAA attempted to obtain the use of the Bavarian Filmkunst studios for the production of films (Norman 63). Instead, the Military Government responded by permitting the showing of German films considered politically safe and by permitting a quadripartite interchange program that allowed the circulation of French, British, Russian, and American films among the occupation zones. Further, under the stated policy of General McClure, German production facilities were not made available to American firms in order to allow German producers to resume production and the re-established German film industry separated production from distribution in order to allow free competition.

One of the major stumbling blocks for the Hollywood studios in entering into the German market was the demands for payment. Under the Military Government's program, revenues from the exhibition of American films in West Germany were held in blocked accounts. In his first year as the head of the MPAA, Johnston established the Motion Picture Export Association (MPEA), a trade organization that merged industry interests in foreign film distribution with the federal government's overseas brand of the OWI. The MPEA enjoyed full cooperation from the OWI because it served the political agenda of the agency while assisting in the expansion of the motion picture industry abroad. Back in Washington, D.C., the OIE established an office for liaison with the private sphere and commissioned a study on the potential for commercial propaganda by the editor of *This Week* magazine, William I. Nichols. Nichols concluded that the weakness of the European currency severely limited the scope for commercial distribution of U.S. films and other media. The Marshall Plan addressed this issue through the establishment of the Information Media Guaranty (IMG), which allowed selected foreign countries to pay for U.S. films and books with their own currency, so they could consume U.S. culture without worrying about the depletion of their limited dollar reserves. The first agreements, concluded in 1949, covered media exports to Germany, Austria, Norway, and the Netherlands. Italy followed in 1950 and France in 1951. The IMGs were renewed under the Mutual Security Acts of 1951 and 1952, at which point a rider was added to require that material exported "reflect the best elements of American life and shall not be such as to bring discredit upon the United States." The program soon expanded into the developing world (Cull, *The Cold War and the United States Information Agency: American Propaganda and Public Diplomacy, 1945–1989* 46). The postwar wave of exportation of American films to Europe reached its peak within six years after the end of hostilities and precisely the time that American film production began to decline.

The overall effectiveness of utilizing Hollywood films to help OMGUS achieve its goals of persuading the German people that the values and ideology of the American way of life was one that they should strive to achieve was quickly called into question by government officials. In July 1946, a group of information-control officers reported that the 35 American films shown to Germans since the end of the war had "no observable effect in the political and psychological re-education of the Germans and have, on the contrary reduced American cultural prestige and probably damaged the future market for American films in Germany" (Schmidt 33). Of the Hollywood features, the most popular genres were the light comedies, while war films were received with widespread disapproval and even hostility. Taken as a whole it soon became apparent that the "Hollywood film was not held in high regard by most Germans" (Norman 67). Again government officials found Hollywood films hindering their attempts to "educate the German people into ways of living and thinking that would make them a world asset rather than a world liability" (Hill, "Our Film Program in Germany II: How Far Was It a Failure?" 131). As commentators at the time noted, the trouble with the Hollywood film was its distortion of the picture of American life. Distribution of commercial Hollywood films in Germany continued to move slowly throughout the late 1940s with only 43 feature films released since the end of the hostilities until 1946, and 39 more added by 1948.

According to officials, the greater number of Hollywood films in circulation continued to undercut the work of the occupation forces. John J. McCloy, the United States High Commissioner for Germany, reported in a letter to Congress in 1951 that he was disturbed by the "harsh" and often "bitter" criticism of the U.S. films from high German government officials and also average citizens. He explained that "judging from the increasing number of complaints reaching my desk, the German people see in all too many American films a serious and immediate threat to their culture" ("Overseas Information Programs of the United States" 240). Widely quoted in the German press at the time was a survey of 400 American and British films that concluded that the films featured "1,952 violations of law, including 405 cases of adultery, 310 murders, 182 cases of perjury, 104 assaults, and 34 cases of arson" (ibid. 240). McCloy warned that

Germans were calling for the censorship of American films in Germany, and the main focus of their attack was the violence and sexuality present in Hollywood films. "The complaints are not limited to anti–Americans," explained McCloy. "Friendly Germans object to the films' presentation of the United States as a land of sadistic violence, criminality, unfettered eroticism, and easy living. That this presentation if false is not, our friends say, at all evident to the average German film-goer, who believes what he sees" (ibid. 243).

As a corrective to the misinformation provided by mainstream Hollywood feature films, the government again turned to documentary films as a key part of the denazification process in Germany. Government-sponsored documentaries produced for American audiences in the 1940s were translated into German and shown in movie theaters, American information centers, schools, and town meetings. Films such as *Tennessee Valley Authority*, *Autobiography of a Jeep*, *The Town*, and *Democracy in Action*, stressed the virtues of grassroots democracy and social cooperation. The documentary film program was considered a political and educational success by the ICD. In August 1947 the ICD created the Documentary Film Unit (DFU) to produce nonfiction propaganda films for the German public that addressed Cold War issues. The unit was headed by Stuart Schulberg, who had directed top-secret training films for the OSS and in 1946 joined the film unit headed by John Ford. Schulberg and his brother, Budd, were sent to Berlin to gather films and photos for use in the Nuremberg trials. Stuart Schulberg remained in Berlin until 1949 and between 1947 and 1949 produced more than a dozen films. Lieutenant Colonel Pare Lorentz, chief of Films, Theater and Music in the War Department's Civil Affairs Division from 1946 to 1947, collaborated with the DFU. The U.S. government's investment in documentary filmmaking was an exception in comparison to the other occupied zones. As Stuart Schulberg explained, "For, unlike the other nations sharing the administration of Germany, the Americans have made the production of documentary films a really integral part of their information program." The primary objective of the unit was the "political, social, and economic reorientation of the German people" (Schulberg 208). The DFU films fell into two distinct categories — anti–Nazi films and Cold War propaganda films. "The anti–Nazi films stressed the causal relationship between German aggression and postwar European misery and insisted on the complicity of the German population with the Third Reich. The Cold War films did not antagonize Germans with references to Nazism but rather emphasized American-German cooperation, explaining the Blockade, the Berlin Airlift, and the Marshall Plan from the American anti–Soviet perspective" (C. S. Goldstein 58).

The construction of a positive image of America for German consumption was not easy because the question of what image to send abroad was highly contested at home; American racism in particular became a central component of Soviet anti–American propaganda. The State Department estimated that 50 percent of Soviet anti–American propaganda in the immediate postwar period focused on American racism. Attempts to distribute anti-racist films such as *The Brotherhood of Men*, an animated cartoon produced by Walter Reuther, president of the UAW-CIO, were vetoed by the War Department. In 1946, Pare Lorentz, chief of the Film and Theater section of CAD's (Civil Affairs Division, U.S. War Department) Reorientation Branch, recommended distribution of the film in occupied Germany. CAD New York purchased more than 200 copies of the film and had them translated into German. Yet heated political debates over the distribution of the film in occupied Germany eventually led President Truman, following the suggestions of his secretary of war, Kenneth Royall, to rule in November 1948 that *The Brotherhood of Man* could not be used in Austria or Germany.

Raymond Daniell, former chief of the London bureau of the *New York Times*, reported in an investigative article in 1947, "What the Europeans Think of Us," that "the disenfranchisement of Negroes in Southern states is cited as evidence of American hypocrisy when it comes to human freedom" (Daniell 68). He concluded that American information efforts had so far been ineffective and damaging. "It would be a tragic blunder if," he wrote, "when we vote billions to help Europe to her feet again, we did not at least appropriate a few millions to tell the people of Europe what we are doing, why we are doing it, what it is costing Americans in labor and in dollars, and what kind of people we really are. They don't know now" (ibid. 71).

Two days before the formal surrender of Japan, President Truman on August 31, 1945, by executive order 9608 established an Interim International Information Service (IIIS) in the Department of State and transferred to it the overseas information functions of OWI and the information activities of the CIAA (Coordinator of Inter-American Affairs) thus reversing for the first time the traditional policy of the U.S. government of nonintervention in overseas information activities and limited or indirect participation in transnational cultural affairs during peace time. The order recognized that the "nature of present day foreign relations makes it essential for the United States to maintain informational activities abroad as an integral part of the conduct of our foreign affairs," thus directly linking public diplomacy efforts with U.S. foreign policy objectives. William Benton was appointed Assistant Secretary of State for Public Affairs and as such was made the head of the new IIIS. Benton drew most of the key personnel for the new agency from OWI and CIAA. The overriding task of the information agencies was to provide "a full and fair picture of American life and of the aims and policies of the United States Government" ("Plans Are Set Up to Sell U.S. Abroad" 9). U.S. national security then became linked to preventive action through the dissemination of "images of America" that were capable of not only capturing the essence of our policies but also, more importantly, convincing others that this was an image that they also share and desire.

As a result of a study requested by President Truman, the Office of International Information and Cultural Affairs (OIC) was set up in the State Department under Assistant Secretary William Benton on January 1, 1946. Like many officials involved in the formation and management of the U.S. information agencies, Benton came from the private industry, having made his fortune in advertising. Benton and Chester Bowles founded their own advertising agency, Benton and Bowles (B&B) in 1929, which proved a runaway success, leading the way with customer research and pioneering the use of radio soap operas (Cull, *The Cold War and the United States Information Agency: American Propaganda and Public Diplomacy, 1945–1989* 24). Though Congressional support for information agencies was slight, Benton found support from the American press, and in the spring of 1946, he persuaded the American Society of Newspaper Editors to establish a committee to investigate U.S. International Information. In an address delivered by Assistant Secretary Benton at a meeting of the American Platform Guild in Washington two days after the creation of the OIC, Benton sketched out many of the key thematic issues that would continue to resonate and shape later discussions and debates about the challenges of U.S. information agencies during the Cold War. The speech was part of a day-long conference on international affairs held in cooperation with the State Department. Fresh on the heels of the collapse of the fascist governments in World War II, fears of the impact of propaganda on a mass audience permeated the meeting. As Benton explained, "Twice in this century the great mass of the world's people, in sad ignorance of each other, have fought wars of rapidly accelerating destruction. Up until the last moment, those who see the issue must keep working for the victory of mutual understanding in this third and last heat of the century's race against disaster" (Benton, "Can America Afford to Be Silent?" 7). World peace could be obtained through an effective public relations strategy that succeeded in building in the "hearts and minds of foreign peoples everywhere a full and fair picture of American life." Implicit in Benton's argument was the idea that national identity can be rendered and made recognizable to a global audience through the means of mass communication, that American national identity has stable and limited contours that can be transmitted to a vastly varied and diverse audience.

President Truman (center) walking to the beach in the morning during his vacation at Key West, Florida, with Economic Stabilization Administrator Eric Johnston (left), Chairman W. Stuart Symington of the National Security Resources Board (right), and other members of his entourage, March 20, 1951 (Office of Presidential Libraries. Harry S Truman Library, National Archives).

The actual qualities that constituted American national identity were never explicitly stated except that Benton argued for an inclusive image of America. "We shall profit most by portraying ourselves frankly, the bad with the good. Our democracy is far from perfect. The United States has its own problems of poverty and maladjustment. We have much to learn ourselves — as we have much to teach" (Benton, "Can America Afford to Be Silent?" 8). For this strategy to be fully functional these messages of American identity must be made understandable to every individual in the world on the levels of both the rational ("mind") and the unconscious ("hearts"), and the target for these messages is specifically not elites but the masses, who have minimal contact with or understanding of U.S. policies and goals. "Fear and misunderstanding of America can cost us the friends and allies we need in time of crisis. We must not rely only on the friendship of governments and rulers. History shows the weathervane characteristics of such friendships. We must seek the friendship of peoples — their understanding of our own peoples and of our free society. It is the peoples of the world in whom we must put our trust" (Benton, "Can America Afford to Be Silent?" 7).

Benton identified throughout his address the sizable task before them because of the damaged image of America abroad that already existed by the end of the war. "The strong nation," he stated, "too readily becomes hated and feared by all the rest — and we are today the strongest nation since gunpowder was invented. Do our returning troops report everywhere a rising tide of war affection and esteem for the United States? I am afraid they report, all too often, just the contrary. Our very virtues, in fact, seem often to be held against us.... In large regions of the globe we are a hazy legend of military and naval power, of wealth, luxury, and carefree irresponsibility" (ibid. 8). One of the primary causes for the "distorted impressions" arising throughout the world was motion pictures. As Benton states, "A foreigner ... who has seen entertainment films but never a documentary film of American life, may have a most distorted view of America" (ibid.).

In a radio broadcast titled "America — As Others See Us," Benton and a panel of "Americans uniquely qualified in the field of world affairs" including C. D. Jackson, managing director of the overseas editions of *Time* and *Life* magazine, who had served as the OWI's top representative with the Army's Psychological Warfare Branch, and would have significant impact on the later formation and development of the U.S. information agencies, and Commander Herbert Agar, former editor of the Louisville *Courier-Journal*, who served as head of the British Division of the OWI, discussed why "the world does not understand the United States, that people of other nations have strange, mistaken notions about is" (Benton, "America — As Others See Us" 11). Peppered throughout their discussion are anecdotes of misconceptions of America expressed by foreigners because of the influence of Hollywood films. A listener in Valguenera, Italy, wrote the Voice of America radio station asking if "American gangsters are really as prevalent as American films and mystery stories have lead him to believe" (ibid. 12).

Norwegian journalists on a coast-to-coast tour of the United States as guests of the U.S. government were "astonished to discover quite a number of really nice girls in New York — having been prepared to find nothing but delinquent bobby-soxers" (ibid. 13). At the close of the radio roundtable, the panelists were directly asked if American movies were an "asset or a liability." Agar responded that he has "no intention of belaboring Hollywood. But the fact remains that films which were designed and made primarily as entertainment for American audiences have created a strange impression of us abroad. At home, we see Betty Grable as a stenographer on the screen, elegantly gowned by Adrian. We know it's simply make-believe because we see real stenographers in the subway every day. Overseas the effect is something else again, and one of the problems we are up against is the popular delusion abroad that Americans live in incredible luxury" (ibid. 16). Importantly, though the panelists were quick to point to Hollywood motion pictures as a direct cause in creating misunderstandings of the American system abroad, none of them called for censorship or regulation of the motion picture industry. Rather, Benton recognized that the government could only function as a corrective to the motion picture industry and that the government would remain dependent on the industry because of its economic power. As Benton explained,

> We in the State Department know that private interests are eager to do more than they have done. They are seeking world markets. The total volume of their efforts represented by news carried by the commercial wire services, by foreign editions of magazines and books, by movies, by tourists, and commercial contacts will amount to vastly more than the Government's contributions. The Government's job will be merely to fill the gaps — though the gaps are important and often crucial [Benton, "Can America Afford to Be Silent?" 8].

To fill the gap created by the motion picture industry, one of the OIC's "channels of action" was in "acquiring, adapting, and scoring in foreign languages a continuing series of newsreels and documentary films about the United States, for non-commercial showing to foreign audiences" (ibid. 10). Because of significant financial constraints and also the perception by government officials that the public was unwilling to use federal money for the production of propaganda, the government information agencies were not in a mutually supportive role with the motion picture industry. Rather the "U.S. commercial media were consistently suspicious of government information activity.... At its most virulent, this suspicion resulted in attempts to close down the entire U.S. information machine but most typically the private media ignored the whole government information operation" (Cull, "Public Diplomacy and the Private Sector" 211).

Benton, though, believed that U.S. film had a vital role to play in the global information campaign. In the autumn of 1945, the newsreel companies agreed to a deal whereby the State Department distributed a United Newsreel (to which they contributed) in countries such as Czechoslovakia and Holland, where they had no commercial interests. Benton's adviser on film, John Hay Whitney, had acted as a wartime liaison officer between Nelson Rockefeller's Office of the Coordinator of Inter-American Affairs and the Hollywood studios encouraging sensitive representations of Latin America, and he recommended expanding this sensitivity worldwide following the war. Benton traveled to Hollywood in March 1946, where he brokered a deal whereby the

MPAA acquired the research files of the Rockefeller Bureau's Hollywood office. The studios agreed to a voluntary system of consultation with the State Department in their representation of international matters. Benton additionally impressed upon the Secretary of State for Economic Affairs, Will Clayton, the political value of helping Hollywood export movies (Cull, *The Cold War and the United States Information Agency: American Propaganda and Public Diplomacy, 1945–1989* 32). During his meetings with the secretary, Clayton expressed his concern about the negative impact of gangsters and racial discrimination in U.S. movies overseas.

Between 1945 and 1947, Benton waged an arduous war to win Congressional and public support for authorizing legislation and appropriations to keep alive worldwide informational and cultural programs. In the fiscal year of 1947, the Congress allocated $20 million with an additional $5,375,000 for the work of the Interdepartmental Committee. 1948 represented a low point for the OIC when its budget request for $31 million was slashed by the House of Representatives to $0. The Senate voted to grant $12.4 million. One of the reasons cited by the House Appropriations for lack of funding was the lack of authorizing legislation. When funds were being considered for the 1948 fiscal year Representative Taber, Chairman of the Appropriations Committee in the 80th Congress, called attention to the fact that Congress was being asked to appropriate money for an agency for which there was no enabling legislation. As a result of congressional action, funds for the overseas information program were drastically curtailed.

Recognizing the need for a permanent international public relations program within the government, Senator Smith of New Jersey and Congressman Mundt of South Dakota lobbied for the passage of the U.S. Information and Education Exchange Act of 1948. The Senate delayed ratification until a Senate-House committee investigated the existing U.S. information and educational exchange programs by traveling to Europe. Almost half the members took trips abroad in 1946 and 1947 and were overwhelmingly astounded by what they perceived to be the deliberate and widespread misunderstanding of the United States abroad. The Smith-Mundt Act, formally called the U.S. Information and Exchange Act of 1948, passed the Senate in January of 1948, legalizing the first peacetime propaganda program in the United States. In order to conform to the language of Smith-Mundt, the Office of International Information and Cultural Affairs (OIC) became the Office of International Information and Educational Exchange (OIE). The act authorized the federal government to employ its own agencies and private organizations to "disseminate abroad ... information about the United States, its people, and its policies, through press, publications, radio, motion pictures, and other information media" (United States Information and Educational Exchange Act of 1948, ch. 36, Title V, 201–202; January 27, 1948). The effort was necessary because America had shortsightedly failed to promote itself to other nations. "From early days, American enterprise, skill, generosity, and zeal made great contributions to the life of other nations which have also enhanced the appreciation of the United States. Frequently, this projection has often been haphazard. No one can estimate fully what differences a greater amount of persistent concern might have made in our foreign affairs" (ibid.).

Senator Smith, cosponsor of the act, expressed the views of many members of Congress in January 1948, when he spoke of the "campaign of vilification and misrepresentation" and the "incessant falsification" of the motives of the United States on the part of Soviet propaganda (Palmer and Carter, "The Smith-Mundt Act's Ban on Domestic Propaganda: An Analysis of the Cold War Statute Limiting Access to Public Diplomacy," *Communication and Law*, Winter 2006, www.lexisnexis.com). The underlying thesis of the act was that "if other people understood us, they would like us, and if they liked us, they would do what we wanted them to do." Legislators argued that the Smith-Mundt Act would create world peace through mutual understanding. "Words of truth can be most powerful weapons of peace if we use them properly and effectively.... It is our conviction that a world-wide understanding of the real America will provide an environment which will contribute definitely to the maintenance of permanent peace."

In January 1948, President Truman nominated diplomat George V. Allen to fill the vacant post of Assistant Secretary of State for Public Affairs. Allen had worked as a journalist, served as advertising manager of the *Foreign Service Journal*, and had been ambassador to Iran. Allen made major adjustments to the OIE's internal structure. The OIE was split into an Office of International Information (OII), which looked after what was termed the "fast media" of radio, press, and motion pictures, and a parallel Office of Educational Exchange (OEX), which administered the "slow media": exchanges, libraries, and links to institutions around the world (Cull, "Public Diplomacy and the Private Sector" 41). Drawing definite lines between information and cultural activities, information was seen as closely involved with politics. Largely unilateral in character, information activities were to be employed as an instrument "to implement the diplomatic policies of the Department of State." Part of the law required that government activities in information were to be reduced whenever corresponding private activities were found to be adequate. Cultural activities were to be nonpolitical and kept clear of propaganda, or else they would be viewed as cultural imperialism designed to impose the culture of the United States on other people.

As the Smith-Mundt Act was being debated, the House Committee on Un-American Activities (HUAC) investigations of Hollywood movies began. The rhetorical battles waged in the hearings revealed both that the state recognized that movies were a crucial ideological tool for the government and yet that movies could cause significant harm to American national identity, that they did not represent the American way of life. Faced with the impending Paramount decision and the implementation of film monopolies and national subsidies by foreign nations, the studio ousted Will Hays as the industry spokesperson and replaced him with Eric Johnston. Johnston was designated as chief Washington lobbyist for the movie studios, spending most of his time promoting the sale of Hollywood films abroad. Asked by HUAC whether the Production Code "checks pictures to determine whether or not they are propaganda for a foreign government," Johnston immediately responded that "there is nothing in here about propaganda. We feel that it is the duty of each motion picture producer to determine what goes on the screen, just like it is the duty of each newspaper publisher to determine what goes into a newspaper (322).

Johnston's overriding concern was maintaining an advantageous relationship with the government in order to protect the Hollywood film industry's economic interests both nationally and abroad as it faced divestiture of its theaters. In his HUAC testimony, he assured the committee that economic interests outweighed any concerns about the political content of Hollywood films. "Please bear in mind," he told the committee,

> that we are doing business on a world-wide basis and when you hurt us you hurt our pocketbooks world-wide and you hurt the American Nation world-wide, too, because the best conveyor of good will between our Nation and other nations, in my opinion, is the American motion picture. One picture is worth 10,000 words, according to the old Chinese proverb. In many countries they get their ideas of America from American motion pictures. We don't want the feeling to go out to these countries that American motion pictures contain Communist propaganda and have them excluded in those areas. It would be bad for us financially. We think it would be bad for the American people and bad for the rest of the world if they went out [328].

The social problem films that raised the ire of HUAC, such as *Crossfire*, *Gentlemen's Agreement*, and *The Best Years of Our Lives*, were also the sort of films that were bad for business and public relations abroad. Efforts to curb these films and to focus on more entertaining and less disturbing or challenging pictures served the studios' financial interests. As Jon Lewis argues, HUAC benefited from and capitalized on studio panic over the Paramount decision by offering a means by which studios might continue to control the workplace despite divestiture and despite the unions. "The working relationship between the MPAA and the committee was less a concession vis-à-vis control of a product line than a strategy on the part of the studio establishment to regain control over the marketplace, itself in the process of postwar privatization" through the leadership of Eric Johnston and the MPAA (Lewis 17).

With the outbreak of the Korean War in 1950, the emphasis of the information service shifted sharply from a "full and fair picture" of America to one with more definite objectives. President Truman embarked on his "Campaign of Truth," which brought a major expansion of information programs and an emphasis on the unification of culture and information as propaganda instruments. The immediate political objectives of the program were to counter Soviet propaganda attacks, prevent the expansion of communism and marshal cooperation between free world nations. Programs were designed specifically to deter further aggression, to help maintain the stability and cohesion of the countries of the non–Communist world, and to inspire in them confidence in their mutual capacity to meet any eventualities (Daugherty 31).

In the military establishment in Washington, D.C., psychological warfare had ceased at the end of World War II. Several months after the outbreak of hostilities in Korea, in June 1950, the Department of the Army created the Office of the Chief of Psychological Warfare as a special staff section. The seemingly ever-growing tendency for various agencies interested in international operations to engage directly in propaganda and information activities, as well as the increasing awareness that acts of governments themselves carry great psychological warfare implications, led to the demand for some coordination at the executive level. Therefore, President Truman announced the establishment of a national Psychological Strategy Board (PSB), whose mission was to coordinate "foreign information and psychological strategy in situations where joint action by more than one agency of the Government is required in this field" (Daugherty 31).

Filmmaking under the OIE focused on the production of documentaries. The International Motion Picture Division (IMPD) was headed by Herbert T. Edwards, who had much experience making and distributing documentaries as the director of motion picture distribution for the Republican National Committee. The division produced some 40 reels itself and released 60 commercially produced films a year in 14 languages. Additionally, the film bureau turned out a weekly newsreel called "News of the World" and a more comprehensive monthly pictorial news magazine. They also maintained a supplementary backlog of more than 1,000 films inherited from the defunct Office of War Information and the Office of the Coordinator of Inter-American Affairs. All these subjects were re-edited and brought up to date with new commentaries. The content of the newly produced films was determined by the State Department policy experts, who were guided by reports from special film officers and other information personnel attached to U.S. embassies and consulates. Frequently the films were filmed at different intellectual levels according to Grant Leenhouts, the associate chief of the IMPD, "One version being aimed at informed people ... while the other designed for the uneducated masses" (Pryor, "Films Aid 'Truth Campaign'" 81). Preparation for the films for the masses was produced in consultation with anthropologists such as Dr. Margaret Mead. The budgets for IMPD increased steadily under the Truman administration. Many of the films were carried into remote areas that lacked theaters through a vast network of more than 1,200 16mm mobile projection units scattered throughout the world. By 1950, the audience for OIE films topped 125 million worldwide. The reception of these films was not always welcoming. Reports from field agents told of instances where the "opposing forces had arranged demonstrations involving physical violence as well as costly vandalism" (ibid.). Theater screens were destroyed by "knife wielding" demonstrators, and theater operators were threatened with physical harm. An important function of the IMPD according to Leenhouts was "to create a closer feeling of kinship between the average foreigner and his American counterpart. In this regard the Government [felt] the need to correct generally the romanticized impression of life popularized by Hollywood's entertainment films" (ibid.).

In April 1950, Edward W. Barrett, Dean Acheson, and the administrator of the Marshall Plan, Paul Hoffman, met with Eric Johnston. The agenda of the meeting was an attempt to get Hollywood's aid in producing documentary shorts with Marshall Plan funds to "mobilize the motion picture industry in this Cold War much as was done in the last war" (Cull, *The Cold War and the United States Information Agency: American Propaganda and Public Diplomacy, 1945–1989* 58). Johnston offered the industry's assistance but pointed to the diplomatic difficulties that Hollywood had already encountered in attempting to assist in the fighting of the Cold War. In 1948, when 20th Century–Fox released *The Iron Curtain* by William A. Wellman, a treatment of the Gouzenko spy case, the U.S. embassies in Paris, Oslo, and elsewhere blocked local distribution on the grounds that "it would stir up too much hostility towards the U.S." (ibid.). Acheson pledged in the future to wire each embassy as necessary to request cooperation with the release of such films. By 1951, the State Department was proposing to underwrite the losses for Hollywood studios agreeing to produce politically useful feature films for foreign distribution (ibid.).

When Dwight Eisenhower delivered his first inaugural speech, he stated that "the future shall belong to the free." The freedom that he called for came at a price. To secure the freedom that America had to offer the rest of the world, a complex web of "institutional control" was established that made it possible to wage the Cold War against the Soviets (Parry-Giles 147). Government officials, academics, and corporations were enlisted to win the ideological battle against Communism. Eisenhower in particular thought that psychological warfare was a key component of his foreign policy initiatives. "Far from being a peripheral aspect of the U.S.–Soviet struggle, Eisenhower believed that the competition for the 'minds and wills of men' was one of its principle battlefields" (Osgood 405). Eisenhower's experiences with psychological warfare during World War II supported his belief in the efficacy of propaganda for waging a war primarily through words rather than military battles. A 1958 casebook, written for psy-warriors in the Eisenhower administration, provides a definition of psychological warfare. It describes the "planned use of propaganda and other actions designed to influence the opinions, emotions, attitudes and behavior of enemy, neutral, and friendly foreign groups in such a way as to support the establishment of national aims and objectives" (Osgood 407). Psychological warfare, therefore, was fought on all fronts, with friends and allies, with the intention of establishing the dominance of the American way of life throughout the world. Though the Soviets were portrayed as the expansionist aggressors, American foreign policy strategies throughout the 1950s show that the United States intended to expand its ideological boundaries.

Eisenhower had vowed when he assumed the presidential office he would improve America's overseas information programs, thus guaranteeing an international network of American propaganda operations. Within weeks of his inauguration, he launched two inquiries into U.S. information overseas: the President's Advisory Committee on International Information Activities, chaired by William H. Jackson, and the President's Advisory Committee on Government Organization, chaired by Nelson Rockefeller. Meanwhile, the Senate Foreign Relations Committee continued its investigation of information initiated by Benton and chaired by Senator Fulbright under the leadership of Bourke Hickenlooper (R-IA). Hickenlooper's witnesses included a delegation from Hollywood, led by Eric Johnston, a witness who was "well known to members" of the committee, and George Weltner, president of Paramount and chairman of the foreign manager's committee of the Motion Picture Export Association (MPEA). Johnston, in his prepared opening statement, articulated the primary discursive positions that the MPAA assumed in its relationship with the U.S. government. The MPAA's foremost concern was the continued intercession of the government in trade disputes with foreign governments that might disrupt the flow of Hollywood films abroad. This concern was becoming even more pressing at this time, as the domestic market began to be seriously eroded by the divestiture of the Hollywood studios and the emergence of television.

In order to maintain a favorable relationship with U.S. government officials, the MPAA continued to argue that Hollywood films were an exceptionally powerful and persuasive means of communication capable of effectively presenting the American way of life abroad. Johnston, therefore, positioned the MPAA as directly engaged in the ideological battles of the Cold War and willing to take on the burdens that were commensurate with the need to present a true and balanced image of America. He described how "the leaders of the American motion-pictures industry have constantly recognized that the power of the film to influence audiences carries with it a commensurate and exacting responsibility. The importance of this sense of responsibility is heightened by the current ideological world struggle for the allegiance of mankind" ("Overseas Information Programs of the United States" 231). As evidence of the ideological force of Hollywood films, Johnston cited the Soviet directive of July 1950 that went out from Moscow to Soviet outposts around the world: "It is imperative to render the American cinema, this weapon of most aggressive imperialism, harmless." This verified Johnston's claim that "American films were doing too good a job of telling the story of freedom to people everywhere.... American films have been called ambassadors for democracy — ambassadors the Kremlin would like recalled" (ibid. 233).

As the senators continued throughout the hearing to read letters and relate reports from government officials abroad concerning the detrimental effects of Hollywood cinema on American foreign policy, Johnston turned to the Production Code Administration as the industry's major wall of protection against content that could damage America's image abroad. With the senators openly debating the possibility of greater government oversight in the production of commercial films in Hollywood, Johnston discussed the creation of the MPAA's own information service on overseas operations headed by Addison Durland in the Production Code Administration. Durland had first joined the PCA when he had been hired by John Hay Whitney to be the industry liaison for the Office of the Coordinator of Inter-American Affairs during the war years. Durland was responsible for checking every script that passed through the PCA office to determine if there was "anything harmful to the country, or any country in which that picture is likely to be shown" ("Overseas Information Programs of the United States" 233).

The International Committee of the MPAA was established to give formal recognition to the work of the foreign experts at each studio who met regularly to exchange information and current problems in their field (Eldridge 154). The only aspect of the Production Code that dealt directly with issues of national identity was Article 10, which stated that "the just rights, history, and feelings of any nation are entitled to most careful consideration and respectful treatment." The function of this clause was to protect the image of the nations outside of the United States from offensive and stereotypical treatment. No aspect of the PCA was explicitly concerned with the image of America being sent abroad. The MPAA's primary reason for setting up an international committee was to protect overseas markets from the possibility of closure due to censorship imposed by other nations. As Luraschi explained, "The idea was to try to make the picture please the maximum number internationally" (Eldridge 152).

Concerns over possible censorship in foreign markets was indeed justified, as both national censorship boards and the U.S. government stepped in to restrict the exhibition of films found to be morally questionable. In 1955, the British Board of Censors issued a general warning to Hollywood to tone down scenes of violence, passion and exploitation of sex or else risk having such pictures banned from distribution in Great Britain (Pryor, "Film Studios Get British Warning" 28). The board did reject six Hollywood films, and two were so cut up that they could not be distributed. The loss of the British market to these films cost the companies that sponsored them $2,000,000 in revenue according to the European manager of the MPEA. German exhibitors placed 30 percent of Hollywood films on the proscribed list for children under the age of 16. "Brutality" was the primary reason for the barring of American films for young audiences and in some cases the cutting of films before they could be viewed by adults (Pryor, "German Outlines Film Censorship" 33). Even U.S. information officials denied the exhibition of 82 Hollywood films in several countries overseas because they were found to "hurt the nation abroad." In 1958 the USIA provided Congress with a list of the "black-listed" films, which they were able to censor because they were scheduled for exhibition in countries that were still participating in the IMG program. Films on the list included *All the King's Men*, *All Quiet on the Western Front*, and *The Sweet Smell of Success* ("U.S. Lists Movies It Limits Abroad" 46). By the end of the 1950s, the PCA had been significantly weakened. When Geoffrey Shurlock became head of the PCA in 1954 he immediately set a different tone from the agency that had been under the leadership of Joseph I. Breen. With the domestic market rapidly shrinking, Shurlock understood that "a significant market awaited more adult-themed pictures and that the studios could not be expected to cooperate with a production code that prevented them from better exploiting the adult demographic" (Lewis 111). Therefore, while Johnston in his congressional testimony claimed that the PCA was effective in censoring material that might be damaging to America's prestige abroad, he simultaneously argued that for Hollywood films to be economically viable they needed to be "entertaining or people won't go to see them. They must have life and action, or you can't get the people into the theaters" ("Overseas Information Programs of the United States" 277).

Testifying to the important functions of motion pictures in the international information program was William Grenoble, acting assistant administrator in charge of the International Motion Picture Service. The USIS had been producing predominantly short, 20-minute, documentaries covering a wide variety of subjects that could easily be packaged into a program by the field agent. Approximately half of the films used were produced originally for American audiences by private organization and agencies in the United States. The remainder were produced to IIA specifications on contract by private motion picture productions, many of which were filmed in the countries for which they were intended. The films were being administered by 50 film officers working in 87 countries and in 135 posts. Firstly, according to Grenoble, "the films are an effective instrument for conveying information and understanding." Due to their ability "visually to portray people in action and events as they occur ... they are the closest approximation to an actual experience that is possible to convey through a communications medium" ("Overseas Information Programs of the United States" 977). Furthermore, a field agent can use film as a means to attract an audience and then supplement the screening with lectures, exhibits, recording, and discussions. "Motion pictures thus provide a flexible medium around which to build a diverse information approach" (ibid. 978).

Part of Eisenhower's presidential initiatives included the reorganization of information services into a more cohesive and centralized agency. With this agenda in mind, Congress on June 1, 1953, removed information services from the State Department and created a new agency, the United States Information Agency, with sole responsibility for the conduct of information programs. The USIA was created with the understanding that the primary and overriding purpose of American propaganda should be "to persuade foreign peoples that it lies in their interests to take action consistent with the national objectives of the American people" (Hogan 141). In 1954, the NSC (National Security Council) agreed to a mission for the USIA, which stated that the "purpose of the U.S. Information Agency shall be to submit evidence to peoples of other nations by means of communication techniques that the objectives and policies of the United States are in harmony with and will advance their legitimate aspirations for freedom, progress and peace." This purpose would be carried out by "explaining and interpreting to foreign peoples the objectives and policies of the United States Government" and also by "unmasking and countering hostile attempts to distort or frustrate the objectives and policies of the United States" (Cull, *The Cold War and the United States Information Agency: American Propaganda and Public Diplomacy, 1945–1989* 102). The USIA would play a prominent role during the years of the Eisenhower administration. With the directive to "present America accurately to the eyes and ears and hearts of the world," the USIA established libraries throughout the world that provided classes, books, radio shows, artistic presentations and films celebrating American capitalism and democracy (Osgood 416).

The first director of the USIA was Theodore Streibert, the former chairman of Mutual Broadcasting System radio network and the president of the station WOR in New York City. Streibert had much experience in communications working with Cinema Credits Corporation, FBO Pictures, and Pathe before joining WOR and Mutual in 1935. Streibert worked to develop the USIA's output of film and television. By the end of 1953, USIA films claimed an audience of 500 million worldwide, and the USIA served 210 film libraries around the world. USIA posts had a total of 6,000 projectors and 350 mobile motion picture units. In July 1954 the USIA launched *Our Times*, a monthly 20-minute newsreel of events bearing on U.S. policy that was shown in 31 languages in 84 countries. Streibert determined that all USIA films should be "hard hitting anti–Communist films calculated to expose Communist lies and distortions or designed to support and clarify American foreign policy" (Cull, *The Cold War and the United States Information Agency: American Propaganda and Public Diplomacy, 1945–1989* 109). Over two-thirds of the USIA's anti-communist films were produced in the field. The creation of a fully functional, centralized motion picture industry for the production of government-sponsored, American propaganda films was continually stymied by the Congress, which was divided over the issue of using taxpayers' money for the production of cultural propaganda. Work tended to be piecemeal, with larger feature-length documentaries frequently contracted out to major educational film companies and independent documentary filmmakers. The USIA also relied heavily on industrial films produced by major U.S. corporations that were made available by those companies for government-backed distribution abroad.

As Hollywood's domestic market dropped precipitously during the 1950s, its overseas market became crucial to the continued growth of the U.S. film industry. Though there continued to be congressional attacks on Hollywood throughout the 1950s on the damage it was doing to America's image abroad, Congress never suggested that they would in any way hinder the industry's worldwide expansion. As Johnston proudly proclaimed in the *New York Times* in 1954, "American movies now occupy 65 to 70 percent of the available screen time in theaters throughout the world. There still is a large market to be explored, he said, because there are 'many millions' of persons in far away countries who cannot see movies regularly because of the lack of facilities" (Pryor, "Johnston Expects New Movie Gains" 27). Therefore, as U.S. commercial films continued to proliferate abroad, foreign audiences would be exposed to both Hollywood films and U.S. government–produced films, causing a dissonance in their conception of American national identity. As one U.S. information officer reported, "A Filipino who recently attended a USIA showing of a film depicting our humane treatment of the American Indian" came up to the operator and said, "How can you expect me to believe what I have just seen after seeing *Devil's Doorway* last evening at the Avenue Theater?" ("Overseas Information Programs of the United States" 239).

In the face of these messages that "Americans live in a cultural wasteland, peopled only with gadgets and frankfurters and atom bombs," Eisenhower stepped up his investment in the arts as an expression of the American way of life. In 1954, he created an Emergency Fund of $5 million annually for musical and dramatic presentations abroad and for U.S. participation in international trade fairs. The program was made permanent in 1956 when Congress created the International Cultural Exchange and Trade Fair Participation Act of 1956. Fairs and exhibitions were ideally suited venues for nation building with both private and public funds combined for the creation of a clearly articulated platform for the expression of American ideology. The Brussels World's Fair was "the most spectacular piece of U.S. propaganda in Europe" in 1958 (Cull, *The Cold War and the United States Information Agency: American Propaganda and Public Diplomacy, 1945–1989* 159), and yet the conflicting representations of American hegemony that defined the relationship between Hollywood commercial cinema and government-sponsored films persisted at the fair.

The Brussels World's Fair provides a snapshot image of Eisenhower's psychological warfare in action. Framed within the goals of the USIA, it presents a uniquely contained example of America's program of propaganda directed toward its European allies, who were considered a key target for their information programs. As Howard Taubman, the chief music critic at *The New York Times*, reported, "It will be the place where the Cold War, fought with the weapons of art and drama, music and dance, architecture, books and films, will reach a climax." The Brussels World's Fair would be "the most concentrated and spectacular, of a grand campaign whose objective is the minds and hearts of men" (Taubman, "Cultural Front" 12).

For the Brussels World's Fair, the USIA enlisted the aid of many of its most important intelligence agents. The initial planning meeting was convened at the Center for International Studies at MIT, a CIA–funded think tank. The earliest planning sessions for the fair included the economist and former CIA assistant director Max Franklin Millikan and the economist Walt Rostow, a former OSS officer and a speechwriter for Eisenhower. Rostow and Millikan were actively involved in many of the covert, psychological warfare operations of the administration. They represented a group of experts who were frequently consulted on issues of national security for the government and the academy (Hogan 153n43). The high level of national security experts called in to assist in the planning of the Brussels World's Fair indicated the serious manner in which Eisenhower viewed the fair and the government's involvement in what was being publicly presented as solely an international cultural event. Culture formed the backbone of the USIA's psychological warfare strategies during the Cold War period. Artistic productions were one of the most important elements of the USIA's efforts to project America for a foreign audience. The USIA's goals, as expressed by operatives in their use of culture as psychological warfare, included:

1. The unfavorable stereotype of Americans as cultural barbarians must be counteracted. Americans are regarded throughout the world as uncultured boors and crude, materialistic people "who have no time for the finer things of life." This impression stems from a lack of information, Communist propaganda, and "sour grapes." (Countries that have lagged behind the United States may salvage their national self-esteem by maintaining the myth of our cultural inferiority.)

2. Cultural activity raises U.S. prestige in backward areas. It demonstrates that the U.S. can compete with European colonial powers that have traditionally been dominant in such areas as the Near East, Africa or Latin America.

3. Cultural activity creates a favorable response because people are grateful for the entertainment or inspiration it gives them.

4. Cultural activity is a means to the end of supporting U.S. foreign policy. It impresses people abroad with the fact that American foreign policy can be trusted and accepted because it is made by cultured and civilized people [Bogart and Bogart 91].

Eisenhower's psychological warfare programs, then, consciously sought to emphasize the cultural achievements of the American people as a way to counteract attacks concerning the United States' preoccupation with materialism and the notion that their only cultural achievements were in the commercial arts. Countering this perception was especially important in negotiating the United States' relationship with Europe, considered, in the West, to be the center of the world's greatest artistic achievements. Questions of both high and low cultural forms were especially centered on the dominance of Hollywood films abroad. USIA officers and the administration officials targeted Hollywood as the main purveyors of false and negative images of America, and so the USIA produced thousands of films during the 1950s for exhibition to millions around the world in order to create a "true" image of America.

Hollywood had an advantageous relationship with the U.S. government. The U.S. government exerted influence on the motion picture industry through censorship or positive engagement, which included the overt sponsorship of films. During the Eisenhower administration, this relationship reaches an unprecedented alignment as a result of the House Un-American Activities Committee (HUAC) hearings. Many film histories have documented the impact of HUAC on Hollywood production, but Senator McCarthy's hearings initially led to the purging of the State Department's propaganda programs, including the Voice of America, which he charged with being soft on Communism. As a result of these hearings, Eisenhower removed the propaganda program from the State Department and created the USIA, which was more directly accountable to the president.

The USIA assigned propaganda a more prominent and permanent place in the U.S. foreign policy apparatus. While the HUAC hearings led to a chill within both Hollywood and the USIA, they simultaneously encouraged the production of films that would uphold the American way of life and fight communist propaganda. The USIA considered film vital in its cultural diplomacy strategy, which included supporting the Free World, convincing neutral countries of the desirability of the American ideology, and subverting communist regimes. The USIA's Motion Picture Division produced hundreds of films by Hollywood directors on short-term contracts. These overtly sponsored media productions were central to Cold War cultural diplomacy. They were also part of the strategic framework of a national security state, designed to promote an image of America that would win a total campaign for the hearts and minds of the world.

As this book documents, even during a period when Hollywood would appear to represent the apotheosis of state business, in fact, the government propagandists under Eisenhower considered one of their primary goals the correction of the distorted image of America that Hollywood projected internationally. As a secret USIA summary of U.S. information since the creation of the USIA revealed, "On the whole, that Agency's influence in regard to specific films has been greater in regard to film sequences having foreign policy and foreign relations implications than in regard to aspects of American life depicted. On these matters the industry prefers to be guided largely by its own domestic code and by moral standards established by importing countries" (Cull, *The Cold War and the United States Information Agency: American Propaganda and Public Diplomacy, 1945–1989* 185).

CHAPTER 2

America's Salesman: *Walt Disney's* USA in Circarama

The U.S. pavilion at the 1958 Brussels World's Fair was an ideological project constructed in order to push visitors toward a positive outlook on the United States at a time when the nation's international reputation was being severely challenged by Soviet propaganda. Eisenhower's second term was also beset with concerns that the administration was not dealing with its diplomatic, military, and domestic problems. Many Europeans feared the rapid militarization of the United States and its concomitant expansion of atomic power and additionally condemned its racial injustice. The Brussels World's Fair offered the U.S. government an opportunity to calm these fears and present an equitable image of the nation. The fair exemplifies the type of soft psychological warfare developed in the Eisenhower administration in order to propagate a positive image of America throughout the world. The U.S. pavilion was constructed to create an actual space that would become America for its visitors, and this was an America demarcated by its ideological imperatives. Even though the 1950s is often characterized as a time of the homogenization of American life and the solidification of traditional values against the onslaught of the communist threat, the difficulty on the part of both state and private entities to develop a coherent and stable national image to put on display for an European audience points to the inadequacy of the conception of American popular culture as a hegemonic force. As Susan Hayward has argued, "Traditionally the 'national' of a cinema is defined in terms of its difference from other cinemas of other nations, primarily in terms of its difference from the cinema of the United States (i.e. Hollywood)" (Hayward 8). What is left out of discussions of national cinemas is the question of what constitutes the "national" in Hollywood cinematic production. This chapter, through the analysis of a film produced specifically to capture the image of America for an international audience, argues that Hollywood as a perceived hegemony in fact did not present a coherent and recognizable image of American national identity and that American propagandists struggled during this period to attempt to articulate and present an acceptable image of America for international consumption.

As recent historians have argued, the Cold War was primarily a rhetorical war that depended upon the newest developments in mass communications as a means of persuasion. One of the central goals of the Eisenhower administration was the implementation of an effective propaganda strategy as an offensive against the Soviets. Shortly after his election, Eisenhower appointed the President's Committee on International Information Activities to study America's propaganda programs headed by New York businessman William Jackson. The committee concluded that America's propaganda programs had failed in the past due to their "haphazard projection of too many and too diffuse propaganda themes" (Parry-Giles 265). Their recommended central goal for America's information program was that "men and women throughout the world on both sides of the Iron Curtain must come to believe that what we are, and what we stand for in the world, is consistent with their aspirations" (Parry-Giles 266). Government officials saw Hollywood cinema as the primary source of the distorted and destructive image of America that foreign audiences were assumed to have accepted as true and correct.

The exhibit that had the most success in attracting and selling the American way of life to Europeans at the Brussels fair was created by Walt Disney. Disney captured a saleable image of America that eluded official American propagandists. Disney's transformation into an ambassador for the U.S. government and the American way of life was shaped by two significant events within the Disney studio. Firstly, the conversion of the Disney studio into wartime production marked Walt Disney's first direct involvement with the production of propaganda films for the government. Twenty-eight percent of the Disney studio personnel were drafted into the war, and seventy five percent of the studio's output was targeted for the government. These films included animated instructional films for the armed forces, such as *Four Methods of Flush Riveting*, along with jingoistic cartoon shorts including *The New Spirit*, which had been commissioned by the Treasury Department to convince the general public to pay their income taxes in order to support the war effort. Additionally, Disney threw himself into producing his package films, *Saludos Amigos* and *The Three Caballeros*, for the Office of Coordinator of Inter-American Affairs, an office created in 1940 under the direction of Nelson Rockefeller, who had significant investments in the Standard Oil subsidiary in Venezuela, in order to promote relations between the United States and Latin America. By the war's end, Disney is estimated to have produced between 150 and 300 hours of government movies. These films kept the studio from bankruptcy and closure. Though Disney reportedly expressed to Treasury Department officials his fear of being labeled a propagandist in the public mind and the damage that it might cause to his reputation as a "whimsical, non-political artist," his extensive involvement in government-backed, pro–American propaganda films provided Disney and the studio with the expertise in the production of effective political messages for a popular audience (Gabler 389). Secondly, the bitter and divisive studio strike in 1941 convinced Disney of a communist conspiracy to destroy his studio. The strike converted Disney into an avowed anti-communist and directly lead to his assumption of the position of the first vice president of the Motion Picture Alliance for the Preservation of American Ideals, an industry organization publicly opposed to leftist influences in the film industry. In September 1947, when the House Committee Un-American Affairs under Chair J. Parnell Thomas began its investigations of communist influence in Hollywood, Disney's name was among a list of 45 "Possible Friendly Witnesses" compiled by the FBI. And Disney was also among the select group of friendly witnesses initially called to testify. In his testimony before the committee, Disney claimed that the 1941 strike had been supported by "Commie front organizations" and that "throughout the world all the Commie groups began a smear campaign against [him] and [his] pictures" (Watts 284).

By the 1950s, Walt Disney was viewed by American intelligence agencies as a singular figure in Hollywood who could be relied upon to spread the officially sanctioned message of the American way of life. Before the CIA–backed overthrow of the Iranian government in 1952, the American Embassy in Tehran sent a classified message to the Department of State suggesting that "if the Department is considering the production of films of more obvious propaganda type, that a short motion picture, probably of ten minutes duration, that pokes fun at the communist system without mentioning it as such, would find an appreciative audience in Iran. Further, if this film were done in the style of Disney, using his technique with the familiar Mickey Mouse, Donald Duck, Pluto, and so forth, the reception would be further enhanced" (Wells, archival document). In 1954, J. Edgar Hoover made Disney a special agent in charge contact for the FBI. In an office memorandum to Hoover, the Los Angeles special agent in charge wrote that "because of Mr. Disney's position as the foremost producer of cartoon films in the motion picture industry and his prominence and wide acquaintanceship in film production matters, it is believed that he can be of valuable assistance to this office and therefore it is my recommendation that he be approved as an SCA contact" (Smoodin 161).

Even with his stellar reputation as a spokesman for the American way of life, the HUAC investigations of Hollywood had significantly altered the tenor

of the popular discourse and the perception of film as a form of escapist entertainment. Questions about the communist infiltration of American film production had transformed film, in the public mind, into a political medium
capable of projecting ideologically significant images that could have a dele-
terious and lasting impact on its viewers. Both the popular press and government officials debated and perseverated over the "distorted image of America"
that Hollywood was popularizing abroad. Norman Cousins, the editor-in-
chief of the *Saturday Review of Literature* and a well-known advocate of liberal
causes including nuclear disarmament, wrote a well-publicized three-part edi-
torial in the *Saturday Review* titled "The Free Ride" in which he argued that
"Soviet propaganda was not nearly as damaging as the grotesquely distorted
view of the American people being created abroad by our own motion pictures" (Cousins, "The Free Ride, Part II" 20). The overriding complaint about
the image that Hollywood was propagating was two-fold and linked. Firstly,
Hollywood films created the impression that most Americans were excessively
materialistic. As Cousins described, "We don't all live in plush duplex apart-
ments with elaborate cocktail bars and retinues of servants. We don't all sleep
in kingsize beds with silk topsheets nor do we all arise languidly at noon for
breakfast in bed" (Cousins, "The Free Ride" 25). Coupled with the decadence
and hedonism of American capitalism that Hollywood films broadcast internationally was the celebration of immorality and criminality. "We have more
than our share of humanity's faults, but we by no means monopolize them,"
Cousins editorialized. "Nor are we predominantly a nation of murderers,
gangsters, idlers, deadbeats, dipsomaniacs, touts, tarts, and swindlers, as Hollywood would have us appear" (Cousins, "The Free Ride" 25).

   The assault by Cousins on Hollywood films and their detrimental effect
on international perceptions of American society elicited a heated response
from Eric Johnston. Johnston, a significant figure in postwar Hollywood, had
been during the war the president of the U.S. Chamber of Commerce. A successful businessman from Seattle, where he owned four electric companies,
Johnson developed lasting ties with Washington administrators and American
business during his tenure at the Chamber of Commerce. He was a member
of the Economic Policy Subcommittee of the State Department's Advisory
Committee on Postwar Foreign Policy and an outspoken foe of the Soviet
Union. In September of 1945 he became president of the Motion Picture
Association of America, replacing Will Hays. Unlike Hays, who had been
hired to exercise his authority within and on the film industry, Johnston was,
from the outset, "designated as chief Washington lobbyist for the movie studios. Spending nearly all his time in the capital, Johnston worked closely with
the Department of State, Justice, and Commerce, the Coordinator of Inter-

American Affairs, the Director of Reconversion, members of Congress, and, often enough, with the White House and President Truman — in short, with anyone who could promote the sale of American films abroad" (Ceplair and Englund 247–48). Johnston found Cousins' arguments too reductive, and he argued foreign audiences were getting "a balanced diet of American pictures," and that the "whole picture of America cannot be unwound from a single reel" (Johnston 11). Additionally, American democracy was necessarily linked to consumerism and materialism, and it was something Hollywood films should flaunt as a means of selling the American way. "What would Mr. Cousins have us do?" Johnston asked. "Can we paint the American scene in film without showing our automobiles, our telephones, our bathtubs, our better clothes, better roads, higher buildings, refrigerators, radios, and household conveniences? ... These 'dazzling gadgets' are products of a democracy, and we have them in such a multitude largely because we work and live by the rule of democracy" (Johnston 11).

Walt Disney's extensive work for the government and his overt stance against Communism made Disney into the one Hollywood executive that could be depended on to assist in the propaganda battle being waged against the Soviets in the 1950s. Walt Disney was the one Hollywood studio executive chosen by the Cambridge Study Group for the Brussels Universal and International Exhibition at MIT, along with a group of America's top business and cultural leaders, to help determine the thematic basis for the American pavilion at the fair. The study group was composed of the key members of the CIA–funded Center for International Studies (CENIS). The Center had been founded in 1950 by W. W. Rostow, an economics professor who served in the OSS in World War II and later as chief of the State Department's Policy Planning Staff in the Kennedy and Johnson administrations. In 1952, Max F. Millikan, another economist, became the director of the center after a two-year tour of duty as an assistant director of the CIA in Washington. The CENIS was contracted by the USIA as the initial planning group for the Brussels Fair and charged them with determining what "should be the message of our exhibit? How is our message best put across?" ("Letter: USIA Washington, Office of Director"). The first action of the group, which included Rostow, Milliken, Eric Hodgins, Jerome Weisner, Ithiel Pool, and Victor Weisskopf, was to contact 50 of America's top business leaders including Nelson Rockefeller, Thomas Watson, Jr., president of IBM, and Walt Disney, to solicit their view of how America should be presented abroad.

The reliance on a CIA–funded think tank headed by economists and their enlistment of corporate leaders to assist in the preparation of a world's fair pavilion is indicative of the state-private relationships that were formed during the Eisenhower administration. Cultural events, like the fair, were viewed as crucial for the successful achievement of American foreign policy goals, including the spread of liberal democratic capitalism. By the middle of Eisenhower's first administration, there was bipartisan support to transform the United States' free market system into a world system. The CENIS's institutional mission to study the dynamics of the communist system and theorize about the economic and sociopolitical evolution of developing countries placed the group in an advantageous position to contend with the circuitous routes through which social scientific theory enlightens policy communities in government (Pearce 14). The CENIS study group for the fair, in a series of meetings conducted between 1956 and 1958, attempted to articulate a comprehensive strategy for the exhibit that would present for European visitors "The Undiscovered Country." "Of all the nations, great and small," the study group argued, "the United States today is probably the most widely known — as also the most widely misunderstood. To this day, ours, to the foreigner, remains an undiscovered country. The fact is disquieting.... Thus beyond the efforts of our statesmen, our diplomats, our overseas information services, there is an urgent need to bring to ordinary men and women abroad the true picture of what we are and what we are after" (Max Franklin Millikan papers, 1913–1969, MC 188, Box 4, f.119; MIT Archives). The group struggled over the challenge of selling the free market system abroad through the use of soft power techniques. In attempting to write a slogan for the pavilion, it argued that "it is believed that the peculiar American characteristics and traditions which have made this nation unique should be emphasized" (ibid.). And the fair planners needed to determine "basically what has set our nation apart, enabling it to achieve in a relatively short span of years a pinnacle of economic and social supremacy and world leadership?" ("Theme Development Staff Discussions" [ibid.]).

Because of his close governmental ties and his espousal of corporate capitalism as the American way, Walt Disney was ideally suited with managing the challenge that faced the Cambridge study group. The group's initial interview of Disney was conducted by Robert Warner, the coordinator of U.S. Building Exhibits, along with John Hench, one of the designers of Disneyland, at the Burbank studio on January 8, 1957. The summary of the meeting stated that "these gentlemen came up with almost nothing" but that they had "asked for time to study the problem." Disney did suggest that "it was important that we emphasize the fact that we are a people who like to enjoy ourselves. He felt we should play down the idea that we only want money and said we must avoid bragging about money and leisure" ("Interview with Walt Disney and John Hench" [Millikan papers, ibid.]). Warner spent a day touring Disneyland during his visit and by the end of January began negotiations with Walt Disney for the production of a 360-degree film comparable to the park's Circarama attraction. With a proposed budget of a million dollars for the new film, the search began for an official sponsor of the exhibit. James Plaut, the deputy commissioner general of the Brussels Exhibition, wrote Howard Cullman, the commissioner general, that "after due consideration, we feel that this would be the ideal vehicle for Ford. This is based on the fact that General Motors will have a big show in the Belgian section and that Ford is very keen to do something spectacular for the Belgian market.... We are prepared to go so far as to call the undertaking 'Fordarama' which ought to interest them" (Plaut). The selection of a major automobile company for sponsorship of the film was a logical choice since the original Disney attraction was paid for by American Motors and was shot with a camera mounted to a car.

The development of Walt Disney's Circarama occurred at a time when movie attendance had significantly declined in the United States due to the marked increase of television viewership and other leisure activities, including the opening of Disneyland in 1955. A considerable amount has been written about the immense popularity of Disneyland for the postwar suburban, middle-class family. Through the use of television, Disney was able to market his park and his stockpile of films to a new and ready audience. In addition, he was able to develop a symbiotic relationship with corporate sponsors that would fund his projects in exchange for the promotion of their products. Disney's reliance on corporate backing for his theme parks was unprecedented. The future envisaged in the park's Tomorrowland was based on the prosperity and progress offered by corporate capitalism. Similar to the New York World's Fair of 1939 and its theme of "Building the World of Tomorrow," images of the future were dominated by a consumer culture that foregrounded the beneficent success of the free enterprise system. The three main exhibitions in Tomorrowland at the time of the opening of Disneyland were American Motors' *Circarama*, the Richfield Show called "The World Beneath Us," and TWA's "Flight to the Moon." All three exhibits emphasized film innovations that combined education and entertainment in order to showcase Disneyfied corporate promotions. Corporate involvement in sites of leisure activity was common throughout the early 20th century especially at world's fairs. But Disney greatly expanded corporate involvement in his theme park by using other corporation's monetary investment in pavilions to create a distinctly Disney-based product that would serve as a source of public relations advertising masked by the lure of entertainment. Although the *Disneyland* television program proved to be an unexpected success, Disneyland itself was considered a risky investment before its opening. Therefore, companies that chose to enter into an agreement with Disney at the park were counting on the popularity of the Walt Disney name to provide them with a distinctly white, middle-class, suburban audience and clientele.

Disneyland, with its distinct vision of America and especially American history, was not unique to 1950s culture. Disney's complete faith in corporate culture as the American way was derived from a sentimental attachment to a bygone America. The Disneyland Main Street that formed the entranceway into the park was grounded in Disney's own reminiscences of his childhood in Marceline, Missouri, at the turn of the century. Though Disney actually spent only a few years of his childhood in a small, mid-western town, it served as a core mythological space for his own conceptions of American identity. This combination of faith in industry leaders, hard work and individual initiative pervaded his other projects as well. The bedrock values were also the cornerstone of the 1950s, with that decade's emphasis on the family, America's divinely appointed manifest destiny, and the rise of a corporate culture. Two of the major inspirations for Disney's Disneyland were John Ford's Greenfield Village in Michigan and John D. Rockefeller's Williamsburg in Virginia. As a Disney-produced book on Walt Disney explained, "Walt Disney clearly loved America and her colorful history. He long held the belief that we, as Americans, should recognize the extraordinary influence of historical events on our present day lives" (*Walt Disney Imagineering*, 62). History for Disney was not something in the past, but it was the living basis of our lives in the present. Disney frequently visited both Ford's and Rockefeller's own reconstructed Main Streets before he created his version in Anaheim. Ford's recreation at Greenfield Village is a living museum meant to give future generations a "tangible picture of the life their ancestors led, especially the men of America's Industrial Revolution" (Bowie, "The Past Is Present in Greenfield Village" 107). Ford sent people around the world to collect artifacts of the industrial age, including a meticulous reconstruction of Thomas Edison's Menlo Park laboratory. As an inspiration and friend of Disney's, it is important to note Ford's conception of the significant events and people of America's past and the roots of American culture. America's great past was founded on independent thinkers, the ones who were willing to go out and search for their own destiny and create their own fortunes. These were men who had initiative, common sense, and core Christian values. Ford's greatest hero was Thomas Edison, and in 1929 he staged "Light's Golden Jubilee" to commemorate the 50th anniversary of the electric light bulb. While proudly displaying the Menlo lab reconstruction at Greenfield Village, Ford asked Edison, "Well, what do you think of it?" Edison shook his head, "Henry it's 99.9% perfect." "What?"

Ford asked incredulously. "There's something wrong?" "Yes," Edison replied, "We never kept the place so clean" (Bowie, "The Past Is Present in Greenfield Village" 109). This was the history that America should be grounded on — technological wonders and products that dramatically transformed our world for the better, but that need to be cleaned up a little for younger generations. The replication of Edison's lab stood alongside Ford's actual family homestead that was transported intact to the property and where he would often sleep on the same bed he used as a boy. Disney would also spend many nights in his own reconstructed Main Street in Disneyland. Disney visited Greenfield Village on several occasions before the opening of Disneyland, and the design of the Village had a clear influence on his own designs and his position concerning the values that his park should instill.

Disney was also a frequent visitor to Rockefeller's colonial reconstruction, Williamsburg. Both Williamsburg and Greenfield Village were intended to celebrate a bygone vision of America before traditional, bedrock values became severely challenged by modern culture — the irony being that Ford, Rockefeller, and eventually Disney were all instrumental catalysts for the transformations that occurred within American society in the 20th century. These villages went back to a time when class, gender, and racial boundaries were intact. None of the cataclysmic events of the modern age had corrupted the specific conception of American national identity that they wanted to maintain. Just like in his many visits to Greenfield Village, Disney frequently immersed himself in the colonial reconstruction at Williamsburg. He enjoyed the low-key historical presentation but not its non-profit status. A park official related that "one evening at dinner at King Arms Tavern [Disney] asked, 'How much do those carriages cost, how many do you have, and how much do you charge riders?' I told him we usually run two or three carriages or wagons with horses; they cost $8,000 to $10,000 each; one fancy carriage cost approximately $35,000 — and all were hand made. As for the price per ride, I told him we were charging $2 per person. Disney looked at me in disbelief. Then quickly he solved the problem in his imaginative, profit making way: What you should do is mass produce wagons. Put a lot of seats in each one, charge every person 25 cents, and keep them going early and late up and down the Duke of Glouchester Street. You'd make a lot of money" (Gonzales 109). A visit to Disneyland today will quickly show how Disney put his marketing ideas into action: one can still pay for a ride up and down his own Main Street. Disney's visits to Williamsburg stretched from the 1940s until his death. When he learned that he had terminal cancer, he made a final pilgrimage during which he sat for hours in the business section near the College of William and Mary. As David Gonzales recounts, "He never sat alone. People by the score recognized him quickly.... Some of his last days were spent pleasantly holding court outside the Williamsburg theater—a final home away from home for him" (Gonzales 110). Disney's ideas for Disneyland were grounded in the nationalistic and patriotic values of both Ford and Rockefeller, and these ideas were the core values of the dominant culture in the 1950s. Disney also added another important ingredient of the time—corporate ingenuity—in order to make his park the most profitable in the world.

In order to understand the evolution of the Circarama phenomenon that proved so popular at the Brussels World's Fair of 1958, it is instructive to chart the history of the "ride" within the context of Disneyland itself. Circarama was designed for a multitude of reasons beyond standard film exhibition. It was part travelogue, part patriotic anthem to the American way, and predominantly an advertisement within a corporate-sponsored playground. By the time Disney's Circarama reached Brussels, it had undergone significant development and refinement as a product of Disney's synergy. The Circarama technology was originally developed by Ub Iwerks, who had been with Disney since the start of their animation careers, but had by the 1950s been consigned to the engineering barns because of interpersonal conflicts. The Circarama exhibition required considerable financial investment for its initial development. A contemporaneous article in *Business Screen*, the industrial film journal, made special mention of the complexity and ingenuity involved in this new widescreen technology. Even considering Disney's well-known perfectionism, his extensive investment in the technological development of Circarama signaled his confidence in the ability of this one-of-a-kind experience to effectively reach crowds of consumers.

The format of the original Circarama film was that of a traditional travelogue, *A Tour of the West*, displayed on a new 360-degree screen. The selection of a travelogue as the source material for the film can be traced to the recent development of Disney's True-Life series of nature documentaries that began with *Seal Island* in 1948. These documentaries became a regular feature of the original *Disneyland* television series, and in the 1950s Disney created another related documentary series, *People and Places*. As Margaret King has shown, these documentaries anthropomorphized nature by transforming animals and their environments into human scenarios. They also used the symbolic landscapes of the United States in order to create films flooded with American optimism and manifest destiny (King). James Algar, who wrote five Academy Award pictures for Disney, including *Nature's Half Acre*, *The Living Desert* and *The Vanishing Prairie*, and also directed several wartime films produced by the studio for the U.S. Armed Forces, was the scriptwriter for *The USA in Circarama*.

Disney's interest in Circarama was a direct product of his desire to compete with the hugely successful widescreen formats that transformed film exhibition in the 1950s. It also provided Disney with the opportunity to establish his own specialized exhibition spaces for his films. Television became one aspect of Disney's expanding role as an exhibitor. With the Circarama films, he was able to turn theaters themselves into attractions. The difference between Disney's widescreen developments and other popular widescreen technologies, such as Cinerama, was that the film was only one element in an integrated theatrical experience that also included dioramas, narration, and the actual integration of products into the show.

Even with the considerable financial investment in the Circarama technology, and the enlistment of many of Disney's most talented Imagineers, the development of Circarama was not without its setbacks. The first prototype of the 360-degree camera consisted of 11 cameras that caused eyestrain and dizziness. In his quest for perfection, Disney challenged his crew to eliminate this visual problem. Engineers discovered that the problem was that "because the entire camera lens faced outwards, they did not share exactly the same focal or nodal point. In order for the system to work properly, the cameras had to be aimed and focused at the same central nodal point." The engineers were able to quickly solve the problem, and the second generation "required only nine cameras, all focused into the same centralized focal point, which was a highly polished, angled mirror. The system worked flawlessly" (Walt Disney Imagineering 62).

The financiers of the Circarama exhibit were American Motors and Kelvinator appliances (the producers of the durable goods par excellence of the 1950s), who invested $350,000 into developing the show in order to "make friends who will eventually become customers for cars or appliances" (ibid.). American Motors needed the potentially vast audience available at Disneyland probably more than Disney needed their investment. In 1955, American Motors had lost nearly seven million dollars, and it lost another twenty million in 1956. Their losses were a result of a price war launched by Henry Ford II in 1953, in which he vowed to beat Chevrolet in sales or "kill the company trying" (Foster). This had, as might be expected, a deleterious effect on other automobile manufacturers. Independent automobile companies struggled throughout the 1950s to survive by merging with other companies. American Motors was the result of the merger of Hudson Motor Car Company and Nash Motors in 1954, which was necessary in order for them to compete with the Big Three automobile companies. Even though the company was experiencing a financial crisis, American Motors recognized the potentially great economic returns that an investment in a ride at Disney's amusement park might mean. They eagerly invested their money into a project that was entirely under the control of Disney. The company would actually run out of money just as Disney was about to start shooting, and the film was completed in two weeks with most of the final footage made up of test shots that were run to see if the equipment worked.

Circarama, with its eleven projectors, showed you simultaneously "where you are, where you are going and where you have been." Not unlike television, the film was one element in a broad display of consumer goods. The theater contained softly lit displays of Kelvinator appliances, and around the open portion of the screen was a sampling of automobiles. Kelvinator, as a manufacturer of home appliances, had devised a series of successful advertisements at the end of the war that showed the transformative powers of its appliances in bringing together the postwar family in their dream homes. Kelvinator, in their ads, made the home into a "kingdom all our own" by presenting to female readers of popular magazines a vision of familial enchantment through appliances. As one ad in *Life* proclaimed,

> We'll follow our noses to the kitchen door. It will be like no kitchen you've ever seen before. It will be an enchanted place ... with a wonderful automatic electric range that will cook by itself while we are away ... or have breakfast ready when we awake. And there'll be the very newest refrigerator, bigger and roomier, with gleaming shelves chock full of cheeses and cold cuts and steak ... and salad and greens that sparkle with dew behind magic compartments of glass. And right beside it another kind of a fabulous chest ... a home freezer, something brand new, that we can store with luxurious things like ice cream, asparagus and brook trout. It's all a part of a lovely dream.... This is not a dream. We believe your hope and finer home can and will come true.... This will be our part in the building of a greater, a happier nation ... where every man and every woman will have the freedom and the opportunity to make their dreams come true ["We'll Live in a Kingdom All Our Own," inside cover].

By the time that Kelvinator was placing its appliances into the Circarama exhibit, the dream that its ads evoked as a possible future reality had indeed become true for many Americans. Not that there were electronic ranges instantly making meals, but the American suburban kitchen had become the dream landscape crafted in their advertisement. The newest refrigerators, stoves, and dishwashers were filling the homes of America, helping to build a strong and robust economy.

The Disneyland Circarama film opened with a "line of Kelvinator appliances presented: one on each screen," supposedly in order to "give the audience the feeling of the medium" ("Techniques at Disney's Tomorrowland" 38–39). This was an audience that had already become familiar with Disney's method of combining entertainment with corporate sponsorship through his television show. The appliances and automobiles were recognizable friends for the fans of the television show, who had been primed for months with regular updates about the building and opening of the park. And yet this blatant commercial placement, though typical of television, was not a standard experience for film viewers. Most Americans held the view that "the cinema was supposed to be a place where you could escape from all those annoying commercials seen on network television" (Bigness D1). But the wonder of the new widescreen technology and the sensory overload that the experience created facilitated audience acceptance of the placement of products within the screen as yet another enchanting Disney creation. As *The New York Times* described two weeks after the park opened, "For the most startling innovation in movie presentation, one will have to visit Disneyland.... Walt Disney and the Eastman Kodak Company have hit upon the ultimate in audience participation or envelopment, via a 360 degree screen.... The effect of viewing a motion picture that is going on all around you is fantastic. Particularly overpowering is the sense of motion, or moving with the picture" ("Techniques" 37–38). No mention or judgment is made concerning the fact that the film was simply part of a large advertising campaign directed to the ideal consumers — the nuclear family — that flooded the park grounds.

Circarama was targeting the predominantly middle-class, Southern Californian audience who arrived from the suburbs in their American Motors station wagons. As car travel became a favorite leisure activity for the postwar middle class, Circarama provided a ready inducement to begin planning next summer's trip to all the great American sights. This tour of America's great parks and historical sites was a crucial rite of passage for most middle-class American families, and Disney knew how to market that desire to his audience through the Circarama experience. As a spectator you were placed in the driver's seat of a Nash automobile. The new design breakthrough for the company's Rambler in 1956 was the "huge glass areas to give the interior a light, airy effect.... The windshield was a wraparound, considered a premium feature, as was the rear window" (Foster 23). Similar to the expansive vision provided by the Circarama screen, the newly designed cars reflected the altered vision of a society now satiated with consumer abundance that gazed with confidence on the vast bounty of the world spread before it. The viewer's trip began with a leisurely tour of the shopper's paradise of Beverly Hills, which then abruptly shifted to a police chase on Wilshire Boulevard accompanied by a loud siren screech. The journey continued on to Monument Valley, the Grand Canyon, and finally Las Vegas. Effectively crafted to fit the mores of Disney's middle-class suburban audience, the show provided the mother with the opportunity to examine the newest refrigerator as Junior got to experience the thrills that awaited him in his own automobile, and sister could envision her next date in the backseat at the local drive-in. For father there was the added treat provided by one of the Las Vegas scenes set at poolside. Here the forward cameras "pick[ed] up two charming young ladies in delightfully form-fitting bathing suits. With the cameras fixed and their lenses trained from knee height on their fascinating subjects, the bathing beauties walk[ed] separately with consummate poise along paths on either side of the battery of cameras, meeting each other again at the rear. As expected, the pop-eyed audience [wa]s beside itself trying to follow the action around the screen" (Lipton 185).

American Motors would rebound a few years after the opening of Circarama at Disneyland. Its financial success was tied to those mothers and sons sitting in the audience who were waiting for an economy car, the Rambler, to appear. As George Romney, president of American Motors, explained to an audience of women's clubs, "'Ladies,' he [said], wagging his fingers at them, 'why do you drive such big cars? You don't need a monster to go to the drugstore for a package of hairpins. Think of the gas bill!'" (Bowie, "The Dinosaur Hunter"). Disneyland was closely tied with the rise of the youth market in the 1950s and the dominance of the female consumer in the nuclear family. And these were the markets that got a first-hand look at the Rambler at Disneyland. As an article at the time in *Time* notes, "With thousands of war babies coming of driving age and crying for their own cars, countless families had found the foreign car [and the Rambler] an inexpensive playmate for Junior — and a less precious article to entrust to freewheeling Mom" (Bowie, "The Dinosaur Hunter").

Disney's first Circarama film was a travelogue of America's most popular tourist destinations. Even though it was a main attraction in Tomorrowland, the only futuristic image provided by the exhibit was the film technology that Disney devised in order to out-do all other new widescreen formats. As *Business Screen* reported, "Bigger and wider screens are the unmistakable trend of movie presentation. The best way to predict the future of movie presentation then, was to go to the end of the line — the widest possible screen is a complete circle" ("Techniques" 37). The Circarama exhibit stood alongside other attractions that similarly incorporated film images with corporate slogans. Overall, Disney's world of the future in Tomorrowland was a corporate park fronted with the façade of a fairground. Disney's conception of the future looked back to the successes of the past in order to pave the way for the new glories of our corporate future.

Though many elites began to attack Disney for his sentimentality and anti-intellectualism in the 1950s, he had become a symbol of postwar American society and its dominant values. And these values were very closely aligned with the USIA. During appropriation hearings before the House of Representatives in 1962, Turner Shelton, who headed the International Motion Picture Service within the USIA, described his belief in the power of motion pictures. He said, "Motion pictures create an atmosphere of receptivity. They create an aura that makes people receptive to what we specifically have to say to them. For example, if you know me well and you know my background and someone says something bad about me, you will be able to discount it, that is, if you understand me thoroughly ... motion pictures can make America understood" (MacCann 178).

The Ford Motor Company was the only corporation solicited for sponsorship of *The USA in Circarama*, and the funding negotiations were contentious. Andrews, the regional executive responsible for English, Canadian and German manufacturing for Ford, believed that the "International Division couldn't hope to get a half million dollars worth out of it from an advertising point of view" (Davies, archival document). Eventually, the Ford Motor Company Fund offered $200,000 to be spent on the production and exhibition of the film with the understanding that Ford would have no rights to the equipment and the film after the fair. The U.S. government provided the rest of the $412,000 total budget, with $100,000 allotted to Walt Disney for the production of the film. The film went into production in October of 1957, and a preview of an hour of raw footage was provided for Robert Warner and Walt Disney in November. The footage shot, per the requests of Ford, included a tour of the River Rouge plant including shots of their test track. Additional footage showed "entrancing shots of the New York harbor, of Vermont, of the copper mine and of the Kansas City railway yard. The shopping center was vividly shown, with its acres of parked cars — perhaps a better demonstration of People's Capitalism than anything we can do in words. The harvest scene was breathtaking, with a sea of yellow wheat stretching flat to the horizon in all directions, and blue sky above it there; then the nine combines came at us, in echelon, and passed on either side amid clouds of chaff" (C. Rand, archival document). Shooting continued through November, with the crew photographing aerial shots of San Francisco, the Grand Canyon and the Southwest. The production was halted in December after the studio requested and failed to secure an additional $100,000-plus to complete the film. Bill Anderson, the executive vice president of Walt Disney Studios, wrote Warner that "this show would be delivered at a real financial loss to Walt Disney Productions but, as always the case, all of the money is put into brick, mortar and furnishings with little or nothing left for the entertainment portion." Warner attended a preview screening of the film in March and wrote to Cullman that he had been told by Anderson that "in addition to the

$100,000 we paid them for the production, they have about $100,000 of their own money sunk into it. Off the record, I doubt it. However, the film is very good and I am sure this is going to be a tremendous attraction" (Warner, "Letter to Howard Cullman").

The USA in Circamara had been filmed across the United States to provide a "continuous panorama" of America. The cameramen traveled in a Lincoln Premier and a modified Ford station wagon, and their shooting schedule was broken into three parts. The first shots were of a wheat harvest in upper Montana, which had a dynamic climax shot from on top of the station wagon as nine combines harvested in unison. After the wheat harvest, shooting occurred at Yellowstone National Park and then at the world's largest open pit copper mine in Utah. With a new remote control in hand, the second shooting segment went on to capture fall foliage in New England, the harbors and bridges of New York, and the bustle of Time Square. Then it was off to Rockefeller's newly restored Williamsburg, now a mecca for tourists. Next came the steel mills of Pittsburgh, and the Santa Fe Railway's vast freight yard in Kansas City. Mounted on top of a caboose, the speed of the cameras was undercranked in order to speed up the action in the yard. A major sequence of the film was shot at the Ford Motor Company's River Rouge plant. After this, it was off to a typical gigantic supermarket, then a modern-day cowboy cattle roundup, ending on a vignette of the oil industry near Tulsa. The last shooting segment required the assistance of a B-52 bomber. Since Disney insisted that no parts of the plane should be visible in the image, the Disney engineers devised a boom that would lower the camera seven feet beneath the plane. This segment was thematically a repeat of the Disneyland attraction. The aerial shots captured the stunning grandeur of the American West. Starting with Monument Valley, several trips were made through the Grand Canyon, culminating with the Hoover Dam and a sunset over the Golden Gate Bridge. It was back to the station wagon for a few trips across the bay bridges, running shots of the San Francisco cable cars, and night shots in Chinatown. In all, more than 100,000 feet of 16mm Kodachrome Commercial film was exposed during a year of shooting. This footage was edited to create the 18-minute film. The film was a hallmark of what Michael Schudson has called "capitalist realist" style in its presentation of American life. As applied by Schudson in the context of American advertising, capitalist realism "simplifies and typifies.... It presents lives worth emulating. It always has a message.... It always assumes there is progress. It is thoroughly optimistic, providing a solution ... for any ill or any trouble it identifies" (Guimond 153).

A literal journey across America, the film was narrated and sequenced in the order in which a European visitor would encounter the landmarks of

The Circarama theater attached to the U.S. Pavilion at the Brussels World's Fair
(*This Is America: Official United States Guide Book Brussels World's Fair*).

America. Opening on a sunrise over the New York harbor, the film journeys to the San Francisco Bridge and concludes with the Statue of Liberty. The film is a recreation of the emigrant journey into the Promised Land of American bounty and leisure. In many ways, the chosen images echoed the displays in the Soviet pavilion. Lines of combines harvested fields of wheat; large industrial plants illustrated the mechanical strength of the nation. Disney's presentational form was very similar to the Soviets' with an emphasis on simplicity of meaning and celebration of productivity. This was the image of America that visitors understood and expected. There was no self-conscious pretense or cynical elitism in these images. America was a country in motion, driven by industry, but also deeply rooted in its heritage, as recreated in Williamsburg and its present-day cowboys. The corporate forces of the Ford River Rouge plant provided the leisure to shop in huge modern supermarkets. This was the iconography of America that was immediately recognizable, and it was based on combining America's modern corporate wonders with a nostalgic and sentimental presentation of traditional values.

Disney's intense appreciation of the American landscape was an expression of nationalism in an era of ideological challenge. In 1957, Eric Johnston acknowledged that film was "America's master salesman despite itself.... Hollywood has portrayed the American family using the newest devices from industry but portrayed the family as people, not consumers; people using and enjoying products in their natural settings ... American mass production ... the American assembly line ... received its momentum and reached full speed in very large degree from the selling power of the Hollywood film" (Segrave 195). The original Circarama film used actual Kelvinator goods to sell products to its specifically Californian, suburban audience. *The USA in Circarama* was also specifically geared toward its European audiences; this time, though, the products were Ford automobiles and other material rewards of the American dream. Presented in three languages — English, French, and Flemish — live narrators would adapt their comments to their respective middle-class, European audiences. As Disney insisted to anyone who would listen, "Through entertainment and showmanship, American industry can reach the public" (Watts and Disney 418).

The film was the smash hit of the fair. Surveys of top attractions at the American pavilion consistently placed the Circarama as number one. Long lines formed outside the theater throughout the time of the fair, causing 20 people to pass out in the heat. Female guides were pulled from the exhibit after getting hurt attempting to handle the crowds. Warner reported to Turner Shelton, the director of Motion Pictures for the USIA, that "this is the finest propaganda weapon I have ever seen" (Warner, "Letter to Turner Shelton"). George Allen, the director of the USIA, after viewing the exhibit, was "quite prepared to take the equipment over on the spot" for use in later USIA exhibits and trade shows. Walt Disney spent four days at the fair, and was initially averse to letting the government use the film and the equipment following the show. "Happily," Warner wrote to the USIA, "Walt Disney is a tremendously public spirited person and he finally agreed, with the understanding that it would not be shown in North America and would only be used by the government" (Warner, "Letter to Robert Sivard").

Descriptions of audience responses to the film emphasized the emotional and sensational impact that the experience provided rather than consideration of the political or ideological significance of the images. The *Atlantic Monthly* exclaimed, "The 19 minute movie, a masterpiece by Disney, sweeps its audience through the United States with one dramatic gesture. Americans walk out, heads high, tears in the eye, still hearing the strains of *America the Beautiful*. Visitors from abroad burst out with their favorite superlatives, Fantastique, magnifique, formidable!" (M. May 70). It seemed as there were no dry eyes after they saw Disney's vision of America. *The Christian Century* reporter exclaimed that "going back to The Hague, among all the hundreds I fell in with the elderly Dutch couple with whom I had shared a compartment coming down. They had had a fine but wearying day. The high point? Circarama! 'It was worth all the standing and waiting,' the wife told me. 'When it ended, I felt I had really seen America and met your people. And then the beautiful scenery, with "America the Beautiful" swelling up at the end — we both had tears in our eyes when the lights came on'" (Frakes 1109). The actual scope of the screen enveloped the spectators and made them part of the vast vistas of a free, vibrant and productive society on the move. This was the image of a world leader that Europeans understood. Technology and industry lead the American people forward into a divinely appointed land of liberty and abundance. After several years of testing Circarama before an American audience, Disney had perfected his technique in marketing the American corporate culture to a middle-class audience.

The visceral experience of the film that caused spectators to cover their eyes, and to sway along with the images, created within them a vicarious sensation of being part of the action. Through his application of the wide-screen format, Disney was able to generate the feelings of sentimentalism and wholesomeness that the American pavilion failed to create. The wide-screen technology created a new viewership experience for spectators that resulted in a "wow" effect. As *Variety* reported, "The auditors stand in the center and thus have the sense of completest audience-participation in the degree that one rollercoaster number had to be excised because of the equilibrium impact. The viewers would lean back so far, because of the overly realistic effect, as

Artist's conception of Circarama Theater at the Brussels World's Fair (*Business Screen* magazine, public domain, Prelinger Archive [Archive.org]).

to fall on their backs. Almost the same thing happens in one scene as the auto-bus climbs a steep grade and then descends on the other side" ("Disneyland Circarama Is Wow as Transported to Brussels' Big Expo" 2). The technology made watching the film into a ride that was driven by the viewer's response to a visual onslaught. Circarama was a "cinema of attraction" that was new and unique for the spectators who were accustomed to the single screen theater with stationary seating.

As film screens were expanding due to the onslaught of television, Disney contrived to control both the medium of television and the advent of widescreen technology. As Tony Bennett shows in his discussion of the new 180-degree cinema shows at Blackpool Pleasure Beach that opened in the 1980s, "Whereas thrill rides take the normally stationary body and hurtle it through space, [these rides] hurtle the vision through space whilst fixing the body as stationary" (Bennett 151). Disney was able to make the particularity of American culture into a universal and also create within the spectator the desire to become part of that landscape and society that the Circarama presented. As the trade journal, *Business Screen*, explained, "The best product we have to sell to the people whose curiosity brings them to the World's Fair is American progress and our way of life. In fulfilling this assignment, movies tell a big story and tell it convincingly" ("Film at Brussels" 32). The best achievement overseas for the USIA was provided by Walt Disney, "whose Circarama tour of the United States seemed to surround the viewer with beautiful scenery and well-scrubbed faces. It was a hit in Casablanca, Moscow and Djkarta" (MacCann 179). This may explain why a recent in-house Disney publication issued as part of educational programs for young people calls Circarama the culmination of film technology. A section titled "From the Silent Movies to Circle-Vision 360: The Art of Filmmaking" explained that "in the Main Street Cinema, the silent film tells a story. In Circle-Vision 360, film not only tells a story, but also communicates a sense of involvement, learning and a whole range of human feelings. Comparing the two films makes it easy to see how film is growing as a form of communication" (*The Walt Disney World of Entertainment* 31).

Walt Disney was one of America's foremost cultural diplomats during the height of the Cold War. International exhibitions were considered particularly important events at which the State Department and the USIA could present a saleable image of American ideology to a waiting audience. But as the Brussels World's Fair illustrated, these government displays, created by panels of American experts, were incapable of moving their audiences. These tastemakers' lack of consensus and misunderstanding of their audience translated into displays that alienated and confused their target audience. Walt

Disney, with his years of experience as America's entertainer, was much better prepared to teach the world the supposed rightness of the American way of life. His combination of corporate skills and entertainment savvy moved the heartstrings of the middle class, and his sentimental nationalism made his audiences weep in understanding. Disney's values were simple and straightforward, his message of a triumphant consumer culture easily sold to the European market. As he explained, "You don't build it for yourself. You know what the people want and you build it for them" (*The Walt Disney World of Entertainment* 171). Disney's *The USA in Circarama* clearly showed who was best equipped to sell America to the world; by the 1950s, Walt Disney had become America's best salesman.

CHAPTER 3

Bug-Eye in South Pacific

Hollywood films dominated the media landscape of postwar Europe. As Reinhold Wagnleitner has written, "Film history is world history and nowhere else is U.S. cultural hegemony as nearly all-encompassing as in the area of movies. Nowhere else has the American Century become so much a 'reality' as in the collective subconscious and communal dreams of the American movie empire, where *reel* history becomes *real* history" (Wagnleitner, "Empire of the Fun" 482). And yet remarkably, at one of the United States' most important public relations events of the postwar period, Hollywood films played a minor role. The Brussels World's Fair of 1958 was the first international exposition following World War II. By the time the fair closed, over 40 million people, the largest crowd ever to visit a world's fair, had come to see the first Atomic World's Fair. Yet, America's most obvious and popular cultural ambassadors — the stars of Hollywood — stayed away from the fair. Innumerable stars had apparently been invited, but according to the *Saturday Review*, "Virtually all complained that they [could]n't do anything besides act and none wanted to come to Brussels for a walk on" (Sutton 30). The more likely reason for their absence was that "Bing Cosby, Bob Hope, Danny Kaye and dozens of other internationally famous stars" who had "plenty of performing talent … were held back by their agents," as Horace Sutton explains. He adds, "It seems clear that as far as Brussels and the American position here is concerned, this is hardly Hollywood's finest hour" (Sutton 30). With the movie industry's dominance in Europe secure, there was little incentive to send over a cavalcade of expensive actors who were already appearing on screens across the continent. The fair for Hollywood was apparently a minor event, and the poor status accorded American films at the fair's film festivals point out the significance of Europe's remarkable postwar economic recovery, and the resulting changes in the European film audience.

The widespread perception by postwar European audiences was that the movies, according to Paul Swann, were a "form of endorsement of life in the United States…. The extent to which movies were believed to be an accurate portrayal of life in the United States is moot, but practically everybody saw them as prominent spokesmen for a set of values and a way of life" (Swann 192). Though the hundreds of spectators that jammed the festival screenings testified to the dominant role that film played in European culture, the spectators' response to those films further signified their ability to read these films as ideological constructions that did not present an accurate or "real" image of America. European spectators at the time rightly understood that American films were part of American propaganda, and nowhere was this truer than at the Brussels World's Fair.

South Pacific and *Touch of Evil* both had their European premieres at the Brussels World's Fair. *South Pacific* opened with the official backing and support of the fair programmers and the Hollywood industry; it received little critical praise from critics and audiences. *Touch of Evil* was covertly submitted without the backing of Hollywood; audiences and critics heralded it as the work of a true American auteur. The different responses to these films can be traced to the state of international relations between the United States and Europe at the time. Though neither of these films was made expressly for the fair, their exhibition at Brussels reveals the important role that Hollywood films played in Eisenhower's program of psychological warfare. During the years of his administration, government officials actively pursued a close relationship with Hollywood in order to perpetuate a positive image of America abroad and thereby to secure the American way of life, though the response of audiences to the films could not be predicted or controlled.

The only film chosen by the Motion Picture Association of America for its European premiere at the fair was *South Pacific*. Released during a time of an international skirmish over leadership in this new atomic age, it exemplifies how the tropes of atomic energy could become suffused with various American cultural themes. As a film, *South Pacific* testifies to the role that the nuclear played in the enunciation of American power and in the establishment of American identity. Its exhibition at the Brussels World's Fair was the product of the role that atomic power came to play in the American national imagination and in the attempt to disseminate a positive image of America throughout the world. Both the film and the facts of its exhibition arise as a result of the development of a specifically American technological sublime that was a central element of American national identity. It was at this particular historical moment that technology — and specifically nuclear technology — could be thrust into the position of sublimity. Though the experience of the sublime theoretically occasions an experience of transcendence, its objects are always culturally determined and relative. According to David Nye, as the "history of the sublime from antiquity shows, if nothing else, that, although it refers to an immutable capacity of human psychology for astonishment, both the objects that arouse this feeling and their interpretation are socially constructed" (Nye 3). *South Pacific* results from the emergence within the dominant discourse of a utopian relationship with the atom at a time when America's nuclear dominance was not assured. As a result, one cannot fully understand the film or the fact of its exhibition in Brussels without a sense of the American public and state relationship with the atom. But the film's celebration of the United States' atomic strength during a time of heightened Cold War anxiety was met with a cold reception among European audiences. Opening the film with the titles "The Producers thank the Department of Defense, the Navy Department, the United States Pacific Fleet, and the Fleet Marine of the Pacific for their assistance in bringing this motion picture to the screen" did little to appease the atomic anxiety of the spectators. After dropping 25 nuclear bombs on the Bikini Atoll between 1946 and 1958, the arrival of *South Pacific,* as Margaret Jolly describes, could only be seen as "the aesthetics of American presence" (Jolly 111).

The Nuclear Context of the Brussels Fair

What better way to welcome in the new postwar era than through the symbol of the atom? The central icon of the fair, the atom had, by the opening of the Brussels World's Fair, become humanity's friend. Only 13 years earlier, the atomic bomb had unleashed utter devastation and terror on Japan, and now a positive aura surrounded the atom. The transformation of atomic power from an instrument of death into one of peace was the result of the American government's successful public relations programming. The atom, with its new scientific pedigree of technological progress and wonder, heralded a new-world order based on an enlightened humanism. The premise of the world's fair was to present a "balance sheet in the creation of a more human world ... far more than an inventory of the conquests of the century: it will be a defense of Man" ("Progress Report" 133). Yet, the peaceful proclamations of the fair's mandate and its presumption of a new and unified world order were much more hopeful than the actual state of nuclear affairs at the time. Indeed, the atomic bomb had ended one war, but the production of more advanced atomic weaponry only escalated after the war and threatened to unleash another one. The Soviets' detonation of their own atomic bomb in 1949 only increased the Cold War tensions in what had now become a war of the atom. In addition, the cries for peace under the auspices of a new humanism in the new atomic age did not stop the outbreak of fighting in Korea, Indochina, Taiwan, and the Middle East. The successful launching of Sputnik in October 1957 brought greater fears that the Soviets could now penetrate American lives with their scientific advancements. America's own perceived status as the world leader in the atomic field became increasingly problematic after the launching of Sputnik I and II. As H. W. Brand explains, "By itself, Sputnik did not alter the balance of strategic power between the United States and the Soviets, but it changed enormously perceptions of power" (Brand 988). And this sense of failure in the face of the Soviets was expressed not only through public anxiety in the United States, but also by a concomitant diminution of America's perceived dominance in Western Europe.

Most Americans and Europeans were not aware of the details of Eisenhower's weapons development program, and most assumed that American scientists dominated the field. Eisenhower intentionally played down the "frantic nuclear weapons buildup" after the Soviet's detonation of its atomic bomb by focusing on the potential benefits of the atom not only for the United States, but also for its allies and developing nations. Few people, including politicians, were aware that Eisenhower had engaged in the greatest nuclear arms buildup in history. When he took office in 1953, the United States had several hundred atomic bombs. When he left office in 1961, "the explosive power of the American nuclear arsenal approached 30,000 megatons, the equivalent of ten tons of TNT for every person on earth" (Medhurst 588). But through the rhetorical strategy of Eisenhower's Atoms for Peace policy, America would now become the global leader through its message of nuclear peace.

Eisenhower presented his Atoms for Peace program in a speech to the United Nations in 1953. This optimistic project was guided by the principle that the atom would be a "powerful source in the service of peace and progress," and it was in this spirit that supposedly "big corporations in the United States [were] building atomic plants for commercial electric power" (Haber 141). Under Eisenhower's policy atomic weapons would move out of the hands of the military in order to become a key element of the free enterprise system. With a supposedly cheap and unlimited supply of energy, the sky was the limit for American energy productivity.

In reality, the Atoms for Peace program was a widespread campaign on the part of the American government to sell atomic energy while it continued to build a nuclear arsenal. As H. W. Brand notes, "By basing American security on possession of the latest scientific and military technology, Eisenhower delivered enormous power over fundamental policy decisions to an elite of scientists, engineers, and defense bureaucrats whose activities the vast majority of Americans could not understand and, not understanding, could not knowledgeably control" (Brand 988). The American government, with its tight control of the flow of information to the media, sold atomic energy as a beneficial and benign force to the American public. Promises of cheap energy and miraculous advances in medicine and agriculture were used to convince many that atomic power could produce a world beyond our imagination. The development of the first atomic power plant, Shippingport, and other experimental reactors was recorded on "dozens of films that the Atomic Energy Commission (AEC) produced and distributed throughout the country to churches, schools, and business and civic groups" (Ford 48). Public displays such as the AEC's "Man and the Atom" were set up to demonstrate how nuclear power worked. Visitors leaving the exhibits received free copies of *Dagwood Splits the Atom* extolling the virtues of the manmade wonder of science. Additionally, through the strategy of the Atoms for Peace program, the Soviets were put into a no-win situation in which they were denied any bargaining leverage in the development of nuclear policy. The Atoms for Peace program was a concerted effort by the Eisenhower administration to demonstrate to the world that indeed the Americans were not the aggressors at the height of the Cold War. And with an America rich with the bounty of the postwar years, most people were eager to abandon the terror of nuclear holocaust in favor of the miracles that the atom could now deliver. Most people were ready to embark on this new atomic age guided by the hand of scientific and political elites.

Probably the most infamous of these sales pitches for atomic energy came from America's greatest salesman himself, Walt Disney. His animated film *Our Friend the Atom* premiered on the evening of January 23, 1957. The film, according to Elizabeth Mechling and Jay Mechling, "helped naturalize the atom in the sense of domesticating it, of making it seem matter-of-fact and unproblematic as an element of our everyday lives.... And, second, the film helped to naturalize the atom in the sense of making it part of Nature, as 'natural' rather than manufactured or artificial" (Mechling and Mechling 436). The project was developed in the mid–1950s and began as a studio-sanctioned book written by Heinz Haber. Both the book and the television show began with the story of the "Fisherman and the Genie" from *Arabian Nights*. The genie in the fable is able to grant three wishes concerning how nuclear power will be used. Removing the scientists and government from their responsibilities as the creators of nuclear power, the magical genie is the one who assumes the decision-making position. As Steven Watts contends, "With great optimism and a torrent of scientific information, *Our Friend the Atom* argued that atomic energy could be used profitably as an energy source, a means of combating disease, and improving biological and agricultural engineering, and as an instrument of peace" (Watts and Disney 312). With the magical genie calling the shots, the show became a huge success. Critics praised the "theme of technological progress and acclaimed its picture as a 'wonderful world of tomorrow, in which the mighty atom will play an increasingly vital part in the daily lives of everyone'" (Watts and Disney 313). The ominous mushroom cloud that only a few years before had been the ultimate representation of destruction becomes in this film something easily managed by the fisherman. Once the fisherman has mastered the power of the atom, the genie superimposed onto reverse footage of an atomic explosion implodes harmlessly back into the lamp (M. Smith 245). The book version ends with the optimistic vision that "the Atomic Genie holds in his hands the power of both creation and destruction. The world has reason to fear those powers of destruction. They could yet destroy civilization and much of humankind. So our last wish should simply be for the Atomic Genie to remain forever our friend! ... The magic power of atomic energy will soon begin to work for mankind throughout the world" (Haber 160). Throughout this period of the Atoms for Peace program, atomic energy is described as "magic," "mystery," and "wonder." The reciprocity between the mass media and the administration in the promotion of atomic energy led to President Eisenhower activating the first commercial nuclear power plant with a wave of a radioactive "magic wand."

By distracting the American public, along with the rest of the world, from the vast development of a nuclear arsenal by the Eisenhower administration, attention could be easily drawn to the utopian potential of this new, magical source of energy. The mobilization of the mass media in an orchestrated campaign to make atomic energy acceptable for future development had succeeded by the late 1950s. Eisenhower's own panel of experts, the American Assembly, reported in 1957 that "the average citizen finds here a subject of which he recognizes the vast importance but in the face of which he stands back bewildered and confused, both by the scientific intricacies of the subject and by the veil of secrecy which has covered so much of the areas of human activity which are being or will be radically affected by the developments of the atomic age. He begins to feel some sympathy for the atom as he finds himself bombarded with strange particles of truth until his head splits" (Jessup 2).

The acceptance of atomic energy was based on a campaign that resorted to simple tales and scenarios that transformed atomic energy into something beautiful and even sublime. Discussions concerning atomic energy mention over and over again the magical power that it possessed. The military complained that "Americans associated atomic energy with something magical, something not entirely subject to human control" (Balogh 96). And yet, the evocation of the splitting of the atom with something miraculous could be found throughout the discourse of the developers of America's atomic energy program. The chairman of the Atomic Energy Commission declared his "faith in the atomic future," which had the additional backing of a "Higher Intelligence [who] decided man was ready to receive" the knowledge of the "atom's magnitude" (Ford 46). Even the films that were produced by the AEC described how "the sure hand of science brings power unlimited from the magic of the atom" but failed to make any mention of the risks involved with nuclear energy (Ford 49). This evocation of the miraculous elements of the atom was intentionally connected by the Eisenhower administration with popular conceptions of America's own global position of power and incorporated into its foreign policy agenda as well. The Atoms for Peace program was thus a key element in Eisenhower's psychological warfare strategy, a strategy meant to solidify both domestic receptivity for America's emerging global atomic dominance and the international dominance of the American way of life in the late 1950s.

A major goal of the program was to secure America's position as the world leader in the development of the peaceful atom. As Klaus Knorr notes, "Connected with this objective is the fear recently expressed by a good many members of Congress and businessmen that 'we are losing atomic leadership' and particularly that we are losing in our competition with Great Britain and the USSR" (Knorr 102). An atomic energy program that emphasized the peaceful use of the atom would undermine the European perception of the United States as an aggressive and domineering nation unwilling to concede its power position to any other nation. This widespread perception would lead to France's decision to develop its own nuclear program independent of the United States. By assuming a leadership role in terms of nuclear power, the Americans also hoped to stem the tide of communist expansion into third world countries. Atomic energy would be a way in which to consolidate nations under the miraculous potential it offered for the betterment of humanity. A major part of this atomic power rhetoric focused on how this power could lead to the liberation of developing countries by assisting them in agriculture, medicine and industry. According to Knorr, "One objective of American foreign policy [was] to aid underdeveloped countries in their effort to become more developed and, eventually, to achieve a more satisfactory standard of living. The rationale of this policy is that such economic improvement will make these countries less susceptible to Communist pressure from within and without" (Knorr 127). The Atoms for Peace program significantly improved European perceptions of the United States. At the end of 1955, a United States Information Agency poll revealed that "substantial pluralities of Europeans felt that the United States had done more than any other country to develop peaceful uses and that United States had shifted its emphasis from military to peaceful uses of the atom" (Balogh 103).

The considerable energy and financial investment by the Eisenhower administration in the Atoms for Peace program helps clarify why the Brussels fair, which was built on the premise of a new humanism directed toward global understanding and peace, would have as its symbol the atom. The actual icon of the Brussels World's Fair was the Atomium, which was built to resemble the nine atoms of a crystal of steel enlarged 160 million times. The Atomium became "a visual metaphor, like a statue of an angel — an image of something the sculptor believes in but cannot see. The Fair authorities [had] seized on it as a symbol of modern science and technology" (Christopher Rand 58). Atomic energy was now the way of the future, part of the fair's theme of a New Humanism — "a declaration of faith in man's ability to mold the atomic age to the ultimate advantage of all nations and peoples" (Funke 88). The Belgium government's choice of the Atomium as the symbolic representative of the fair can be linked not only to the success of the Atoms for Peace program but also to the fact that the best source of uranium at the time was the Belgian Congo. The American government's desire to have complete dominance over the world's atomic industry, including the supply of uranium, the technical knowledge of nuclear science, and the development of nuclear weapons and reactors, was undercut by Belgium's control of the uranium supply. Their control of the Congo led to a Belgian-American agreement in 1955. The agreement gave the Belgians the "right to have nuclear materials processed in plants other than those located in the United States if the plants were acceptable to the United States" (Helmreich 403). The Atomium with its massive dominance of the fairgrounds signified Belgium's own powerful position in the development of an international atomic community. Additionally, the Congo was accorded special status at the fair. There were actually eight units that illustrated the various facets of Belgium's African dominions. These units emphasized the "benevolent paternalism" of the colonizers in a country that may have had "no political freedom in the sense accepted in the West, but ... certainly a considerable amount of technical, professional and academic training, health services and social services, a nascent Negro middle-class; a sense of peace and prosperity; and a circle of limited, but estimable goals to achieve, and of means leading to them, and open to all" (Jesman 486). A large part of the Belgian goals in the Congo were defined by Belgium's own atomic plans. Standing at 360 feet, the Atomium called to mind the "prodigious force of atomic energy and the latest conquest of man over matter" (De Wouters D'Oplinter 11). Forty-one million visitors from all corners of the world crowded in to witness this celebration in which "all the industrial nations, irrespective of ideology, accent the importance and promise of technology, and particularly of atomic energy for peaceful uses.... All nations capable of manufacturing machinery convey the message, well understood by the underdeveloped peoples, that in the atomic age mastery of modern techniques is essential for internal prosperity and internal security" (Dean, "The World's Unfinished Business" 7).

In reality, both the Atoms for Peace rhetoric and the Atomium obscured the fact that the commercial development of nuclear power was still years away. There was little private investment in nuclear power in the United States throughout the 1950s, and nuclear development remained primarily focused on weapons of mass destruction. In the United States the government insisted that nuclear power should be controlled by private industry, and there was extreme concern that the nuclear industry might indeed become publicly owned. A public opinion study entitled "Free Market versus Socialist Thinking" strove to determine the demographics of who opposed the privatization of nuclear power. Foster's Opinion Research Corporation found that in 1956 "those with only an eight-grade education, low-income individuals, and the foreign-born were in the strongly socialistic column (because they approved of public ownership), whereas business executives, upper-income individuals, Republicans, college teachers, and government employees favored the free market (that is, government subsidies without government control)" (M. Smith 243). The majority of funding for research and development did in fact come from public sources. The nuclear agencies of the federal government assured that discussions concerning the possibility of a nuclear accident remained classified. Scientists at the Brookhaven National Laboratory released a report to the Atomic Energy Commission in 1957 that hypothesized the potential impact of a nuclear power plant accident. They estimated that the release of radioactive materials could cause 3,400 deaths, 43,000 injuries, and $7 billion in damages (M. Smith 240). The public was never informed of this report, and instead the Price-Anderson Act of 1957 set aside an arbitrary sum of $560 million for any liability after a nuclear meltdown.

The driving force behind the Atoms for Peace program was the need to create a positive image for nuclear power, not simply for a domestic audience but abroad. A National Security Council review in 1954 revealed the actual intentions of the public relations battle over atomic power. It stated that "the U.S. should continue to take the initiative in advancing proposals for constructive settlements and international cooperation (i.e., atoms for peace) in order to put the Soviets on the defensive and win popular support on both sides of the Iron Curtain" (Osgood 431). The irony of emphasizing the peaceful atom as a part of Eisenhower's psychological warfare strategy at the height of the Cold War did not escape comment by some visitors to the fair. One commentator noted that it was "rather unfortunate that the Brussels' World's Fair should take place in as war jittery an atmosphere as did the New York World's Fair in 1939" (Simons 27).

Even though the Atomium formed the symbolic center of the fair, atomic energy played a very limited role at the fair. While the Soviet pavilion was dominated with models of Sputnik and its success in the battle for the realms of space, the American atomic energy exhibit was lost in "the wolf-whistling stampede toward the fashion models" in the center of the pavilion ("All's Fair" 29). In the spirit of supposed international cooperation in the field of science, an International Science Pavilion was constructed with the collaboration of 16 nations including the United States. The guiding principle of the pavilion was that "at the level of pure science there are no confines: scientists speak the same language; they are objective and disinterested. Science belongs to man" (Simons 26). There is no doubting what language the American scientists involved in the construction of the pavilion thought was being spoken at this international site. A cooperative spirit was meant to guide the construction of the International Science Pavilion, which was structured as a museum to show the progress made in science during the past 25 years. As an indicator of scientific concerns during the height of the Cold War, the museum was broken into four areas: the atom, the molecule, the crystal and the living cell, with each of these areas corresponding to physics, chemistry, solid state physics, and biology. For an atomic world's fair, physics appropriately dominated the Science Pavilion. The American effort for the pavilion was arranged by "a brilliant array of our top scientists, including several Nobel Prize winners" (Simons 26). Ernest O. Lawrence, the Nobel prize winner and director of the Radiation Laboratory at the University of California, Berkeley, headed the sub-committee on the atom. The U.S. atom display included exhibits demonstrating solar power, particle accelerators, anti-protons and anti-neutrons, and a "swimming pool reactor." The International Science Pavilion received minimal coverage in the press; apparently the scientific displays did little to unmask or dissipate the magic of the atom that had been created in popular culture.

Even though American officials had worked aggressively to assure America's position as the world leader in nuclear technology, a year before the fair, a treaty was signed in Brussels creating the EURATOM and the General Common Market. Made up of six nations, including Belgium, France, the German Federation, Italy, Luxembourg and the Netherlands, the EURATOM (the European Atomic Energy Commission) and the General Common Mar-

Actress Mitzi Gaynor demonstrates the electro-mechanical hands in the Nuclear Energy Exhibit of the U.S. Pavilion at the Brussels World's Fair with the assistance of an unidentified tour guide (National Archive).

ket were created with the goal of "changing the structure of Europe, basing it on the federal principle instead of on the principle of national sovereignty" (Kohnstamm 143). The EURATOM was a move against American dominance and its control of the nuclear field and the assertion of the European nations' new sense of power stemming from the recovery of their economies in the postwar period. American policymakers, who believed that a unified Europe would present a more manageable and dependable front against Soviet incursions into individual nations, supported the treaty. The EURATOM treaty provided for the "pooling of scientific abilities and industrial resources, the exchange, unhampered by tariffs or quotas, of all goods and materials necessary to build reactors, and the exchange and opening of a complete common market for the nuclear industry" (Kohnstamm 144). Not wanting to "miss the atomic bus," the European nuclear confederation also signaled a weakening in the image of America as the scientific leader, especially following the technological victories of the Soviets. Max Kohnstamm, who was the Secretary General of the Action Committee for a United States of Europe, revealed in his address to the Twelfth American Assembly that the EURATOM's greatest asset "which nobody has thought of looking for in Europe for a long time. Believe me or not, from now on people are going to find it there nevertheless: It is a growing sense of confidence" (Kohnstamm 149). The European community of scientists was ready to create its own industry outside of the ideological and market directives of the United States. With the Atomic Energy Commission's own difficulties in getting the nuclear power program off the ground in the United States, the creation of a separate European nuclear organization was a strategically powerful move. Not only did a European nuclear confederation challenge America's leadership role in nuclear affairs, but it also would present a threat to the market for nuclear hardware that American industrialists planned to exploit.

Bug-Eye in South Pacific

It is against the backdrop outlined in the previous section that one can begin to appreciate the significance of the reception of the *South Pacific*. Through the history of the production of this film and its construction within the context of the fair, we can begin to see the underlying popular anxiety and ambivalence regarding the nuclear arms race. The tropes employed by this film, their suffusion with the dilemmas of racial and imperialistic strife, evoked in viewers a sense of America's role in these international developments.

South Pacific was originally adapted from several of the stories in James Michener's Pulitzer Prize–winning *Tales of the South Pacific*, published in 1946. Rodgers and Hammerstein adapted the stories into an acclaimed musical, and, as Ethan Mordden notes, "If prize winning is a measurement, *South Pacific* was without question the most successful Rodgers and Hammerstein show" (Mordden 121). The awards earned included eight Tonys, nine Donaldsons, a gold record for Columbia's cast album, and the Pulitzer Prize, all during the season that saw the opening of Arthur Miller's *Death of a Salesman*. When Michener's *Tales* finally reached the Todd-AO Technicolor screen, the production had been inscribed with the visual tropes of atomic power that had proliferated since the end of the War. As Peter Hales points out, "The central icon of the atomic culture is the mushroom cloud, rising above the lush tropical atolls of the South Pacific" (Hales 12). It is this image that functions above all to unify the story in *South Pacific* under the specter of the glowing, radiant island of Balai Hai.

Michener's own connections to the military made him particularly well equipped at projecting a sublime image of atomic power that was intimately aligned with national identity. Michener's long career as a best-selling author was "punctuated by a spell with the Agency. In the mid–1950s, Michener used his career as a writer as a cover for his work in eliminating radicals who had infiltrated one of the CIA's Asian operations. To this end, he was placed in the CIA's Asia Foundation. He later said that 'a writer must never serve as a secret agent for anything or anybody'" (Saunders 246).

As Peter Hales has persuasively shown, popular media images of the atomic bomb immediately following the war were still closely tied to the horrific destruction of Hiroshima and Nagasaki: they tended to be rendered in grainy black and white, which portrayed the early evolution stages of a modern weapon. With time, however, as the American government launched a virtual blackout of information about the development and stockpiling of nuclear weapons, a campaign of re-education concerning the atom bomb began. This campaign intentionally emphasized the bomb's positive aspects and used cartoon characters like Dagwood to reverse public fear of the bomb and its destructive potential. The strategy included the aesthetization of the bomb in its popular representations, and its transformation into a modern American version of the sublime. This process of aesthetization needs to be considered further in light of America's foreign affairs strategies and its drive to maintain its global dominance in the field of atomic power.

The transformation of atomic energy into a sublime concept could already be heard in the voices of those who had early access to the bomb and were instrumental in its representation for popular consumption. The only journalist who flew along with the bombers as they detonated the bombs over Japan was William Laurence, the science writer for *The New York Times*. His coverage of the bombing was widely distributed, and it reveals an image of the bomb as something beyond the previous understanding of traditional warfare. He portrayed the explosion as a "giant flash ... a bluish-green light that illuminated the entire sky ... a giant ball of fire ... belching enormous white smoke rings ... a pillar of purple fire.... As the first mushroom floated off into the blue, it changed its shape into a flowerlike form, its giant petal curving downward, creamy white outside, rose colored inside" (Lawrence, "Nagasaki was the Climax of the New Mexico Test," 30ff). Predating Disney's magical genie by many years, Laurence's representation of the atomic bomb already helped to transform it from terror to tourism, from holocaust to parlor show, and responsibility to mere response (Hales 12). Even the first atomic bomb explosion on July 16, 1945, elicited responses that spoke of a sublime experience. General Leslie Groves wrote in a "Top Secret Memorandum for the Secretary of War":

> The effects could well be called unprecedented, magnificent, beautiful, stupendous and terrifying. No man-made phenomenon of such tremendous power had every occurred before. The lighting effects beggared description. The whole country was lighted by a searing light with the intensity many times that of the midday sun. It was golden, purple, violet, gray and blue. It lighted every peak, crevasse, and ridge of the nearby mountain range with a clarity and beauty that cannot be described but must be seen to be imagined. Words are inadequate.... It had to be witnessed to be realized [Feis 381].

As David Nye has explained, an experience of the sublime is enhanced when viewed as part of a group. And indeed watching the detonation of atomic weapons became a very popular activity for Americans in the 1950s. Between 1945 and 1962 two hundred bombs were exploded above ground with witnesses always present. Nye notes, "Natural wonders are usually surrounded by tourists, and virtually every technological demonstration, such as a world's fair or a rocket launch, provides a sublime experience for a multitude.... The presence of a crowd can enhance the interest in the object, confirming its importance" (Nye 27). Bearing witness to the glorious power of the atom became part of America's tourist trade. Las Vegas became a popular viewing location. And when a giant hydrogen bomb was exploded over the Pacific, tourists lined the beaches in Hawaii. The nighttime explosion was timed to coincide with a fireworks display to entertain the spectators. *Life* magazine provided coverage of the event for "the millions so unfortunate as to miss the pyrotechnic display." The reporter described how "the blue-black tropical night suddenly turned into a hot lime green. It was brighter than noon. The green changed into a lemonade pink ... and finally, terribly, blood red. It was as if someone had poured a bucket of blood on the sky" (Nye 234).

Disney's *Our Friend the Atom* also not surprisingly described the splitting of the atom in equally otherworldly language. The film's narration explains, "The billions of splitting atoms combine their bursts of gamma-rays.... The glowing, suddenly expanding gases leap upward into the high sky.... Behind this awe-inspiring cloud we recognize the terrifying form of the Genie of our fable ... with eyes blazing lie torches, and fiery smoke whirling about him like the simoom of the desert ... and his thundering voice promising us death in the most cruel form" (Haber 133). According to Immanuel Kant, the experience of the sublime induces "pleasure as well as pain." While the mind is "alternately attracted and repelled by the object, the satisfaction in the sublime implies not so much positive pleasure as wonder or reverential awe, and may

Personnel viewing the detonation of Project "Open Shot," Nevada, April 1952 (General Records of the Department of Energy, 1915–2007, National Archives).

be called a negative pleasure" (Kant, *Critique of Judgment* §23). This is just the sort of "negative pleasure" found in the above descriptions of the atomic events in the Pacific. The Pacific is saturated with blood-red hues, and Disney's genie promises us a wonderful, horrible death. Through Eisenhower's Atoms for Peace campaign, the magic of the atom became tied to American national identity and most importantly its manifest destiny. "The atomic explosion

The atomic cloud formed by the detonation seems close enough to touch, and, tension gone, Poth and Wilson do a little clowning for the camera, May 1, 1952 (Department of Defense. Department of the Navy. U.S. Marine Corps, National Archives).

became not a purely human circumstance (for which we must accept responsibility), but rather a part of that benign collaboration among man, nature and divinity that has defined American destiny, a predetermined, even foreordained event" (Nye 13).

The rhetoric surrounding the technological sublime and the atomic bomb was constructed within gendered terms. The atomic scientists frequently conceived of their work in terms of virility. "A successful explosion was a birth and a powerful weapon was a son that they had procreated" (Nye 229). Laurence, the *New York Times* reporter, described the first successful detonation of an atomic bomb as a male birthing rite:

> The big boom came about a hundred seconds after the great flash — a first cry of a new-born world. It brought the silent, motionless silhouettes to life, gave them a voice. A loud cry filled the air. The little groups that hitherto had stood rooted to the earth like desert plants broke into a dance — the rhythm of primitive man dancing at one of his fire festivals at the coming of spring. They clapped their hands as they leaped from the ground — earthbound man symbolizing the birth of a new force [Easlea 97].

Ernest Lawrence, who was responsible for America's atomic energy display at the Brussels World's Fair, had also been involved with the early development of the atomic bomb. When he received word in December 1942 about the splitting of the atom, he sent the following telegram: "Congratulations to the parents. Can hardly wait to see the new arrival" (Easlea 107). "If women made the sublime their own, it was as observers. Works of the technological sublime were decidedly male creations" (Nye 31).

The linkage of female sexuality with military weaponry was another aspect of the atomic discourse. The term "bombshell" appeared in the 1930s, associating a woman outside the household with uncontrollable sexual desire that represented a threat to the domestic sphere. The bombshell would continue to play a dominant role during and after the war. Her manifestation in the form of the pin-up became a crucial component of the World War II soldier's life. "Despite the concerns of religious groups and some officials about the immorality of pin-ups, the United States government and the film industry co-operated closely during the war in the production and distribution of millions of photographs of Hollywood's leading ladies and rising starlets, and these pictures decorated the walls of barracks, the bulkheads of ships, and the fuselages of planes on all fronts" (Westbrook 592–94). The most popular of the World War II pin-ups was Betty Grable, who with her wholesome all–American looks represented the American way of life our boys were fighting to protect. *Time* captured this sentiment when it stated that Grable can "lay no claims to sultry beauty or mysterious glamour.... Her peach-checked, pearl blonde good looks add up to mere candybox-top prettiness" ("Daydream" 40). As Westbrook points out, Grable's popularity was tied to her normal looks, which could fill in for the girlfriends and sisters left at home. She did not present the erotic challenge of difference personified in other popular pin-ups like Rita Hayworth. Grable's apple-pie looks became especially significant in the war in the Pacific, which was being waged within the government's military discourse as a race war. Grable's "obvious whiteness gave her an advantage over competitors such as Hayworth (née Margarita Cansino) in the eyes of white soldiers waging a brutal struggle against a racial enemy as they often complained, white women — especially women as white as Grable — were in short supply" (Westbrook 599). *Time* magazine even reported that Grable's popularity with servicemen grew "in direct ratio to their remoteness from civilization" (quoted in Westbrook 599). In the postwar period, female sexuality continued to be portrayed as destructive to the nuclear family. The South Pacific was a crucial locale for the conflagration ignited by the collision of military hardware with the "bombshell." The hydrogen bomb dropped on the Bikini Islands carried a photograph of Rita Hayworth. And the island itself "provided the name for the abbreviated swimsuit the female 'bombshells' would wear. The designer of the revealing suit chose the name 'bikini' four days after the bomb was dropped to suggest the swimwear's explosive potential" (E. T. May 110–11).

The South Pacific symbolism was particularly instrumental in the con-

Harvesting bumper crop for Uncle Sam. Movie star Rita Hayworth sacrificed her bumpers for the duration. Besides setting an example by turning in unessential metal car parts, Miss Hayworth has been active in selling war bonds (Wide World, ca. 1942) (Office for Emergency Management, National Archives).

Atomic cloud during "Able Day" blast at Bikini. First picture of atomic shock wave, July 1, 1946 (General Records of the Department of the Navy, 1804–1983, National Archives).

struction of the bomb as an instrument of peace in popular culture. By the time Michener's *Tales of the South Pacific* had appeared, Bikini had become the site of Operation Crossroad, the first public atomic test of the postwar era. "The effect of this conjunction of the South Pacific Eden and nuclear holocaust cannot be too heavily emphasized, for it was successful in continuing, even amplifying the strain of aestheticism that had characterized the earliest attempts to anchor the atomic sublime. Terror and beauty, together, begot a terrible beauty, and one that was being lead by the hand of a powerful military American father figure" (Hales 19). Kant's conception of the sublime was clearly a masculine conceit. Women had a natural appreciation for the beautiful, while men had an "innate appreciation of the sublime." In his essay "Observations on the Feeling of the Beautiful and the Sublime," Kant writes, "The fair sex has just as much understanding as the male, but it is a beautiful understanding, whereas ours [the male] should be a deep understanding, an expression that signifies identity with the sublime" (Kant, *Observations on the Feeling of the Beautiful and Sublime* 78–79). By placing the Bikini test site in the location of the mythical Bali Hai, of paradise, the bomb would be distilled into the natural Eden and purity of the South Pacific. And with this cleansing would also come the transformation of the bomb into the "new heroic Grail quest that came to dominate American discussions of America's purpose in the global community" (Hales 20). Journalists writing about the Bikini tests in their reports aided the continued aesthetization of their experience of the bomb. *Business Week* editors intoned, "How little there is in it of the horror or shock its historic importance would lead you to expect, how much of the sheer breathtaking beauty and magnificence.... You think fleetingly, is that all? And then you suck in your breath and hold it because — welling up from the center of the cloud and spilling in easy, leisurely magnificence down the side comes wave of glowing pink foam ... one of the most strangely beautiful of human creations" (Hales 23–24). Waves and waves of pink foam glowing along the Bikini beaches; the discourse of the atomic sublime was suffused with the erotic charge of the "bombshell."

This charge can also be found within the film version of *South Pacific*. Walter Metz's explanation of "the concept of cultural distancing helps explain the relationship between Hiroshima and American cinema. Quite simply, Hiroshima does not exist.... This is why an incipient criticism about nuclear anxiety must locate itself within the unconscious structures of the popular, non-nuclear films of the Cold War period" (Metz 47). The visual design of the film is a direct reflection of the atomic sublime as discussed by Hales. Critics of the film at the time all made note of its unnatural, saturated colors. *Commonweal* commented that "for some inexplicable reason, the film uses a visual glow, bathing the singers every now and then in a mist of artificial colors that are meant to set the mood: blue, purple, green, yellow, gold, etc" (Hartung 50). The *Saturday Review* discussed the "mood of fantasy" that had been "inculcated into the vast, sunlit expanses.... There are at times stunning uses of filters, haze, smoked color" (Alpert 35). Note how these reviews echo the same language utilized by Laurence in his coverage of the first atomic explosions and also the magical language of Disney's *Our Friend the Atom*. The *New Yorker* called the film a "polychromatic jumble" that is full of "technical razzle-dazzle" with "endless color effects to intensify the moods ... and many blurred landscapes" (McCarten 99). *Newsweek* called it a "misty, dream-like kaleidoscope of changing hues" ("Enchanting but..." 96). *Time* also joined the chorus of perplexed critics, explaining that the filmmakers "gave it some of the smoothest Technicolor that has ever creamed a moviegoer's eyeballs; but, then, gripped by the fear that all this would be too subtle, they decided to smear 'mood' all over the big scenes by shooting them through filters. Result: too often the actors are tinted egg yellow, turtle green — and sometimes phosphorescent fuchsia" ("The New Pictures" 85–86).

Richard Rodgers of Rodgers and Hammerstein, who received a $1 million advance for the movie rights, strongly disliked the movie, calling it awful since it was overproduced and the use of color was "atrocious." The widescreen technology of the Todd-AO lens and the expressive use of Technicolor would seem to be the ideal equipment to capture the atomic sublime. The *Saturday Review* critic called the experience "bug-eye," and one in which the lens itself made the film "almost frighteningly all seeing, and while it's a wonderful invention, maybe its danger is that it tends to boomerang." The director, Joshua Logan, who had directed both the stage and screen versions, actually compared the "opening up" of the film in the terms of the military and also used awe-inspiring descriptors. "Opened up is a Hollywood expression, very handy for describing the way a movie can show vast crowds, aerial combat, and entire naval task force at sea and various other spectacular pleasures in the very same story, where on the stage these exciting moments could only be described in dialogue" (Skouras 36). Again in Buddy Adler's, the producer's, description of the film we hear the sublime nature of the film. "We hope that we have provided the way to some enchanted evenings in a world bigger, better and brighter than life" (Skouras 13).

There is a remarkable similarity between the images in *South Pacific*, the film, and the documentary footage of atomic explosions in the Pacific shot at the same time. These documentaries are notable for their extreme and even unnatural reds, yellows and oranges, a use of color that, although it reflects the state of color film technology at the time, were often shot with the specific purpose of highlighting the spectacular beauty of the events. However, not only does the similarity in intense and unnatural color schemes in *South Pacific* seem to reflect eerily the iconography and aesthetic sensibility of these documentaries, but additionally the film uses a technique of color saturation in which various scenes are colored from left to right or right to left. That is, the color actually sweeps across the screen — an image that resonates with the scenes of blast waves sweeping across the landscape. The film is replete with various other formal elements that mimic the aesthetic qualities of the earlier documentaries, which, as I have noted, were designed to convert the image of the bomb into one of sublime beauty. For instance, the island of Balai Hai, which serves as the edenic core of the film, looms ominously on the ocean horizon, enveloped in both a polychromatic spectacle of Technicolor and a mushroom cloud halo of deep reds, oranges, and pinks. And in an opening sequence, as a native sings of the enchantment and beauty of Balai Hai, the mysterious island seems to beckon the colonizing American troops. Its otherworldly glow literally calls out for them to come and be absorbed within its sublime power. The humans in the film are overwhelmed and overpowered by the atomic splendor of the mise-en-scène. They move as mere mortals in the face of this "bigger, better, brighter than life" world. While Balai Hai remains the unknowable for the soldiers — that which they cannot transcend — the native people remain part of the scenery. Similar to the documentary footage of the Bikini bomb tests, in *South Pacific* the native islanders are ciphers that embody the inscrutable countenance of the eager and willing colonial subject.

The literal translation of the atomic sublime in the production design of the film bolstered America's sense of national supremacy and nuclear leadership at a time when the more immediate bomb in America's international reputation was the escalating race wars. By the time of the fair, the racist policies of the United States were well known abroad, and served as a major source of anti–American propaganda for the Soviets. "The foreign reaction to the desegregation crisis in Little Rock was intense and generally negative..." (Krenn 593). However, a report by the USIA evaluating public reactions to Little Rock in major world capitals admitted that the Little Rock crisis had had no major effect on world opinion of the United States, since "America's standing in the area of race relations was already in a very depressed state prior to the Arkansas desegregation incidents, and hence not readily susceptible to further decrease" (Krenn 593). Things couldn't get any worse for America's image builders. Considering the actual conservative and nationalistic theme underlying the film, it is interesting to note that the musical version of *South Pacific* had been attacked by "two members of the Georgia legislature" who saw it "as propaganda and announced their intention to introduce legislation to prohibit the showing of movies or plays that had an 'underlying philosophy inspired by Moscow'" (Hyland 237). The charge of propaganda was provoked by the song "You've Got to Be Carefully Taught," which the legislators believed urged interracial marriage. Rodgers' condemnation of the film version may testify to how the atomic sublime had subsumed the liberal ideals of the original musical. The later film was no longer about crossing racial boundaries, but rather about celebrating America's sublime destiny. The American troops in the film become tourists lining the beaches as they testify to the might of America's atomic sublime. And this sublimity is brought to the third world nations in need of the magic of the American way of life. Remember that a key aspect of Eisenhower's Atoms for Peace program was the gathering together of developing nations under the leadership of the United States. The islanders are there to eagerly welcome the American troops, like they were supposedly eager to welcome the new miracle of Western science when the Bikini atomic tests occurred.

At the time that the film premiered in Brussels, the racial harmony it was supposedly offering paled in comparison to the desegregation protests that were occurring in Little Rock. Mitzi Gaynor, who plays the nurse Nellie

Forbush in the film, and overcomes her "learned racism" in *South Pacific,* is actually from Little Rock. But Forbush is another Betty Grable–type whose white, wholesome, all–American looks compliment the sublimity of America's atomic power. She is not the bombshell who threatens the sanctity of the nuclear family. In fact, she secures the continuation of American dominance in the third world by marrying a white industrialist who will ensure the continuation of a market economy lead by the colonizers of the South Pacific. His greatest crime is not that he is a murderer (which he is) but that he has fathered mixed-race children. It is the horror of miscegenation that she must come to terms with before entering into the bond of marriage. Her fiancé is only able to prove his masculinity and suitability after jeopardizing his life for the American forces. Now that we know he is a willing and eager supporter of the American way of life, Mitzi is able to marry him.

The discourse of gender that inflected the development of the bomb continues in *South Pacific.* As in the World War II's Pacific war, in which the most popular pin-ups were the whitest, Mitzi is the embodiment of the girl next door. Bright and blonde and bouncy, her sexuality, even while she "washed that man right out of her life," was tightly contained. Her wholesome activity and sincerity throughout the film was that of a tom-boy from the Midwest. She was a safe harbor for audiences to identify with, and indeed the soldiers in the film show little sexual interest in her. Their desire is directed to the mystery contained within Balai Hai — the atomic island. The central role of the American military in securing the Pacific for its own technological warfare is charged with the eroticism of Balai Hai, whose beckoning is suffused with the saturated colors of an atomic explosion. Within its verdant and virgin shores throbbed the sexual threat of the mysterious and dark Other, Liat, the local native girl. Ironically, the woman who represents the threat of sexuality and who causes the death of an American soldier is a young, innocent island girl. She is dark, inscrutable, and as part of the mythical Balai Hai, she seems eager to sacrifice her virginity at the command of her mother. The journey of "waspy" Lieutenant Cable into the Dark Continent of Liat could only lead to his death. Miscegenation was not part of America's atomic sublime, especially considering the necessary maintenance of America in the power position of both the paternal protector and strong leader. During Eisenhower's period of containment, contamination was always from sources external to America. To attempt to move into the space of sublimity that the film evokes could only lead to death. Balai Hai, like the atomic sublime, becomes a necessary ingredient in Eisenhower's Atoms for Peace campaign. The concern was not with presenting the facts of America's atomic program or the actual state of affairs in America; rather psychological warfare was concerned with securing

an image of America that would persuasively convince the world of the sublimity of the American way.

Simultaneous with the premiere of *South Pacific* at the fair, another
racially charged exhibit opened in the American pavilion. Recognizing that
racism was seen as a serious problem for America's image abroad, the Time
Corporation's *Fortune* magazine was responsible for the construction of an
exhibit titled "Unfinished Business," which was funded by the State Department. The exhibit was meant to illustrate the United States' acknowledgement
of its problems and its search for a better democracy for all its citizens. The
exhibit was divided into sections that used photographic montages and newspaper clippings to document the problems of segregation, slums and environmental destruction that Americans faced, and it then provided strategies
that were being used to solve these problems. The exhibit caused an immediate
uproar of protests from the American government, which was attempting to
secure a positive image of America for its European audience. Every element
of the American pavilion was part and parcel of Eisenhower's psychological
war and was dominated with the concern to present a positive image of the
American way of life. As Robert Rydell explains, "What bothered the government was the existence of shots of mob violence at Cairo, Illinois, and
Little Rock, and headlines, full and specific, such as WHITE PUPILS JEER
NEGRO STUDENTS; LITTLE ROCK POLICEMEN DRAG A DEMON-
STRATOR DOWN A STREET WHEN A NEGRO FAMILY MOVED
INTO CICERO ILLINOIS THE NATIONAL GUARD HAD TO BE
CALLED OUT TO CHECK A MOB." Rydell adds, "Equally offensive in
the eyes of the USIA were photographs of mixed groups of school children
at work and at play, especially a photograph of a colored boy dancing with a
white girl, and a photograph of the dome of the Capitol with three colored
children in the foreground playing in a slum" (Rydell 209). Several members
of the world's fair staff were sent out to examine the exhibit and report back
to Congress. Eisenhower was hesitant in closing it down, but Vice President
Richard Nixon showed no such hesitation, arguing that we tended too much
in our overall U.S. propaganda to show the "seamy side of America" (Krenn
606). The exhibit was soon closed for supposed renovation — that renovation
resulted in the opening of a new exhibit on Health and Education. The closure
of the exhibit lead to protests by many who had seen the exhibit as a demonstration of a free nation powerful enough to acknowledge that it, too, has
difficult challenges to face. As *New Republic* described the exhibit at the time,
"It said in a few words and pictures that 17 million American Negroes do not
yet have the full rights promised them by American democracy.... This little
exhibit is an admirable attempt by a great nation to admit, publicly, that it

has shortcomings and will not try to hide them. In this way it is the only honest national exhibit in the fair" (Brinkley 8).

A frank exploration of America's racial problems was not part of Eisenhower's psychological warfare strategy at the Brussels World's Fair. This was an atomic fair that would require similarly atomic images to win the contest of ideologies that was being waged. Within the arena of the world's fair, America's Cold warriors saw the construction of a powerful and positive image of America for foreign consumption as an issue of the highest order. It is not difficult to understand, then, why an exhibit that focused on racism was pulled, while a film that was only apparently about racism was premiered and highly celebrated; in fact, it was *the* major Hollywood exhibition for the event. The critical reviews of the film, which echoed earlier responses to the explosion of the atomic bomb, revealed the awesome power of American national destiny that *South Pacific* displayed for a mass audience. They recognized that in the bug-eyed images being presented on the 4,000-square-foot screen, there was something "almost frighteningly all-seeing," something that would "make even your enemies feel romantic" ("Enchanting But..." 51). In *South Pacific* the racial difficulties became insignificant in the face of the awe-inspiring power of the American sublime: this looming otherworldly force for mystical harmony.

At the height of the Cold War, the image that was chosen to represent America's atomic power was not only optimistic, but also sublime. Racism was removed from the "Unfinished Business" exhibit in order to assure that the only acceptable construction of America was one that was problem-free. The Atoms for Peace program was a crucial aspect of Eisenhower's psychological campaign against the Soviets, and *South Pacific* bolstered this strategy by nullifying European fears of American dominance through its spectacle of the sublime. When American dominance seemed to be challenged, Balai Hai beckoned, but it beckoned only those who were willing to recognize the "terrible beauty" of America's destiny. This was a terrible beauty premised on the maintenance of clearly delineated positions of power in terms of race and gender that were meant to guarantee America's continued position as the natural and divine leader of the global nuclear community.

CHAPTER 4

Ribbon of Cold War Dreams: Touch of Evil's *European Premiere*

One Hollywood film at the Brussels World's Fair did open with great fanfare and celebration on the part of its European audience. While hailed as a masterwork abroad, the film had just been universally panned and condemned in the United States. The applause and acclaim that greeted the European premiere of Orson Welles' *Touch of Evil* represented a radical departure from the reception the film had received from American critics. French critics in particular were the ones who surrounded Welles at the Brussels World's Fair, and they were the ones who designated him an *auteur*. One explanation for such a wide divergence in critical opinion can be traced to the Cold War environment out of which the film arose. An examination of French-American foreign relations provides an explanation for the two very different versions of *Touch of Evil* that different critics saw on screen. Furthermore, a consideration of the reception and reading of the film at the time repositions the *politiques des auteurs* as a critical discourse directly arising out of, and shaped by, the political and cultural forces of the Cold War.

American and French relations were tense throughout the 1950s. According to Frank Costigliola, "In their hearts and minds, the French people simply stood further from the United States than did other European allies" (Costigliola 84). The French government resented the dominant position that the American government assumed in European affairs. They furthermore questioned the supposedly peaceful intentions of the U.S. government as it flexed military muscle in Korea. The executions of Ethel and Julius Rosenberg additionally inflamed widespread anti–American sentiment in France. The media and French intellectuals compared their trial to the show trials that had been so harshly condemned in the Soviet Union, and there was widespread protest against the American government. As one French citizen explained, "Real democracies do not execute spies in peacetime" (Brands 125).

In the United States, officials considered a unified Western Europe military and economy essential in containing any potential Soviet expansionism.

They expected their European allies to "build powerful military forces yet still accept Washington's strategic leadership, to become confident and prosperous nations yet still remain loyal helpmates of the United States" (Brands 119). While the Eisenhower administration pushed for the rearmament of West Germany as part of a European Defense Community (EDC) ostensibly under the guidance of American advisers and directors, the French demanded a leadership role in the negotiations and successfully defended the creation of the EDC in 1954. The 1950s was a time a national crisis in France. Colonial conflicts in both Indochina and Algeria erupted throughout the decade. The Algerian War, waged from November 1954 to April 1961, lead to the death of one million Algerians and the return of hundreds of thousands of European settlers to France. In the rhetoric of American foreign affair officials, France was often portrayed as "womanish, emotionally unbalanced and susceptible to revolution. This 'weak sister in the Western alliance' suffered 'selfish, nationalistic, or stubborn contrariness,' 'delusions of grandeur,' and an individualism so extreme as to be 'almost fatal in organizing the disciplines and restraints' necessary for effective government" (Brands 101). The French unwillingness to bend to the demands of the American government, and their clear antipathy toward American culture and propaganda, led to serious questioning of the reliability and dependability of France as a western ally.

The strain of French-American relations finally came to a head with the Suez crisis in 1956. The French blamed the Americans for the debacle, feeling abandoned at the front of an international crisis. Christian Pineau, who had been the French foreign minister in 1956, commented a decade later that "memories of Suez still poisoned French feelings about America." A RAND study at that time concluded that "Suez convinced French legislators of their deep differences with the United States and the necessity of acquiring an atomic arsenal if France was not to be compelled to align her policies with the United States" (Brands 115). In terms of atomic matters again the Americans failed to provide the French with any support in developing their own technology and industry. The British and Americans controlled the industry, forcing France to develop its own, independent nuclear arsenal. This was also undertaken in the face of strong American opposition to France acquiring the atomic bomb. Thought to be unpredictable, unstable, and unreliable, France was not to be trusted by the Americans. By the time of the Brussels World's Fair, the Paris head of the CIA revealed that "this place is going to blow up very, very, very soon. De Gaulle [wa]s getting stronger by the day.... The only thing that the extreme left and right mobs would agree upon ... would be anti–Americanism" (Brands 119). Polls conducted by the USIA throughout the 1950s consistently found "a disturbing proportion" of anti–American sentiment in France. The concerted propaganda campaign that was waged by the United States in France in order to bolster support for American democracy was apparently ineffective. American prestige in France, particularly in influential non-communist intellectual circles, had dropped to the lowest point ever, State Department officials reported (Brands 119). While thousands were attending the Brussels World's Fair, de Gaulle came to power, creating the Fifth Republic. De Gaulle vowed to end the fighting in Algeria, to build up France's nuclear industry, and to become the leader of Western Europe. His assumption of power led to a major transformation in American views of the French leadership. On July 5, 1958, de Gaulle told Secretary Dulles, "At this critical moment there is nothing more important for the French people than to be made to believe again that France is a great power" (Brands 121). With de Gaulle as leader of France, Americans stopped feminizing France in recognition of the patriarchal power that de Gaulle brought to foreign relations and that Americans could recognize in their own leadership. France had become by the end of the 1950s a force to be reckoned with.

Much of the critical writing on *Touch of Evil* has discussed the film as representative of the border crossings between American and Mexican culture. I suggest that a more apt metaphor may be to see the film as a reflection of American relations with Europe during the Cold War period. The film opens with an explosion as multiple forces collide. A bomb literally explodes open the relations that will drive the narrative. At the height of the Cold War, atomic bombs were omnipresent in the minds of most spectators and clearly also in Welles'. He had reportedly intended to end his *Don Quixote* with an atomic mushroom cloud. The atomic bomb lay at the heart of East-West relations, with Europe, the game board, between them. The explosion of the bomb in *Touch of Evil* also marks the death of the father. As Stephen Heath observed, "The beginning of the film, again quite literally, is thus the murder of the father, his annihilation, his dismemberment; the father prohibits the sexual relation of daughter and boy: they kill him" (Heath 92). The film's central theme is the replacement of the old, entrenched system with a newer, more efficient bureaucracy. It signifies passage into a postwar world with new rules and new sons to lead. And the point of exchange between the old, symbolized by the rich industrialist, Linnekar, who is blown up in his convertible, and the new, Vargas, the Mexican bureaucrat, is the blonde female. An icon of American identity recognizable around the world, the body of the female is the figure around which the film's action pivots.

Quinlan, the lumbering behemoth American cop, gorges on the candy bars and the donuts of American consumer culture. A grotesque caricature of self-indulgence and gluttony, he dominates his foreign neighbors. As an out-of-control tyrant, Quinlan's self-assured sense of power and position unravels in the film. While he sinks farther and farther into the morass of his own corruption, his struggle seems to center on maintaining some sense of dignity or self-respect. His foreign neighbors, the Mexicans, are like the French: feminized, nefarious, and unreliable. They scheme with their own set of rules and with utter disregard for their colonizer's rules.

An intricate network of bureaucrats supports Quinlan's individualized style of justice. These leaders of the nation's institutions rule without any sense of justice or moral certainty. They hearken back to an earlier America, of power institutions supported by nepotism and cronyism. Coming out of the McCarthy era, Welles' portrayal of institutional power as corrupting was clear. Strangely, the most dangerously ambiguous character in the film, the one of whom we feel the least confident, the one whose motives we least understand and whose purpose we feel to be the most pliable, is Schwartz, the assistant district attorney, who appears the most normal, least corrupt of the bunch. Joseph McBride observes, "His complacent acceptance of Quinlan disturbs us, but it is not until he asks offhandedly, 'Who do you like as the killer?' that his moral blindness becomes fully apparent" (McBride 137). Quinlan props up his judgments with a native common sense, that is, with good-old American "intuition," rather than with alien ideologies. Full of racist intolerance and preconceptions, he supports the bureaucratic manipulations of his higher-ups who have exploited for years the people across the border for their own personal gain. But the town over the border, America's satellite, has learned to thrive on its own terms.

In fact, the figures of Quinlan's past that he encounters during his journey back into heart of his darkness, which lies across the other side of the border, are distinctly European not Mexican. The instigating event for Quinlan's slide into his moral torpor is the death of Quinlan's wife, who was "long ago murdered by a man who got off free because Quinlan, then a rookie cop, could not prove the cause" (McBride 132). For Quinlan, retribution was served on the battlefields of World War I. In the film, he reveals that "in some mudhole in Belgium in 1917, the good Lord done the job for me" (McBride 134). The most powerful psychic lure for Quinlan in his passage into his past is the clearly German Marlene Dietrich playing the gypsy, Tanya. Tanya conjures up European decadence of a bygone era; she is never a part of the Mexican dust town. She lives in a world removed from the churning wells of American expansionism that surround her. In one of the most compelling images of the film, we gaze up with him at an oil derrick, the camera rocking hypnotically from side to side as the machinery pumps up and down: "Money, money," Quinlan whispers in time with the movement, acknowledging the power of greed but remaining awesomely detached and self-righteous (Naremore 182).

Enclosed within a world filled with "Victorian bric-a-brac," Dietrich inhabits a space divided between faded European, imperial grandeur and the accouterments of American consumer culture. The pianola, tinkling in the background, lures Quinlan into its exotic folds, while atop of it perches a television set. Dietrich's lost cottage is the ruin of Old World Europe that has been rapidly displaced by the influx of American capital and its attendant vices of crime and corruption. As James Naremore has described, "Tanya herself is both mother and whore, both mystic and cynical realist, whereas Quinlan seems to have stepped into an ironic childhood.... Quinlan is so aged and fat that Tanya doesn't recognize him" (Naremore 182). Quinlan and Tanya interact in a dance from the past accompanied by the music of Henry Mancini, which is "synthetically sweet, perfectly appropriate to a place where everything has become 'so old it's new'" (Naremore 183–84). The icons of European femininity haunt the dark passageways of the film. Along the way, we meet up with Zsa Zsa Gabor, a prostitute, again clearly out of context in the Mexican bordertown. Gabor, who was once called by a congressman "the most expensive courtesan since Madame de Pompadour," also inhabits Quinlan's psyche, which is grounded in the exoticism and eroticism of a European past. Playing counterpoint to the past of Quinlan's journey are the bordellos and drug trade — the illicit products of the incursions of American culture and products into developing economies.

This journey takes us into a world strangely reminiscent of a postwar Europe, where the ruins of culture feed off the influx of American aid. This was also a Europe, though, that had vanished by the end of the 1950s with the stabilization of European markets and the emergence of Western Europe into a booming postwar economy. When toward the end of the film Quinlan asks Tanya to read his future for him, she replies balefully, "You haven't got any ... your future's all used up." Indeed, not only was the old-style America that Quinlan represented used up, but also European dependency on their American liberators was used up.

The future of America that Welles imagines in the film is personified in the Mexican detective, Vargas, played by Charlton Heston. In the original story, the detective was described as an American, but Welles intentionally switches his identity. Welles presents a progressive vision of a new America made possible only through the explosion of the entrenched ideology of old. But Vargas' ethnic identity does not necessarily make him the most exciting or dynamic representation of what America's future holds. Even with his ethnic identity, he is the new American white-collar male in the gray flannel suit, and even more so, he is clearly Charlton Heston. In a letter to Heston after the completion of the film, Welles sums up his own view of Heston's character, which is also an apt description of the Vargas character. "There's this character—(known and loved by all)—he might be called 'Cooperative Chuck'.... He is not merely well disciplined in his work, but positively eager— even wildly eager—to make things easy for his fellows on the set and for the executives in his offices.... In a word, he's the Eagle Scout of the Screen Actor's Guild" (Welles, Bogdanovich, and Rosenbaum 307). This is a description right out of the pages of Dale Carnegie's hugely influential *How to Win Friends and Influence People*. Heston's Vargas thrives in his position as chief of the "Pan American Narcotics Commission."

Very much the icon of the new corporate man in an international economy, Vargas follows company procedures rather than his own individual intuition. Unlike Quinlan, he is not willing to let a hunch—commonsense— interfere with the law. He plays by the rules and is willing to use the newest technology to assist him in his quest for the "truth." "Vargas is the holder of the correct ideas; he speaks up for the right principles; he is played by a man who embodies stoic incorruptibility and sincerity.... But his posture is stiff, humorless, and self righteous. When he stands up to Quinlan we know that we are in the presence of a prig" (McBride 136). His assumption of the status of a solid, middle-class American citizen is guaranteed by his marriage to Suzie, a blond pin-up of an American wife, who erotically inhabits most of the movie in her lingerie. Welles' declaration, "I hate women but I need them," substantiates the sadistic treatment that Suzie undergoes in the film. She is the one who distracts Vargas from his professional obligations and ambitions. She makes him obsessed with her purity. Vargas cries out in the film, "How can I leave until her name is clean! Clean!" Her name is his name; he has assumed the name of the father. Vargas sets off the chain of events that result in Quinlan's fall, and Suzie's degradation. As the head of his new nuclear relationship, Vargas fails terribly at protecting his wife. The core of American national security during the Cold War was the protection of the family from alien contamination. In *Touch of Evil*, the clear degradation of the American body politic is enacted up on Suzie's body. The film presents an erotic fantasy of violation and rape played across the exposed body of the "innocent" Suzie. He, the foreign husband, along with the foreign Grandis and the audience, gaze upon Suzie, the white woman representative of their unconscious desires for America. Suzie is contrasted with the foreign, jaded Tanya. Together they are perfect examples of the fair lady/dark lady imagery that runs throughout American literature and Hollywood cinema, an imagery that suggested latent tensions of race and social class, as well as the underlying American ambivalence about "wilderness" versus domesticity. "Hence they are in exact visual contrast: one is blonde and youthfully voluptuous, the other is dark and ageless; one is spunky, rational and naïve, the other is mysterious and world-weary; one is a wife, the other a prostitute" (Naremore 187).

Reading the film through the perspective of America's relationship with Europe is not so far afield when considering that the film was made on Welles' return to the United States after spending many years in Europe. At the end of 1955, Welles returned to America after his exile in Europe, which had resulted from a period of few job prospects and political persecution during the period of the blacklist. He returned to the United States in order to direct for a season at the City Center Theater Company under the guidance of Jean Dalrymple, who would later become the arts coordinator for the Brussels World's Fair. His first enterprise with the company was *King Lear*, which went extremely badly (Wollen 23). In debt to the IRS and constantly scrambling for funds for his projects, Welles was frequently forced to take acting jobs for the money. He reportedly first signed on to *Touch of Evil* as an actor, and it was through the intervention of Heston that he actually got the directing job. Due to the immense popularity of *The Ten Commandments*, Heston had the power to get Welles signed onto the project as the director. The production went extremely well, ending on budget and on schedule. Like other Welles projects, the conflicts began in the editing room. Eventually the studio completed the editing without Welles' input. Welles viewed his experience making the film as yet another instance in which his work had been undermined by the studio heads. Years later, he related to Bogdanovich the horror of his experience.

> Welles: I was so sure I was going to go on making a lot of pictures at Universal, when suddenly I was fired from the lot. A terribly traumatic experience. Because I was so sure. They went out of their way to compliment me every night for the rushes, and "When are you going to sign a four to five picture contract with us? Please come and see us." Every day they kept asking me to sign the contract. Then they saw the cut version and barred me from the lot [Welles, Bogdanovich, and Rosenbaum 322].

Welles' planned homecoming after so many years abroad was quickly cut short. The America that Welles had returned to at the end of the 1950s was radically different from the one he had left after completing *Macbeth* in 1948. *Touch of Evil* presented a world that was anathema to the satiated consumer complacency that pervaded American culture in the late 1950s.

Without the studio's support of the film, the film did not receive widespread distribution or marketing in the United States or abroad. It was given its New York premiere as half of a double bill at a Brooklyn theater. In London the critics were not even invited to review the picture. Gerald Weales reported that "*Touch of Evil* came creeping quietly into the theaters a few weeks ago. No fanfare. No publicity. Universal-International dumped *Touch of Evil* into the neighborhood theaters in New York (it played first run houses in some other cities) as though they wanted to get the film off their hands in a hurry" (Weales 33). Stanley Kauffmann also noted in his review the poor treatment that the film received. He explained that "quick 'liquidation' of a film is frequent nowadays to reduce advertising and promotion overhead; that might — just possibly — explain New York's behavior. But London's fear of the critics remains inexplicable. Indeed the *Sunday Times* critic there sought it out and praised it. Are there so many pictures available today that this one has to be released furtively?" (Kauffmann 23). This was one film that the studios clearly did not want to be seen. And by this time the name of Welles held absolutely no clout for audiences or critics.

The majority of the critical reception of the film compared it negatively to *Citizen Kane*. The popular perception concerning Welles at the time was that his tremendous artistic abilities had diminished along with his standing within the Hollywood power structure. "Whither Welles?" Kauffmann asked in *The New Republic*, and *The Reporter* led with "The Twilight of an Aging Prodigy." Though *Touch of Evil* was no *Citizen Kane,* the few critics who did bother to review the film thought it was still worthy of notice. As Kaufmann argues, "The common response was that in 1941, Welles had directed, wrote and starred in what many considered the best serious film made in this country. In 1958 he is the screenwriter, director and star of *Touch of Evil....* The immediate, incorrect conclusion is that Welles has declined sharply in powers. But his new picture, while not in the same galaxy with *Kane* is an exceptionally good thriller stunningly directed" (Kauffmann 22). Kauffmann proceeds in his review to give his analysis of Welles' personal flaws. Psychologizing Welles was a favorite past time for the critics, who obviously had not heard Welles' proclamation; "I'm fanatically opposed to psychoanalysis. Freud kills the poet in man. Freud kills man's contradictions" (Heath 107). Instead, they asked,

> Why hasn't Welles had one of the greatest directorial careers in film history? The answer may lie more with a psychoanalyst than a critic, but one can hazard a sympathetic guess. His innate gifts brought him so much success so early that he lacks the discipline of failure. He has never developed a sense of responsibility to the audience — not to the mass audience but the most demanding audience he could envision. Without that sense, no matter how talented, one always remains something of an amateur [Heath 22–23].

The critics stated repeatedly in their reviews that Welles' film was a "brilliant bag of tricks," full of surface technical panache but lacking any deeper significance.

> There is a critical bromide, one for which there is plentiful evidence, that American writers hit young and decay quickly.... Orson Welles is ordinarily explained (or explained away) by the same formula.... The long descent from *Citizen Kane* goes on, and yet *Touch of Evil* need not have been treated so shabbily. I cannot pretend that Welles' new film is a good one. It is not. It is often laughably bad, often pompously bad. Yet it has its virtues. For one thing, it is not dull; and that, in a decade of big-budget, wide screen, many starred extravaganzas, is a pleasant surprise. It has made an attempt — a fruitless one it turns out — to deal with a serious theme.... *Touch of Evil* is pure Orson Welles and impure balderdash, which may be the same thing.... *Touch of Evil* is not a good movie, but it is a good bad movie, which is more fun than the mediocre or even the adequate [Thompson, "Screen: 'Touch of Evil'" 25:2].

Considering the current esteem in which the film is held, the smug condemnation of Welles by the critics and their unwillingness to accord the film any meaning beyond the surface appears an intentional denial of the ideological challenges toward the American system that the film presents.

Interestingly, Arthur Knight in his review uses Hitchcock's *Vertigo* as a point of comparison to *Touch of Evil* in order to illustrate the phenomenon of brilliant directors gone astray. The critical perspective now added Hitchcock to the list of directors whose films were devoid of content and just virtuoso displays. "What has happened in these two films by two enormously talented directors is woefully symptomatic of the failures of many a less gifted man today. They have given us surface cinema, the externals of excitement, invention and tempo without concern for rhyme or reason" (Knight, "Sweet Smell of Success" 25). The denial of meaning in *Vertigo* might also reflect the critics' unwillingness to engage with the manner in which "Hitchcock's films participated in a regime of pleasure that was specific to the postwar period and that helped to consolidate the emergence of the national security state" (quoted in Corber 11). The focus on the formal aspects of the film by the critics signaled an inability or unwillingness to engage with the ideological implications of the works. Knight continued in his review, "Both pictures are replete with thrills and chills created by a knowing use of the camera.... In both there is an unpleasant awareness that technical facility is being exploited to gild pure dross — and the suspicion that the dross was chosen because of the opportunities it afforded for virtuoso display" (Knight 25). The studio heads and the American critics in evaluating the film drew a sharp distinction between the formal components, which are considered exemplary, and the content, which is seen as dark, disturbing, "at once repellant and fascinating," and yet held this to be nothing more than "surface cinema." What were these American viewers seeing when they viewed *Touch of Evil* that was so markedly distinctive from the European reception? In order to begin to answer that question we need to take into consideration the effect of foreign relations on both the American and European film industries during the Cold War.

That the film actually received a European premiere at the Brussels World's Fair was in fact fortuitous. According to Welles, the studio "saw the whole thing put together [and] they just hated it. And there was a man who'd been in charge of part of their European sales for years, and he put the film in the Brussels World's Fair at a special festival. The studio had other pictures that they wanted instead of that and said no. He insisted. And the picture got the prize, and they fired him" (Welles/Bogdanovich 303). The film was virtually ignored in every other country except for France, where it received the Cannes Grand Prix for that year. In fact, the film was popular not only with French critics but also with the French public. Welles explained that "they put it into a theater in Paris for a couple of weeks and it ran a year and a half. It did tremendous business.... [Bogdonavich:] Except in America, where they snuck it out" (ibid.).

The arrival of Welles at the World's Fair generated considerable excitement with the European press. Not the pariah that he had apparently become in the United States, Welles was treated like a star by the European critics and cinephiles. When Welles did not inform the fair's film festival committee of his arrival, they sent out scouts to the airport and train stations to wait for his appearance. His arrival was greeted by an "oversize press conference." He revealed to the waiting fans that "he could not afford to do what he would like to do and must accept any job offered. As for *Touch of Evil*, he said he had had complete freedom while shooting it but was not allowed to edit it or even to see the final result. 'I am going to see it for the first time tonight,' he declared, 'and am as curious as you are'" (Koval 356–57). The immense welcome that greeted Welles upon his arrival and the receipt of a special award at the world's fair film festival was certainly in startling contrast to the reception the film had received in the United States. The writer for *Films in Review* expressed the surprise of American critics of the film's overwhelmingly positive reception. He found it incomprehensible that "the best actor prize went to Orson Welles in *Touch of Evil*.... The International Federation of Film Journalists forced through by a very small majority a prize for *Touch of Evil*. They tried to obscure the absurdity by alleging it was meant as a tribute to Welles for the whole body of his film work" (Koval 360).

Welles was provided the star treatment throughout the variety of film events that occurred during the fair. Similar to previous world's fairs, films played a significant role not only within the pavilion displays but also as part of the arts programming. The major film events at the Brussels World's Fair included an Experimental Film Competition (April 21–27); World Film Festival (May 30–June 13); Festival of Children Films (September 19–21); and a contest for the "best film of all time" (October 12–18). As can be imagined, the competition to determine the "best film of all time" generated its own outbreak of cultural dispute and diplomatic skirmishes. In the Europe of the late 1950s, film had become an art form par excellence. Serious cinephiles considered questions such as designating the "best film" of particular significance. The Belgian Cinematheque, which had organized this event, apparently had not anticipated the "huge enthusiasm" that was aroused among the general public. In fact the "2,000 seats of the Grand Auditorium filled for each performance. On some overcrowded evenings, quite extraordinary scenes developed as the determined public elbowed and jostled their way in, suffering bruises and at least one bloody nose in the process" (Gillett 20). One hundred and twelve historians finally made a selection of 12 films from 26 countries. The final films chosen represented a "safe, conformist and academic approach. *Battleship Potemkin* was an easy winner with 100 votes." *Citizen Kane* came in ninth with 50 votes (Gillett 20). The vote demonstrated a clear preference for what would be considered European art films including several Soviet films and no mainstream Hollywood productions.

The judges for the competition consisted of diverse group of young filmmakers who were chosen so that they might specify the films that most effected their own work. Those assembled for the judging included Robert Aldrich, Alexandre Astruc, Juan Antonio Bardem, Michael Cacoyannis, Alexander Mackendrick, Francesco Maselli and Satyajit Ray. The directors spent ten hours debating how to classify the films according to their intrinsic value for today's generation. An excited and volatile audience assembled on the last night to hear the "prophetic announcement: at last, the Best Film of All Time!" and what they received was a statement admitting that the style and content of the 12 contestants defied classification. Instead, the judges had chosen to assemble a list of the six films that emerged as having, for them as filmmakers, a living and lasting value. The six films selected were *Potemkin*, *The Gold Rush*, *La Grande Illusion*, *Bicycle Thieves*, *Mother* and *Jeanne d'Arc*. The audience did not find the judge's choices consistent with their own, and the final announcement was met with "a barrage of cheers, hoots, suggestions of incompetence and shouts of 'Ou est *Kane*?' from the back. The omission of *Kane* came as a great surprise and disappointment. The judges greeted the outcry generated by their decision by commenting on their individual choices. 'It became clear that *Jeanne d'Arc* and *La Grande Illusion* were the prime favorites for almost everyone. Aldrich defended *Kane*'" (Gillett 20). Given the dominance of American films in the European market, and their extensive popularity with the public, it is interesting to note that when faced with deciding which films would have lasting value, that is, films that could be considered art, Hollywood films were clearly and intentionally absent. Art films for Europeans, or at least young directors, were European films.

And then there was Welles. Welles was a favorite of the *Cahiers du Cinéma* critics. Andre Bazin in particular championed his work, and he eagerly interviewed Welles at the fair. The high esteem with which Welles was held at the fair had a significant effect on his own relationship with *Touch of Evil*. As Welles' relationship with the studio had soured and the editing of the final cut was taken away from him, Welles did not believe that the film was really his own any longer. This point of view changed, though, during his visit to the Brussels World's Fair.

> Much to the surprise of the studio, which had shown little interest in seeking the proper distribution/publicity for it in America, the film won top prize in the international competition, and Orson cheerfully accepted. The award was particularly gratifying to Orson in light of the film's having virtually disappeared in the United States. But, however much he seemed in public to have changed his tune about precisely whose picture it was, still his gratitude for the award was mingled with a secret sense of loss, of alienation from a work of art that both was and wasn't his [Leaming 435].

French critics, in their analysis of Welles, position him outside the mainstream of Hollywood filmmaking and even outside the boundaries of America itself. "Orson Welles would never become an entirely American filmmaker," Truffaut wrote, "for the good reason that he wasn't an entirely American child. Like Henry James, he would benefit from a cosmopolitan culture and would pay for this privilege with the disadvantage of not being able to feel at home anywhere; an American in Europe, a European in America, he will always be, if not a man torn, at least a man divided" (Bazin 4). For the French, Welles has transcended the limitations of national and political boundaries through his artistry. His filmmaking was not limited by Hollywood conventions and in actuality, though "many supposedly 'international' films are made ... only those of Orson Welles are truly international in spirit" (Bazin 19). Typical of the adherents of auteur theory, Welles was described as an artist who has moved beyond political and historical considerations in the pursuit of his own artistic vision. Auteurs were those who had "supposedly transcended the ideological conditions that governed artistic productions at the particular moment in which they worked" (Corber 139).

Descriptions of Welles' artistry frequently evoked comparisons to other authentic artistic forms such as poetry and music. Truffaut wrote that "Orson Welles [wa]s a poet in spite of himself.... His conception of cinema being above all musical ... Welles has always been a musical director, but before *Othello*, he created music within the shots. Starting with *Othello*, he would make music at the editing table" (Bazin 9, 17). He later explains that "through his ability to conceive of film as a duration or as a 'ribbon of dreams'" (quoted in Whitebait 164), Welles "transforms vile reality into poetry" each time he says, "Action!" (Truffaut 27). He is someone who has abandoned the "vile reality" of the present state of affairs to explore his own inner psyche. As Sarris explained, "If directors and other artists cannot be wrenched from this historical environments, aesthetics is reduced to a subordinate branch of ethnography" (Corber 139). The auteur critic's celebration of the individual artist who through his work transcends his own historical and ideological limitations is similar to the manner in which America's Cold Warriors turned to Abstract Expressionism as reflective of American values. They celebrated these works for their reflection of an individualized and independent spirit that was able to flourish under the freedom that the American way provided. These artists were capable of giving free reign to their innermost desires in direct opposition to the repressive forces of totalitarian states. While under the Soviet system art was a political tool of the state, in the free West the artist/auteur was no longer bound by the restraints of politics. Only the free individual, the true auteur, was able successfully to produce art outside of dogmatic ideologies.

The French celebration of American auteurs arose from the complex role that American films played in Europe following World War II. The Hollywood film industry and the American government immediately following the end of the war worked to establish an infrastructure that guaranteed an open market in Europe for American films. Part of this market was defined by the recognition that films were a key element in the important battle to sell the American way of life abroad to an audience that might fall prey to the ideologies of the Communist nations. There was then a two-pronged attack in the distribution of American film abroad — both economic and political. It is quite clear that the symbiosis between Washington and Hollywood was extremely advantageous for both parties, not only in the Cold War period. Washington had direct control over the selection of film exports, as only movies with positive propaganda messages were subsidized. Because of the government's involvement, Hollywood began to produce less "provocative" films, and in return for this self-censorship they received further support through the net of information of U.S. diplomatic missions and USIA stations, which — with more than 200 film libraries and 500 million visitors annually — itself constituted by far the largest film propaganda organization globally. The USIA regularly surveyed the local audiences in the regions where they were stationed for their reactions to films, and they would pass this vital market information to the Hollywood studios. In addition, the studios would receive the necessary insights into local customs and tastes, national prejudices and cultural values, which again helped to avoid the production of films offensive to foreign audiences (Wagnleiter, "Cultural Diplomacy" 207–8).

By the time of the release of *Touch of Evil* at the Brussels World's Fair, Hollywood's dominance of and dependence on the European film market was extensive. In 1939, as the beginning of the war decreased opportunities abroad, 65 percent of their profits were made on the U.S. market; by 1959, it was only 50 percent. The profit share from foreign markets grew proportionally, from 30 percent to 50 percent. By the end of the 1950s, American films enjoyed 50 to 90 percent of all film days globally. While the U.S. government attempted to control the images of America that were flooding the European screens, the most beloved genres for European audiences were those that tended to reinforce stereotypes of American materialism and violence. In addition, as America's psychological warriors attempted to project an image of America that highlighted its high cultural pursuits, it was the cinema that attracted the attention of European intellectuals. U.S. officials felt that, of all people, Europe's intellectuals should realize how much their own survival was at stake in the conflict between freedom and totalitarianism, between the American reverence for civil liberties and the Stalinist repression of dissent. Instead, as Edward Barrett (the assistant secretary of state for public affairs) complained, the Europeans focused on America's materialism and its lack of high culture, its "movie queens" and "gangsters" rather than its "universities, libraries, museums and symphony orchestras" (Pells 68).

An article in *Fortune* emphasized the disparity between the government's intended representation of America abroad and the widespread popular perception of American culture. "By our asinine emphasis on the material goods we have seemed, by implication, to deny the existence of anything else in American life worth bragging about. Even during the most desperate days of the war we got our message so tangled up with refrigerators and cars that, as one Office of War Information worker put it, we could have billed it as 'The War that Refreshes.'" The writer went on to explain the disparity between the official work of the government intelligence programs and their investment in creating a positive image for America, and the adverse effect of commercial Hollywood films. "While our information people spend millions trying to demonstrate that we are really cultural after all, the biggest information agency in the world, Hollywood, has been exporting films that seem to demonstrate the opposite — so persuasively, it might be noted, that in Austria the Russians have been saving their breath by letting several of our gangster films quietly circulate in their occupation zone" (quoted in Wagnleiter 222). There was a clear dichotomy between the USIA's attempts to construct their sanitized image of America and the competing Hollywood images that were being hailed by the majority of foreign viewers. In very broad outline, international audiences shared some common impressions of the United States as a dynamic and violent place, a wealthy society where opportunity and aggression were inextricable. This mixture of hedonism and social Darwinism crops up constantly in public opinion polls conducted in Europe in the 1940s and 1950s (Swann 188). These same polls found motion pictures culpable for constructing these impressions. As one European student studying in the United States responded in a survey: "The most damaging factors to the prestige of the United States are not so much Russian or other anti–American propaganda, but items from the United States itself. The deplorable trash emanating from Hollywood has already succeeded in convincing increasing numbers of Europeans that America consists of gangsters, sadists, pinup girls, cowboys and skyscrapers" (Swann 188).

This popular impression of American culture that was supposedly being reinforced by Hollywood films can be further explained by the need of Europeans, following the devastation of the Second World War, to preserve their own sense of cultural superiority. Financially dependent on the economic aid of the United States, the one way in which Europeans maintained a sense of dignity and pride was to emphasize the quality of their high culture over that of American popular culture. Europeans were not interested in hearing about American excellence in the high arts; that was an image that was too close to their own cultural identity. It was much easier to accept the images of America as a nation of greed and bad taste. Ironically, the core of the State Department's cultural programming focused on bolstering American high art abroad. America's psychological warriors could have soothed the feelings of European resentment that resulted from the relationship of economic dependency following the war by downplaying America's position of dominance in all spheres. But instead they exacerbated these feelings by continually bragging about America's great high cultural endeavors. In an article in *Look* magazine, William Attwood, who lived and traveled abroad from 1946 to 1954, wrote that foreigners believed in a set of cliches about American life that included the claims that "Americans are materialistic. They are too busy chasing the almighty dollar to appreciate the finer things of life, such as culture" and that "Americans are immature and overbearing spoiled brats ... who think they have a right to push other people around" (Attwood 6). Attwood argued that the way to overcome these misconceptions was to show that in America "culture is bursting out all over." His conception of the culture that needed to be shown was "amateur drama societies, symphony orchestras, ballet dancers, art groups and sculpture classes" (Guimond 160). This was exactly what Europeans did not want to see — they much preferred an America undermined by its own cultural problems, as revealed through the popular cinema.

This backdrop of European perceptions of American culture helps explain aspects of the reception of *Touch of Evil* at the Brussels World's Fair. In fact, by the time of the release, America's position as global teacher and leader appeared to be slipping. In addition, many European nations were experiencing their own economic boom, which now placed them squarely within the type of consumer culture that they had previously been criticizing in America.

> Two polls conducted by the USIA in 1960 revealed that for all of Washington's information and cultural efforts over the previous fifteen years, neutralist sentiments were still high in Western Europe. If anything, America's prestige seemed to be declining. Eighty-one percent of the respondents to the polls in Britain, seventy-four percent in France and fifty-three percent in West Germany thought that the Soviet Union's advantage in the space race signaled the end of America's postwar supremacy in science and technology. Many also believed that the Soviets were catching up economically with the United States. The results of these polls indicated, at the least, that America's cultural diplomacy had been ineffective [Pells 87].

The French *Cahiers* critics were writing at a time when France was again on its own independent footing. It was about 1957 that French observers first noticed the fact of their own economy's remarkable growth. The French standard of living had improved markedly by the mid–1950s, and France itself seemed headed toward its own consumer society. This economic change necessarily made American society seem more relevant. The Soviet launching of the Sputnik satellite further "contributed to the new appeal. Now the United States was no longer omnipotent, and its vulnerability made it less menacing" (Kuisel 129). The French pavilion at the fair was one of the most daring architecturally and was a reflection of the new sense of international power that France was experiencing. Modernism was the unifying stylistic choice of the majority of the fair buildings. However, the French one stood out as it "jutt[ed] and soar[ed] into a space like some steel and glass pterodactyl, scream[ing] "I am a Great Power!" (Mannes 19). With de Gaulle's assumption of the leadership of France, the French were presenting a newly masculinized French challenge to America, while U.S. dominance was slipping.

The auteur theory critics reflected the position of power that the French population was experiencing in the 1950s, and its celebration of American films furthermore revealed a cultural elitism that stemmed from a recognition of their own national identity. Firstly, the B-quality of *Touch of Evil* and its reliance on gangsters, violence and hooliganism were All-American filmic tropes that European spectators celebrated. This was their preferred image of America. The America that Welles creates in the film, with its bullying, self-righteous, materialistic and obese presence, was consistent with French sentiments toward the United States throughout the Cold War. In contrast to America's decline with the death of the father, the hope for the new generation is found in the foreigner, Vargas, whose stand against American injustice generated immediate empathy. With his white-collar sentiments and beautiful, sexualized wife, his presence signaled France's own transformation into a consumer-based economy. The film exposed an America in decline, torn apart by its moral laxity, materialism and racism. The United States was no longer able to control the allies that it had dominated, and the developing countries had acquired their own skills in order to compete and succeed.

Like the U.S. critics, the *Cahiers* critics never consider *Touch of Evil* in terms of its political or cultural significance. The text was read as an exploration of human nature and the moral ambiguity of the modern age. Unlike the American film critics, though, Bazin chooses to read the film as art, reflective of the greater aesthetic issues that arise out of its formal elements. There was a presumption that the French intellectuals possessed the superior ability and cultural capital to discern what constituted "art." For Bazin, the film became a drama play between good and evil. During his interview with Welles at the fair, he stated that "we'd like to extricate a certain ideal character who runs through all your films, from *Citizen Kane* to *Touch of Evil*. Is he the man of whom Truffaut spoke, in *Arts*, apropos of *Touch of Evil*; that is to say, the man of genius who isn't able to restrain himself from doing evil? Or is it necessary to see a certain ambiguity in him?" (Comito 204). The interview questions proceeded to focus on the parable of the frog and the scorpion as told in Welles' *Mr. Arkadin*. Bazin said,

> We are struck by the theme of character in your work, from *The Lady of Shanghai* to *Mr. Arkadin*, and perhaps a little less explicitly in *Touch of Evil*. "It's my character"—isn't that what the scorpion said? Is that an excuse the scorpion offers the frog? We'd like to know what the connection is between your own views and the story of the scorpion, because basically our whole conversation has been raising the question of the relation between the frog and the scorpion, don't you think? [Comito 209].

Notice the marked difference in the route of questioning that Bazin employed in comparison to the American critics. His focus on the moral implications of the film was consistent with the rhetorical strategies employed by the West during the Cold War. By emphasizing morality, he was engaging in the political divide that was set up between the God-fearing West and the atheistic communists. The parable of the scorpion, which forms the core of their entire interview, was a parable of Cold War relations. Framed in this manner, it was not difficult to answer: Who played the role of the Scorpion? Who could we trust? Who had been stung by the deceit that was a natural part of their character? I would argue that the French critics' glowing reception of *Touch of Evil* at the Brussels World's Fair was shaped both by France's changing relationship with America and by Cold War ideology. Andrew Sarris has explained that auteur theory was "concerned with interior meaning, the ultimate glory of the cinema as art. Interior meaning is extrapolated from the tension between a director's personality and his material" (Corber 138). This emphasis on interior meaning in auteur theory was set up in a dialogic relationship with the ideological discourses of the Cold War that the critics chose to disregard.

The French critics' discussion surrounding the moral dimensions of *Touch of Evil* differed significantly with the reception by American critics, who considered the film lacking of any thematic content. As one of them stated, "While good versus evil remains the text, the lasting impression of this film is effect rather than substance, hence its real worth" (Thompson, "Screen: 'Touch of Evil'" 25). What was it that the critics and the studio found so unacceptable in Welles' picture? And what also was it that made *Touch of Evil* do so poorly at the American box office? Welles' explanation was that

> the picture was just too dark and strange for them.... Not just an awful story—a mystery. There's something missing there that I don't know about, that I'll never understand. It's the only trouble I've ever had that I can't begin to fathom. The picture rocked them in some funny way.... They were deeply shocked—they felt insulted by the film in a funny way. And hurt and injured—I'd taken them for some kind of awful ride. It was sad for me it turned out that way, because I was ready to settle down in America [Welles, Bogdanovich, and Rosenbaum 322].

Though the critics appeared to focus primarily on the technical pomposity of the film, the critical direction of these reviews was undercut by hints of the darker implications beneath the "bag of tricks." Explications of the film abound with implications of darkness, perversion and degradation. The studio's disgust was coupled with descriptions of the film as a "wild, murky nightmare," and that "Welles' mastery of hurtling movement, of rhythmic variety, of light and depth, his unerring sense of the dramatically ugly, took the eye from point to point as if a hand were on your neck forcing you to look there, then there, then there." There runs throughout the reviews an acknowledgement that "there was a manic intensity to *Touch of Evil* that made it at once repellant and fascinating" (Knight 25). In Vargas' emphatic statement to Quinlan that "a policeman's job is only easy in a police state. That's the whole point, captain. Who's the boss, the cop or the law?" it is the United

States which has become the police state. When conformity and consensus had become the bywords of this "age of peril," which nation, the United States or the Soviet Union, was the actual police state? Not only was Welles' America full of corruption and deceit, but he also created a world in which sexual boundaries were crossed. America in the 1950s "experienced the emergence of an increasingly heterogeneous and antagonistic social field in which the proliferation of differences threatened to lead to a generalized crisis of identities" (Corber 7). The film was a nightmare vision of America collapsing under the panic and fears produced by the racial, sexual and gender changes transforming the outdated America of Quinlan and his cronies. "Everything turns round the mise en scene of Susan's body and the panic images of its sexuality. The line from Night Man to Zita is crossed by the line of the fantastic sexual brouillage of the Grandi family — homosexual, lesbian, hermaphrodite" (Heath 74). This panic of sexualized difference can be heard seeping through the comments of both the American critics and the studio. "Welles clearly wanted to make the film a political and moral fable, its centerpiece the denunciation of Quinlan for racism and for framing suspects, irrespective of whether they were guilty or no" (Wollen 23). This was an America that Americans did not want to see — this was an America that haunted their dreams not their screens. As McBride writes, "Quinlan dies in a world so foul that his malignity seems, because of its unsparing candor, to be a virtue" (McBride 139).

CHAPTER 5

The Visual Jazz of Shirley Clarke: Avant-Garde Cinema and the Department of State

In 1958, Wham-O sold 25 million Hula-Hoops, and America's postwar economic boom appeared to ease the anxieties of the Cold War. Yet, the widespread concern expressed by government, business and cultural leaders about America's image abroad was reflective of the anxieties created by the significant social transformations occurring within the United States. The cultural crises of the 1950s, which reached their apotheosis during the McCarthy hearings, centered on ferreting out the various un–Americans who were portrayed as internal threats to the stability and security of Eisenhower's consensus government. The civil rights, women's, and youth movements presented serious challenges to American hegemony by the late 1950s. Therefore, significant bureaucratic energies were employed to guarantee that only the most appropriate, dignified and positive images of America be projected abroad.

This chapter examines the role that race played in America's cultural hegemony, on both the domestic and the international level, through an analysis of the use of jazz in the American fair planners' cultural programming. The programming choices reflected broader concerns about American high culture and aesthetic modernism. On the one hand, there was significant anxiety about the status of American high culture. With the vast expansion of the mass media following the war, and, in particular, the unprecedented growth in television, the United States was increasingly seen in the public imagination aboard as a pop-culture wasteland. At the same time, there were significant sources for high-cultural admiration, especially in the emergence of distinctly American forms of modern art and architecture. The pavilion planners wanted to highlight these elements of American culture and its ability to rival the European aesthetic tradition. One particularly salient implication of this concern for aesthetic excellence was ethical; the capacity to produce works of art that are significant and of enduring value was traditionally seen as an indication of moral excellence. On the other hand, there was the tension generated by the implications of race and class prevalent within the popular discourses of the time. The United States was wrestling with an international image of moral failure, due to its ongoing racial conflicts. It is not surprising that the locus of the conflict at the fair became a series of loop films by Shirley Clark that dealt with these racial issues in terms of jazz, a contentious image of a genuine American contribution to the arts. As we will see, the planners of the fair attempted to confront this issue of racial discord in the United States directly and openly, but in examining the discourse surrounding the construction of this exhibit, and in the official reactions to its presentation, it is clear that there was little consensus (moral, political, or social) regarding the racial crisis in the United States.

The issue of racial tensions in the United States at the time of the fair and, in particular, the international controversy and negative publicity provided by the desegregation crisis in Little Rock, Arkansas, created one of the major conflicts at the fair. Due to the withdrawal of a considerable amount of federal funding for the American pavilion, corporate sponsors were sought to enhance the government's plans. This intersection of corporate sponsorship with extensive government planning on the part of the State Department and the USIA lead to controversy over the "Unfinished Business" display. In order to illustrate that America was strong and free enough to address some of the problems that the nation was still dealing with, the Time-Life corporation provided "buildings and exhibits dealing frankly with America's unsolved problems, race relations, juvenile delinquency and the waste of natural resources" ("So Short at the Fair" 941). Early discussions with the fair consultants repeatedly addressed the need for America to certify its position as a global leader by revealing that the United States was a nation in "ferment," one that was willing to look head on at its problems, and be prepared to discuss solutions. The *New York Times* reported, "Originating the idea, a conference at the Massachusetts Institute of Technology last year advised the State Department to play down at Brussels the self-righteousness and boast-fulness often associated with the United States. Dr. Walt Rostow, an economist at MIT suggested then that a candid report on 'unfinished business' be presented at the fair" ("Fair Exhibits to Symbolize U.S. Problems" 12). After some negotiations, "It was finally decided that the State Department would pay for the design, and that *Fortune* [another Time corporation publication] would furnish the time and talent" (Krenn 597). The *Fortune* staff then set about planning the exhibit. The exhibition, eventually designed under the guidance of Leo Lionni, the artistic director of *Fortune*, grouped three of America's most pressing problems under the following categories:

"The American Negro." One American in ten is descended from African slaves. These 17 million Negroes have yet to win all the equal rights promised them by American democratic theory. 2. "The Alliance with Nature." The American continent was settled with little thought for the future of its seemingly unlimited supplies.... Now nature needs help from man's management to husband and renew trees, soil and water; 3. "The Crowded City." In less than two generations, American have changed from a country to a city people. 3/4ths of them live in urban areas, whose rapid growth has brought problems of conglomeration and of housing that is not yet up to the other standards of American life.

The final section of the exhibit contained a plaque that read:

American communities, like American individuals, like to emulate and surpass each other. By this process democracy's unfinished business, already partially mastered, will get done on a national scale. To be followed no doubt by other (and perhaps nobler) challenges. The goal that draws us is not Utopia, but larger freedom, with more justice. Democracy is our method. Slowly but surely it works [Dean, "Policy Spotlight" 7–8].

Considering how the Brussels World's Fair was seen internationally as one of the more overt displays of ideological warfare between the Soviets and the Americans, the frank nature of the "Unfinished Business" display, with its presentation of the flaws and difficulties in the American way of life, was exceptional. In comparison to the forced optimism of the Soviet pavilion, the "Unfinished Business" exhibit reflected the perspective of America's power elites, who, because of their confidence in the American way, were capable of recognizing the challenges that American democracy faced. Their recognition of racial intolerance as anathema to American democracy, though, did not represent the dominant racial ideology at the time. This significant gap in racial views was laid bare during the controversy over the "Unfinished Business" exhibit at the fair.

The exhibit was housed in "three architecturally symbolic buildings," which consisted of multicolored pavilions raised on stilts and separated from the main U.S. pavilion. A suspended runway passed through the center of its three sections. The other attachment to the pavilion standing opposite "Unfinished Business" was Disney's Circarama Theater, which presented a clearly contained and stable image of America at the fair. At the start of the "Unfinished Business" exhibit, visitors were greeted with a sign in English, French and Flemish stating that "America is a society in motion." Multilingual guides led visitors into the first pavilion, which was crystal shaped and contained a maze of enlarged newspaper clippings telling about Southern school difficulties, bus boycotts and discrimination. The less chaotic walls in the second section were filled with photographs and charts that documented moves

Adlai Stevenson and the unidentified tour guide visit the Unfinished Business exhibit at the United States Pavilion (National Archives).

toward the "improvement of the Negroes' status" ("Fair Exhibits to Symbolize U.S. Problems" 12). The section dealing with segregation carried the caption, "Not since the Civil War, which freed him and made him a citizen, has the Negro made such strides toward full equality as he is making now.... As a result, the doom of the American caste system is in sight" (Krenn 598). The walls of this section were also covered with quotations from President Eisenhower, Adlai Stevenson, and Martin Luther King, Jr. The final building was constructed with "simple, angled panels" which would be "calm in contrast. Inside, three large photographs present[ed] the ideals that a sometimes slow democracy works toward. In one enlargement, white, Negro and Oriental children play[ed] together.... The exhibit [was] titled 'American Idealism in Action'" ("Fair Exhibits to Symbolize U.S. Problems" 12).

Soon after the opening of the pavilion, there was an outcry from members of Congress. "A new storm was brewing today," *The New York Times* reported. "Representatives Prince H. Preston of Georgia and L. Mendel Rivers of South Carolina expressed their feelings at a private meeting with Mr. Allen, Howard S. Cullman, United States Commissioner General for the fair, and John C.

Folger, United States Ambassador to Belgium. They made no secret of their outrage that the pavilion would be telling the world that segregation was a problem we must solve" ("Brussels Exhibit on Bias Is Decried" 17). The one aspect of the exhibit that was specifically cited as problematic was the photograph of the children of different races holding hands. Burke Wilkinson of the State Department's Office of Public Affairs traveled to Belgium to study the exhibit and report back about the controversy that it had caused. In the second building, another problematic photograph showed a college dance with "a colored boy dancing with a white girl who seems to be reluctant to join him" (Krenn 602). After suggesting that the photograph should be removed, he stated that he had "very seriously explained our reservations about one of the photographs, which happens to be the most appealing of the whole exhibit: a mixed group of children dancing in a ring in a field. They include white, colored and yellow.... The trick here, if the exhibit as a whole is to be saved, is to label this scene of the dancing children correctly. This does *not* represent any national objective defined by law, but freedom of choice to play as one wishes" (Krenn 602).

Edward Steichen's "The Family of Man" exhibition of photographs, which had already been touring the world under the auspices of the USIA since its opening at the Museum of Modern Art in 1955, had an entire section of photographs of multiracial children around the world clasping hands. "The Family of Man" exhibit would also play a central role in the following year at the American Exhibition in Moscow. The art director for the exhibition catalogue of "The Family of Man" was Leo Lionni, who also was the designer of the "Unfinished Business" exhibit. Lionni, who was known for his distinctive European style in design, had been artistic director for *Fortune* magazine from 1948 to 1959 and had also been art director for the Container Corporation of America's landmark "International Series" campaign. His connections both with the advertising world and Time-Life were complemented by a modernist European upbringing and his support of leftist politics. The conflicts that crossing this divide caused Lionni would eventually result in his departure from *Fortune* magazine in 1959 in order to pursue his career as a writer and illustrator of award-winning children's books.

The use of the photograph of the multiracial children within the context of a national problem highlighted the racism that permeated all aspects of American society. And this was not deemed to be an acceptable image of America for international consumption — the Eisenhower administration did not want people to think that the American system actually condoned the crossing of racial boundaries. But when the same image was placed within the global and humanist context of "The Family of Man," the threat of racial difference became dissipated and unproblematic. The rapid response toward and critical attack of the "Unfinished Business" pavilion indicated the level of sensitivity of Americans toward charges of racism and an unwillingness to view racism as America's problem. The primary driving force behind the changes in the pavilion was a result of a series of individual complaints by American tourists who had a clear notion of national identity, which did not include social injustice and inequality. In comparison, "The Family of Man" exhibit, which opened at the American exhibition in Moscow, was restricted to Russian citizens, and so there was no possible input from American tourists.

The majority of USIA information programs abroad were never seen by Americans, and the major concern of these programs was shaping local perceptions of the East-West ideological divides of the Cold War. The considerable economic investment in these programs was not for simple altruistic ends, but was seen instead as a necessary cost of the cold war and the efforts to sway the hearts and minds of nations that might fall prey to communist influence. USIA officials would regularly interview and survey local people in order to judge their responses to exhibits, and alterations would be made if there were perceived misunderstandings of the ideological goals of the exhibits. Unlike most USIA events, the Brussels World's Fair was caught in the double bind of attempting to create a persuasive presentation of the American way of life to a specifically middle- and upper-class European audience while also handling the flood of American tourists in Europe who had their own understanding of the discursive battles of the Cold War. Evidence of this conflict of interest can be seen in the caption for "The Family of Man" photographs of children grasping hands, which was chosen to illustrate the theme: "Clasp the hands and know the thoughts of men in other lands" (Steichen 94–95). At the Brussels fair those same images now were read to mean that the American government was condoning, and perhaps even promoting, miscegenation rather than supporting racial tolerance.

Though many American tourists were vocal in their complaints about the "Unfinished Business" exhibit, it was extremely popular with many visitors. It "drew praise even from visitors who had come prepared to condemn the United States for its treatment of its Negro citizens. Some said, "You are very courageous to do this," or "Only a great country can recognize its faults" (Dean, "Policy Spotlight" 7). *Newsweek* called it "one of the real surprises" of the fair, which dealt "frankly and graphically with U.S. efforts to solve such problems as floods, droughts, juvenile delinquency, and racial tensions. (Georgia's Senator Herman Talmadge ha[d] dubbed this exercise in national candor — sight unseen — a 'gross insult to the South'" ["Where East Meets West: The U.S. At the Fair" 53].) President Eisenhower's response to the criticism of the exhibit was to require that racism be placed within the context of a wide variety of problems facing American democracy that could be "rotated" throughout the summer. George Allen, reiterating the administration's position, stated, "There is a great deal of unfinished work in the United States. If we want to be broadly representative, we should go into as much as we can" (Mooney 1). Now that we had admitted that America was actually a society in ferment, one way to dissipate that ferment was to make racism not a uniquely American challenge, but one of a whole long list of social issues that all nations must confront.

The Southern representatives who had come as "guests of an airline" to examine for themselves the controversial exhibit "asserted privately that there were other national problems such as crime and the influx of Puerto Ricans, that might have been included if 'Unfinished Work' had not been intended to give a one-sided picture" ("Brussels Exhibit on Bias Is Decried" 17). Because of the attack by Southern politicians and Eisenhower's wavering position on the race problem in the United States, the exhibit was in fact closed, and the "Unfinished Business" displays were removed in early August. Even though the exhibit had made "deep impressions on visitors from Europe, Asia, the Middle East and Africa, as well as on many American visitors, [it] was removed and replaced by a public heath exhibit" (Dean, "Policy Spotlight" 8). Public health was a more ideally suited problem to choose to illustrate the freedom and diversity of the American system. Vera Dean, writing about the exhibit for the *Foreign Policy Bulletin*, ended with the observation that "one is left with a challenging thought: in the international competition of the future, what nation will assume the responsibility of leadership in nurturing a humanism which admits that no one person has a monopoly of virtue — or ever will?" (Dean, "Policy Spotlight" 8).

By the time of the fair, the U.S. government had already quite actively used cultural ambassadors that were sent to other countries not only as representatives of America's artistic excellence but also as spokespeople for the American way of life. Originally these ambassadors were drawn from the more traditional high arts such as classical music and opera. As other historians have documented, these ambassadors of the high arts were not warmly welcomed, especially by those European nations (Germany, Austrian, Italy) with a long history of dominance in the high art (see, for instance, Wagnleiter, "Cultural Diplomacy"). With the destruction of their national infrastructure following the war, the cultural domain was an area where Europeans could maintain a sense of superiority in relation to the Marshall Plan and the onslaught of American popular culture into their nation's media outlets. One of the unexpected outcomes of the U.S. government's strategy of flooding the

European markets with Hollywood films as part of their Americanization programs was the perception of many Europeans that American culture was defined by Hollywood movies and American popular culture. American foreign policy strategists by the 1950s were extremely conscious of this and worked to dismantle the European perception that Americans lacked any "real" high art forms that were distinctly American.

The major art forms used to strengthen America's artistic position abroad tended to be modernist and included Abstract Expressionism and jazz. Though these movements generated considerable opposition within the political debates over the ideological significance of modernism, by the mid–1950s these forms became the most important forces in the U.S. government's cultural ambassadorship programs. "The abstract expressionists could serve as an advertisement for American values in the Cold War.... They were free to 'express' their individuality, their subconscious emotions and private visions, without having to answer to cultural commissars," Richard Pells has observed.

> They were "action" painters: their work was improvisational and spontaneous [like jazz], like America itself. And to make this point unmistakably clear, modernism (so its defenders claimed) could flourish only in a society that was open, democratic and capitalist, a society that believed in non-conformity and competition as catalysts to artistic and economic achievement. Thus, in the eyes of anti–Stalinists in the intelligentsia and liberals in the State Department, abstract expressionism should be welcomed as an essential ingredient in America's cultural diplomacy, another way in contrasting the vibrancy of life in the United States with the monotony of totalitarianism [Pells 78].

Within Eisenhower's propaganda programs, the arts were a necessary ideological tool of the Cold War. Aesthetic considerations were reduced to issues of political intention and significance. Questions of form were reduced in their official translation into messages of national ideology.

While jazz lacked high art status, it would be more productive in the end to utilize jazz's potential as an ideological force that could best speak for the nation, rather than fight the popularity of America's popular culture. By the mid–1950s, this strategy had been adopted in full force: jazz had become a major element in the cultural programming of the State Department. An article in a 1955 edition of the *New York Times* titled "United States Has Secret Sonic Weapon — Jazz" explicitly discusses the propaganda value of jazz. The article reveals that "all Europe now seems to find American jazz as necessary as the seasons.... In Paris ... Sidney Bechet and his soprano saxophone drew 15,000 Frenchmen to demand equality of opportunity to share 3,000 seats. Not to be deprived of their chance to demonstrate enthusiasm for his individual artistry, the unseated majority 'wrecked the joint,' just as the Germans did at Hamburg" (Belair 1). The article goes on to reveal that "the popularity of jazz and the market for it is a phenomenon that strikes Americans who returned to the continent after a long absence. Men actually have risked their lives to smuggle recordings of it behind the Iron Curtain and by methods that the profit motive cannot explain" (Belair 1). A German Swiss who was interviewed in the article reveals that "jazz is not just an art. It is a way of life" (ibid.). The reason given for the widespread popularity of jazz was tied both to its emphasis on individual and free expression and to its roots as a folk music for the oppressed. Jazz was seen as an indigenous form still not corrupted by the mass market. In addition, during a time when the "Negro Question" was so prevalent within the European media, jazz served as a clear demonstration of successful integration in the United States.

After the rise of bebop in the late 1940s, jazz became established as a modernist form that was elevated into the realm of high art. America had a way to compete with the dominance of European classical music. As *The New York Times* stated,

> American jazz has now become a universal language. It knows no national boundaries, but everyone knows where it comes from and where to look for more. Individual Americans will continue to pack them in and the reasons for this are clear.... There is not a wide difference between the best symphony orchestras of the United States and Europe — not where the masses of the people are concerned. But nobody plays jazz like an American [Belair 42].

The jazz musicians that became America's cultural ambassadors, though, did not typically see their music as a form of political propaganda. Louis Armstrong in a 1955 interview was described as "outdrawing opera, smashing box-office records all over Europe. Fans slip out from behind the Iron Curtain just to hear it" ("They Cross Iron Curtain" 54). Asked if he thought that "hot jazz will end the 'cold war,'" Armstrong replied, "Well, not knowin' about politics — but I know that hot jazz can do a whole lot for a lot of fans that don't care so much for that. If it's left to people that's peaceful for music, there wouldn't be no wars. Wouldn't be none. It comes from people that probably don't care so much about jazz, but, I mean, music has done a whole lot of friendships, and everything" (ibid.). This is not exactly the response you would hope from someone who was being viewed as a spokesperson for America. Though the interviewer keeps attempting to draw Armstrong into a political discussion, he maintains a clear separation between his artistic production and questions of politics. Asked if "the atomic bomb has made people go to music more than they did before," Armstrong responds, "Well, I don't dive into politics. Like in Geneva — that guy with the mike, you know. He would rush you with it. 'Well, what do you think of the Big Four Conference?' I say, 'Well, I jus' hope that combo has a good time and straightens out that jive'" ("They Cross Iron Curtain" 62).

Eisenhower's psychological warfare programmers who saw all forms of art — both low and high — as a means of persuasion, were certainly aware that most Europeans considered jazz to be an African American musical form. They, therefore, tried to use jazz to counter the adverse effects on public opinion abroad that the ongoing violations of African Americans' civil rights had caused — and which they sought to track carefully, for example, in opinion surveys on the case of Emmett Till, an African American boy who had been brutally murdered by whites. In addition, jazz was stringently suppressed in the Eastern bloc countries, especially in East Germany, and so it made jazz into an attractive messenger for American democracy. In fact, jazz, like modernism in art and literature, could become part of the anticommunist battle (Poiger 163). But though jazz musicians were accorded a prominent role in cultural exchange programs throughout the world, they were still considered unreliable in terms of their worth as government operatives. C. D. Jackson, a main proponent of Eisenhower's psychological warfare project who was also a writer for Time-Life, wrote in a memo to Nelson Rockefeller warning his "CIA colleagues not to get the 'smarty pants' idea of using these artists as intelligence sources — 'I don't think that these people are emotionally capable of playing a double role.' He did think though that 'after they return they can of course be skillfully debriefed'" (Saunders 428n42).

Considering the huge popularity of jazz in Europe in the 1950s and the recognition by the State Department of its political significance, it is not surprising that jazz was accorded center stage in the performing arts programming for the American pavilion. The responsibility for the arts programming at the Brussels World's Fair was assigned to a good friend of Howard Cullman's, America's fair commissioner, Jean Dalrymple. Dalrymple had begun her career as a vaudeville comedienne, became a theatrical publicist and producer, and later helped found the New York City Center (now part of Lincoln Center), which opened in 1943 with the aim of presenting plays and musicals at popular prices. In her autobiography, Dalrymple relates that

> the most rewarding work I have done has been at City Center and at the Brussels World's Fair of 1958 and it was Howard Cullman who made both possible. When Eisenhower appointed him high commissioner of the United States for the fair, he asked me if I would be his co-ordinator of the Performing Arts program. As it turned out, we never could have accomplished such a full and varied program at the fair without the link with City Center [Dalrymple 287].

In both of her autobiographies, Dalyrmple's recollections of the fair center on the theatrical and classical music presentations. "Each country had its 'national days' when the attention of all forty-nine contributing nations was drawn to that particular one. Ours were July second, third and fourth," Dalyrmple relates.

> But we had such a plethora of talent available at this time that the United States had not national days but a national week, beginning on Monday with a piano concert by Bryon Janis, attended by Queen Elisabeth of Belgium, followed by the opening of *Carnival on Ice* on Tuesday (this was a purely commercial venture, but Morris Chalfen, the producer of the glamorous and popular spectacle, had obligingly switched his July engagement from Barcelona, Spain, to Brussels for the occasion), the first night of *Wonderful Town* at our American Theater on Wednesday, the American Ballet Theater at the Grand Auditorium on Thursday, the Philadelphia Orchestra with Isaac Stern and Ormandy on Friday and on Saturday an extra concert by the Philadelphia Orchestra with Van Cliburn as soloist [Dalrymple 290].

Though her recollection focuses on the more middle- and high-brow events at the fair, in fact the most popular performances were the jazz and popular music events.

An early list of performers reveals a large number of African American performers including "Harry Belafonte ... Leontyne Price, the great Negro soprano ... Louis Armstrong ... Robert McFerrin and William Warfield, two superb Negro baritones" (Funke 88). Why the heavy emphasis on African American performers? The Little Rock crisis made State Department officials very conscious of the need to dispel racist images of America at the fair by emphasizing cultural programming that showcased America's tolerance and diversity. One of the African American performers, though, who did not make it to the fair stage was Louis Armstrong. Although Armstrong had already toured extensively throughout the world as a goodwill ambassador for the American way, in 1957 Armstrong became politicized for the first time in the mainstream media. While in Grand Forks, North Dakota, in September of that year, Armstrong saw footage of the Little Rock, Arkansas, school desegregation and heard that Governor Orval Faubus intended to use the National Guard to prevent desegregation. At the time, Armstrong was preparing to go abroad again on "another international goodwill tour in the guise of Ambassador Satch, the personification of the American dream, and the American way of life and all its freedoms, but after watching these traumatic events in Little Rock, he was damned if he was going to stand up and grin hypocritically before foreign audiences, pretending that his country was the land of the free with equality for all" (Bergreen 471).

By the time of the fair, Armstrong had become significantly politicized to make a public statement about his own personal experiences with racism in America. "The way they were treating my people in the South, the government can go to hell," he told a reporter as he shaved in his North Dakota hotel room. "It's getting so bad, a colored man hasn't got any country" (Bergreen 471). This was not the type of press that America needed to repair an image already besmirched by charges of racism, and so the international goodwill tour was off. "The people over there ask me what's wrong with my country, what am I supposed to say?" Armstrong asked (Bergreen 471). Armstrong, who had been primarily responsible for the spread of the gospel of jazz internationally, was now under the surveillance of the FBI. Whatever his views about jazz, J. Edgar Hoover was willing to grant on reviewing Armstrong's file that his "life is a good argument against the theory that Negroes are inferior" (Bergreen 472).

While Armstrong had become an international symbol of American integration and equality, he still could not perform in his hometown of New Orleans, which continued to prohibit the performance of integrated bands even after the law was ruled unconstitutional in 1956. Armstrong was quite aware of the irony of his situation in the midst of the Cold War, one in which America's own ideology of tolerance and freedom was severely curtailed for many of its citizens. "I don't care if I ever see that city again," he insisted. "They treat me better all over the world than they do in my hometown. Ain't that stupid? Jazz was born there and I remember when it wasn't no crime for cats of any color to get together and blow" (Bergreen 472–73). Armstrong's absence at the fair was not to the detriment of the American pavilion. *Newsweek* described that "with considerable imagination, hard work, and very little bragging they have gone a long way toward their stated goal: To give 'the feel and smell' of the land, and to suggest that 'something happens to men living in America ... which can be called progress, real freedom and better living'" ("Where East Meets West: The U.S. At the Fair" 54). Though he did not appear in person at the fair, visitors using the voting machines put on display per Eisenhower's request unanimously chose Armstrong as their favorite American musician.

Since the Soviets frequently used the racial tensions in the United States as an example of the hypocrisy and inequalities of the American system, C. D. Jackson felt that it was crucial that American foreign policy experts launch a counterattack to these charges. There were serious concerns in the Eisenhower administration that the race issue was mobilizing European support away from the United States. C. D. Jackson argued that it was time we stop explaining in terms of "this dreadful blot on our scutcheon" and to look the whole world in they eye. To this end, psychological warfare experts on the Operations Coordinating Board (in close collaboration with the State Department) established a secret Cultural Preservation Committee whose chief activity was to plan and coordinate tours of black American artists. The appearance on the "international stage of Leontyne Price, Dizzy Gillespie, Marian Anderson, William Warfield [who sang at the world's fair], the Martha Graham Dance Troupe [also at the fair], and a host of other multiracial and black American talent during this period was part of this covertly supervised 'export' programme" (Saunders 291). The broad representation of both classical and modernist artists signaled again the administration's understanding of the arts as a necessary part of the government's ideological battles and their willingness to support performances that could fit into their political agenda.

Unlike the political controversy that led to the cancellation of Armstrong's performance at the fair, the jazz acts that did appear fit comfortably into the State Department's agenda. One of the biggest hits was the Benny Goodman band. Goodman, like Armstrong, had already proved himself an able spokesperson for the American way. In December 1956, the State Department sponsored a tour by Goodman in eight Far Eastern countries. This trip included a two-week engagement at the Thailand International Trade Fair, where it was reported that "Goodman had seen more of the King, and on closer terms, than any other visiting Americans" (Saunders 291). The tour achieved its political purpose admirably, leaving behind a wake of good feeling toward the United States and an impression that "America is not only great in modern plumbing and fancy cars," as one American official put it, "but in things of the spirit and the arts." The Goodman band also received positive press for its multiracial composition. The band stood out as an exemplary example of America's integration during a time when the world was closely watching the civil rights struggle. Many Europeans were especially horrified by the violence utilized to squash the protests. "I was constantly asked by the press over there about the colored people here," Goodman reported. "They were quite concerned. I didn't really have anything particular to say, other than we've had colored musicians in the band for twenty-five years. That was probably more than enough to offset what they had been hearing from the other side" (Saunders 291).

By the 1950s, the swing music of Benny Goodman had become a widely commodified form in the United States and was seen by many jazz critics as old-fashioned and out-of-date. Though Goodman had attempted to incorporate more modern and bebop jazz renditions in his performances, overall he continued to depend on his now-popular favorites from the prewar period. Goodman's popularity at the fair and the lack of opposition to his appearance is not hard to understand. Goodman's performance received backing from the Westinghouse Broadcasting Corporation, which announced that "as a public service" it would strengthen the almost non-existent performing arts

The Benny Goodman orchestra performs at the Brussels World's Fair (National Archives).

program at the American pavilion by underwriting a week of concerts by "the great Goodman orchestra." Westinghouse's president explained: "In sponsoring these performances of American jazz, we will add a dimension to the Brussels Fair in which the Soviet Union cannot compete. American jazz has been shown to be a great good abroad" (Firestone 397). For their public service abroad, the Westinghouse Corporation in addition received several days of broadcast on the local radio and television shows of the Goodman performance, which was sure to bolster the already-booming record sales in Europe. Westinghouse, in fact, picked up "the $85,000 tab for the concert in the hope it would be a top attraction for Europe's jazz aficionados. It was — Goodman literally had his audience jumping in the aisle" ("Business Packs Them in at Brussels Fair" 29).

Europeans loved jazz. Goodman's first night performance in the American theater shook the U.S. world fair cultural effort out of the doldrums. Playing to a full 1,100-seat theater, Goodman and his band brought a sedate first-night audience to life whistling and shouting. There was concern on all fronts that the Americans were losing the battle of the arts with the Soviets, who had invested significantly more in their programming. Therefore, Goodman's performance was "not only a triumph for Mr. Goodman and his musicians, it was also a long overdue assist for the American performing arts program. Nothing has been needed more than good, live talent to bolster United States morale and prestige badly sagging until now because the Soviet Union has already scored a number of musical successes here since the fair opened April 17" (Waggoner 6). The culmination of the Goodman performance was a performance to celebrate his 49th birthday. For the event, "he took over the stage in the ninth century old Grand Palace (Market Place) and gave a capacity crowd of 10,000 a program of the music he made famous.... The crowd gave Mr. Goodman and his band a tremendous reception" ("Benny Goodman Scores New Brussels Triumph" 60). The week that Goodman spent at the fair was an unqualified success for the band and also for the American arts programming, but this was not a performance that was in anyway challenging or experimental. Most European jazz fans had become enthralled with bebop in the late 1950s, which was seen as authentic, non-commercial, and more closely aligned to its African American roots than swing. "The band Benny assembled for the occasion certainly had the potential to be something more than another pallid recreation of the past.... Though Benny said he planned to restrict himself to playing swing because 'bop and progressive jazz was not our cup of tea,' he had in fact commissioned some interesting new arrangements by more contemporary writers like Gil Evans and Bobby Gutesha. But to judge from live recordings issued by Columbia and Westinghouse, very little of this potential was realized in performance" (Firestone 398). Goodman took his role as an ambassador for America seriously, and while at the fair, he applied for a visa to travel to Russia. His application was turned down on the grounds that "the Russian people were simply not interested in jazz." However, "Nothing could be farther from the case. A member of the Philadelphia Symphony fresh from a tour of the Soviet Union reported that 'Every Russian youth I met listened to the Voice of America jazz show' and 'Everyone in Russia [wa]s crazy about Benny Goodman'" (Firestone 398). Goodman would finally get his chance in 1962, when he took his band for the first government-backed "mission to Moscow" by a jazz performer.

While Goodman was indeed one of the most prominent and popular performers on the U.S. roster, there were several other jazz performers that also attracted considerable notice. They also clearly fit well into the forms of jazz deemed appropriate by the State Department for cultural diplomacy. In July, the Sidney Bechet sextet saved the day for the U.S. arts programming. Bechet had been living permanently in Paris and was considered a star in

France. His Dixieland jazz, like bebop, was considered by many critics as arising from the authentic roots of an African American folk form. According to Howard Taubman, Bechet's sextet's performance "saved the evening. It played with a sense of rhythmic momentum and a gusto that are the liveliest tradition of American jazz.... At last American jazz woke them up. The audience that turned out for this program had come virtually begging to be stimulated" (Taubman, "Jazz Arriues" 19). This audience was markedly different from the more staid and mature fair audiences. Jazz was one of the main products American record companies were selling to the burgeoning European youth market. "This was not the usual gathering of very important people who turned out for premieres in Brussels. It was a 'hep' international crowd. Many were youngsters, and their desires were thoroughly informal. For them the music was the thing" (ibid.). These headliner performances were the exception during the summer of programming that, because of limited federal funding, was forced to rely on many amateur performances. The *New York Times* coverage of the Bechet performance confirmed the lack of consistency or quality in the American arts program. "For Brussels it should have chosen its performers more discriminatingly and concentrated its programs to better purpose. If Americans cannot do better than this with a jazz concert, of all things, they might as well throw in the sponge" (ibid.).

Even though Bechet attracted a large audience of jazz lovers, by the late 1950s, jazz no longer represented a threat to established cultural institutions. Previous concerns about the illicit nature of jazz quickly dissipated as rock 'n' roll rapidly spread into Europe and caused considerable distress among parents and social critics. The one performer at the fair who reflected the transformation in popular musical tastes and the impact of the youth market on the commercialization of popular music was the calypso performer Harry Belafonte. Calypso, especially a toned-down, commercial variant, became a worldwide craze with the release of Belafonte's rendition of "Banana Boat Song" on his 1956 album *Calypso*. *Calypso* was the first full-length record to sell more than a million copies. Belafonte stopped at the fair as part of his first European tour. He was already earning up to $10,000 a night but gave four free performances at the fair. *The New York Times* thought that he gave the American program a marked lift. His recordings had created a public for him all over Europe, and there was a big demand for his performances. His act was broken down into three groups of songs: "Moods of the American Negro," "Songs of the Caribbean," and "Around the World." Taubman noted that the best thing about his program was the intensity he brought to such numbers as "Cotton Fields" (about Little Rock, Arkansas), "Jamaica Farewell," and "Danny Boy." "The packed theater seemed to relish everything Mr. Belafonte did.... Among those who joined in chanting the perfidy of 'Matilda' and 'Went Venezuela' was Mrs. Franklin D. Roosevelt" (Taubman, "Belafonte Sings" 200).

Belafonte's repertoire displayed a willingness to overtly tackle pressing racial issues through song. So, why was Belafonte's performances granted clearance by the State Department even though he was singing about social injustice in the United States? Belafonte's political position became even more clearly expressed following his performance at Brussels. He held a news conference arranged by the U.S. Embassy in Italy in order to denounce Governor Faubus. How was it possible that the U.S. government was sponsoring a public proclamation about America's racial injustice at the exact moment when they were supposedly attempting to downplay the "Negro problem" in the United States? The content of Belafonte's press conference suggests why he was chosen to assume this public role as a spokesperson for the American government. Belafonte told Italians that "America will survive Faubus in the same way as Europe survived Hitler." He added that "most white Americans disliked Faubus ... [and the] situation after the Supreme Court's stand on integration, represented 'progress and not regression'" ("Belafonte in Rome Denounces Faubus" 19). Newspapers throughout Europe were daily carrying reports about the escalating violence in Little Rock with considerable dismay and uncertainty over the U.S. government's actions. Belafonte's "impromptu" press conference was meant to put a positive face on a problem that continued to cloud America's image abroad.

Belafonte represented exactly the kind of image of African Americans that the government hoped Europeans would associate with the American dream of the melting pot. Looking back, it's interesting to take note of Belafonte's popular persona during the 1950s in order to understand how race played a significant role in the ideological debates of the Cold War. Belafonte was acceptable as an African American spokesperson because he embodied many of the ideals that were understandable to a white audience. The *New York Times Magazine* actually featured Belafonte the year after the fair in an article that emphasized his skills as an "organizational man." In the article he is celebrated for the fact that he is "a corporate enterprise." Belafonte's financial wizardry was of considerable more significance than his artistic abilities. The *Times* gushes that "the financial rewards of such corporate activity have been notably impressive. At 32, Belafonte is the highest paid Negro entertainer in history.... His album titled 'Calypso' was the first by any single artist to sell more than one million copies" (Coleman 35). The *Times* writer does posit the question of the possible source of Belafonte's fame and fortune. Her own investment in Belafonte's successful career is revealed when she asks,

What is this mysterious ingredient that sends both men and women — young, middle-aged, and old — running to the box office and into the record stores? That a good part of it centers around his handsome head and lean, lithe body is undeniable. Most women, for example, will take an oath that the colored shirts he always wears on stage are open all the way down to the leather belt and brass rings which buckle in his well-cut black trousers. In reality, this shirt is open only to the center of his chest, or to about where the third button comes on any ordinary man's dress shirt [Coleman 35].

Belafonte's fair complexion and traditional good looks coupled with his slick, commercial renditions of "exotic" music made him, like his good friend Sidney Poitier, acceptable to a white audience. And, in fact, his audience was primarily a white one. By 1953, Belafonte began to appear regularly on the *Ed Sullivan Show* and went on to become the most frequently heard singer

Eleanor Roosevelt and Harry Belafonte in Brussels, Belgium, September 6, 1958 (Franklin D. Roosevelt Library, National Archives).

on the show. Belafonte received his greatest popular exposure so far, but he was also — and not for the first time, either — experiencing the bitterness of being shunned by his own people. In a later interview, Belafonte revealed that "a lot of people on the left turned against me, because they thought there was no way I could get on the Sullivan show if I hadn't talked to the Committee, or whatnot. I had to live for a long time with the pain of rejection from people who were in the same camp" (Gates 136). That he succeeded where so many others failed was, in the eyes of some, no real mystery. Belafonte's friend and collaborator Bill Attaway observed in the late 1950s, "At the present stage of the struggle for human freedom, the need is for a bridge Negro — one who serves to connect white and Negro. Harry fills that need remarkably. Although he is brown skinned and unmistakably Negro, he is acceptable in terms of white standards of beauty. Brown up Tab Hunter and you could hardly tell him from Harry Belafonte" (Gates 139).

Harry Belafonte surrounded by young fans at the Brussels World's Fair (National Archives).

The State Department's heavy reliance on African American performers at the fair became an effective way to avoid the controversy surrounding the "Unfinished Business" exhibit. Rather than approaching the civil rights crisis in the United States as something that needed to be remedied, the African American performers were ready evidence that the desegregation crisis was an exceptional event and that race injustice was not a widespread problem. At least in the arts it appeared that there was no color divide in the United States. Besides the conscious use of African American performers on America's stage, guides working in the pavilion were intentionally chosen in order to represent America's diversity. During a meeting of the NAACP in March 1958, one of the members of its board of directors noted that "twenty percent of the U.S. representation at the Brussels World's Fair is supposed to be non-white" (Krenn 602n22). The presence of African American guides did not go unnoticed by visitors. One guide mentioned that "an Englishwoman shocked me when she burst out with the remark, 'You really are trying to push your colored people, aren't you?' I explained to her that Negro guides were included in the group as a representative part of the American population" ("We Open in Brussels" 69).

Avant-garde film, along with Abstract Expressionism and jazz, was also brought on board in order to express the individualism and freedom offered under the American system. Though the State Department was not generally considered to be the backers of experimental filmmaking in the United States, with the removal of the "Unfinished Business" exhibit at the American pavilion, the only African American images in the pavilion could be found in the loop films of Shirley Clarke. Clarke photographed and edited, along with D. A. Pennebaker, a large number of the 25 loops that were produced for the fair. The loops were scattered throughout the pavilion and were incorporated into the various displays. Many of the films were at first ineffective because of their small screens, which were originally placed at six-and-a-half feet above the floor and often were bleached out by external light. The films played without the benefit of the spoken word or music and sound effects, and they were edited in kaleidoscopic and quick takes in order to maintain interest purely through vision. What excited many onlookers was that each loop screen "fit" the decor of the exhibit. Each was designed to be as natural to the exhibit's appearance as a static picture on the wall ("Film at Brussels" 30). The films contained no beginning, middle, or end, and they played continuously throughout the day with the expectation that they had to make sense wherever the spectator wandered in on them (Knight 15). The integration of the loops into the pavilion structure only further enhanced the domestic emphasis of the American pavilion decor, which included a full-size home and an endless stream of fashion models. Many visitors confused the loop films with television sets, again emphasizing the home-like atmosphere of the building. With a screen size of 27 by 36 inches, these "light boxes" were specifically located to highlight aspects of static exhibits. Others, grouped in threes and fours, presented in three-minute swatches (color, but no sound) candid studies of American life (Koval 358).

Independent films were brought center stage at the fair during an international experimental film festival that screened 133 films including works by Stan Brakhage, Kenneth Anger, Maya Deren, Len Lye, Agnes Varda, Peter Kubelka and a prize-winning short by Roman Polanski. As the British filmmaker Karel Reisz reported for *Sight & Sound*, "No one could complain that Brussels did not bring us face to face with the avant-garde" (Reisz 231). Reisz's critical position reflected the diminished stature of avant-garde filmmaking in postwar Europe. As founding member of the Free Cinema documentary movement, Reisz reported that the

> inevitable haggling about what really constitutes an experimental film was ... not very fruitful.... The successful experiment has a way of not seeming experimental at all: it comes over as the inevitable way of saying something fresh. And the more pioneering — images of oscillating sounds, dance films in negative and so on — is new enough and easy enough to justify as experiment, but who cares? [Reisz 231].

For Reisz the festival illustrated that "the obverse of the rigid and exclusive financing systems of the larger film-producing countries [wa]s the self-enclosed, sterile avant garde. From this — the evidence of Brussels [wa]s quite clear — one can expect little more than films as a hobby for the makers. One bears these filmmakers no ill-will, but I for one do not want to see any more of those montages of neon lights, or undulating reflections in water or low-angled views of pylons. And I don't want to see any more films which can only be justified on the grounds that they 'Use the Medium'" (Reisz 233). Reisz, like many European filmmakers, had turned to realism to explore urgent social issues. Comparatively, the formal concerns of avant-garde filmmaking in the postwar period had removed any of the original political impetus of the movement. So, even though it at first it would appear unusual that the American fair planners would choose an independent, avant-garde, female director to create the only government-sponsored films in the pavilion, Clarke's films, like the jazz performances, fit well into the modernist pavilion.

Clarke's films matched the theme set up originally at the start of the "Unfinished Business" exhibit: "American is a society in motion." By the late 1950s, motion was an apt term to describe American culture. The abstract expressionists brought movement to painting, the Beats made their poetry "bop," jazz had the world grooving, and Clarke brought that same drive toward movement into her films. Drawing on her extensive background in modern dance and her experiences with Martha Graham, in one of her earliest films, *In Paris Parks* (1954), she found a way to use editing in order to create movement. Her choice of a jazz accompaniment by LaNoue Davenport further reflected Clarke's development of a rhythmic signature that more closely corresponded to the "abstract poetry of city motion." Shortly after completing the film, Clarke asserted, "[Movies are] predominantly visual, rhythmic experiences" (Lauren Rabinovitz 98). An article in *Film Quarterly* in 1960 described her as an

> instinctual filmmaker, whose feeling for movement generally seems to have carried over into her feeling for the camera.... As in *Bridges*, there is an astonishing lyric quality [*Skyscraper*], even when dealing with mechanical processes. Not only are the shots edited dynamically ... but the changes of tempo, the pauses, accelerations, retards and even visual glissandos — such as a shot looking up an elevator shaft as the elevator ascends — work with a remarkably complex correctness and grace. One is tempted to suggest that, like Jazz, *Skyscraper* simply "swings" [Breitrose 57–58].

Clarke embodied the urban ethos of the late 1950s with its hip reliance on modernist codes found in abstract expressionism, jazz, and modern dance. In a later interview, Clarke recalled the loops that she worked on for the Brussels World's Fair as "little, jazzy, dance-like films" (Berg 54). She also revealed she had been planning on making an entire film on jazz but had been dissuaded by her producers, who thought the idea was not commercially viable. After more than a decade of making films that drew on the 1950s culture of movement, Clarke reported that she was "ready for my mature period. I've learned the craft, and now I should really swing — so, Shirley, swing, already!" (Berg 55).

Clarke was solely responsible for three shorts: *Melting Pot, Bridges*, and *Occupations*, but she worked on a total of 19 of the loops. Told by the State Department officials that the "one subject we couldn't do was jazz," Clarke decided to make "them all jazzy" (Rabinovitz Clarke papers). When discussing the production of the loops, Clarke revealed that she "quickly found that our problems on these loops were very similar to those which every dancer must face — to abstract, condense, direct and rhythmatize the movements of life. And I also saw that here we were dealing with elements completely familiar to any dancer — rhythm, movement, symbols or abstractions and what we call in both dance and film 'montage,' the organization of all these elements into a meaningful whole" (Knight 15). For Clarke, the loops became an exper-

Loop films played throughout the U.S. Pavilion at the Brussels World's Fair (Business Screen, public domain, Prelinger Archive, Archive.org).

iment in form dependent on editing in order to create abstractions and distortions of perception. Her film *Go-Go-Go* provides a good example of how the abstraction of jazz got translated into these shorts. "In this frenetic suggestion of a nation constantly on the move, Mrs. Clarke assembled shots of cars, buses, and people in a bustling potpourri, but included a constantly recurring glimpse of a small child skipping across a schoolyard. Its effect is to establish a rhythm, a pattern in the midst of confusion" (Rabinovitz, Clarke papers). With *Melting Pot*, she translated one of the grounding principles of American society during the 1950s, with a brief investigation of American types. It "illustrates its thesis completely in terms of abstractions — the characteristic gestures of cowboys, businessmen, shopkeepers, housewives, policemen and children at play in various parts of the country. The thrust of a hand, the shrug of a shoulder, the wild gesticulation of a child's arm cry dance from each frame" (Knight 15).

With the serious concern about the race question in the United States, and the desire by the State Department to present an image of an integrated and undivided America, it is interesting to note the recommendations of the fair planners for images that should be chosen to illustrate America's melting pot. Their sole recommendations for specific shots of ethnic diversity included a "Negro wedding in front of Harlem Church, Black Pullman porters, University campus (all negro, or mixed), Indians (?), Mexicans (?)" (Clarke papers). The short was initially given the title, "Melting Pot-au-feu," and Bernard Rudofsky suggested using various shop signs in a multitude of languages in order to display the diversity present in America rather than segregation. Recommended token shots included a "Chinese food shop, San Francisco, Chinese Lettering, from a speeding car — signs announcing a highway eatery, Vienesse café, Yorkville, NY, German letters, Spanish grocery store signs, Kosher shop, Hebrew letters, Greek restaurant or shop sign and pizzeria" (Clarke papers). Even though the propaganda goals of the world's fair were to demonstrate that America had dealt with its racial issues, particularly in terms of its injustices toward African Americans, the fair planner's conception of diversity in the United States was still predominantly European, white and productive. For their image of the melting pot of America, they sought out images of small businesses that were supporting the American economy, and were the mark of the first step towards assimilation into the American system. Native Americans, African Americans, and Latin Americans were not accorded a position in America's melting pot. Other instructions in the list of possible images that was sent to Clarke and the other film producers stated that when putting together on film this collection of America's diverse food signs, it was "important that the environment and people in this sequence are characteristically American; that there be enough English words in the pictures to convey the fact that the foreign language signs were photographed in the U.S.A." Again, emphasis should be on a population in the process of incorporation and not separation.

"The Melting Pot" short was one of the few that was solely Clarke's, and it showed a clear deviation from the guidelines of the planners. But Clarke's notes for the shorts also revealed a sense of ethnic diversity based on type. A starred notation to herself stated that she needed to "remember, America[ns] are human beings." She also reminded herself to "Get — negro mother, father and child, negro talking with hands, negro and white kid together." Clarke's shot lists are short note cards that reveal a production process that is in accord with the government planners' suggested lists. She also turned to stereotypical and iconographic images in order to express ideological assumptions about what constituted American identity. What is significant in Clarke's pre-production process is her reliance on types to convey ethnic and racial identities with a glance. Even though Clarke's primary concern appeared to be with the experimental and formal properties of film, she brought into her shorts many of the mainstream conceptions of diversity shared by the State Department. Though Clarke saw herself subverting the fair planners' guidelines by making her shorts jazzy, in the end her selections of shots were still locked within a reductive and simplified understanding of the racial issues confronting America. Clarke provided the only images of diversity within the American pavilion, but her presentation did little to challenge that dominant racial ideology of the State Department. And in actuality, Clarke's stylistic experimentation did not prove particularly popular with visitors. The most popular shorts were *Sports* and *Farm Machinery at Work*, "a seemingly dull subject to most Americans," yet they attracted and interested crowds (Koval 358). Other popular ones included *American Supermarkets*, *Food and Drink* and *Life on the Highways*. "Large groups [also waited] to see *Pageantry* and *People at Work*. Some school children seemed transfixed by *Natural Disasters*" (Koval 358).

The confusion with many visitors over the actual medium of the films highlights the effect of the fair displays and the feminized space of the pavilion building on viewers. As television was becoming a major force in Europe, the abstract, rhythmic, and endless streaming of the loops played more as a televisual event rather than a filmic one. Clarke's reliance on types within a very slick and modern façade called to mind for many visitors television rather than experimental or independent film. "Obsessive in their rhythms, the short collection of images are bursts of humanity caught at its most mundane — whether eating, playing or engaging in sports. These are acerbic, tightly edited films that gain their power not so much from their subject as from the filmmaker's willingness to play, to manipulate and to layer the film until it becomes the visual equivalent of jazz" (Auerbach 82). The films were uncredited fragments that were meant to "stress that which is colorful 'Americana,'" and as Howard Thompson noted, "Their real achievement lies not only in the content but also in their superb professionalism" (Thompson, "Loops" 7). The loops epitomized the whole design philosophy of the exhibition along with the advertising techniques that had become prevalent on television. They were extremely short and vivid. Their purpose was to produce a flash of insight, convey a flavor, a revelation — not to exhaust any subject. Extremely important was their independence of captions and other verbal crutches, their exploitation of the psychological advantage of surprise. This was the key to the pavilion ("United States Speaks" 140). Even though the intention of the loops was to present to the audience glimpses of an America that would challenge assumptions and misconceptions about American culture, they actually fit squarely within the dominant and mainstream conceptions of a white, suburban, middle-class society. The films, even with their formal experimentation, clearly complimented the consumerist, soft-sell approach of the pavilion. As Clarke revealed, "I was an experimental filmmaker only in the sense that when I finally felt I had control of the medium, I didn't really have anything burning I want[ed] to say. My personal 'women's' experiences seemed unimportant. Yet by refusing to go deep into my soul, I [felt] that my work [was] not really significant. And in that state of mind, I kind of [made] sure it isn't" (Rosen 110). It is not surprising, then, as Lauren Rabinovitz reveals, that "such intense cinematic expression was so successful in these short pieces [the Brussels loops] that it was adapted for television commercials and was widespread industrial practice by the 1960s" (Rabinovitz 100). The avant-garde techniques employed by Clarke were readily adopted by television advertisers as the newest way to capture and hold consumers' attention. Even though the loops were never released in the United States, the State Department continued to permit their release for political events. The dominant ideological position expressed in the film was later revealed when Clarke related that "one day during a Republican convention, the phone rang and someone said, 'Quick, look at the TV. They're playing your loop'" (*Dramalogue* 13).

CHAPTER 6

Selling Good Design: IBM and the Films of Charles and Ray Eames

Much of the criticism directed at the American pavilion at the Brussels World's Fair centered on the lack of adequate representatives from industry and business. American officials sought to instill in the European audience a desire for the American way of life and the conviction that the American economic system was preferable to Communism. Fundamental to these efforts was the portrayal of a lifestyle of leisure and consumption that could be obtained by Europeans, if they adopted the American model of corporate capitalism. Given such a goal, the lack of displays and exhibits that adequately celebrated America's corporate achievements was seen by American tourists and critics immediately as problematic. This was a concern particularly in comparison to the Soviet pavilion's heavy reliance on images of industrial productivity as a sign of the successes of Communism. Many noted that the Russians treated the exposition as a giant industrial show in which they were "putting on display their heavy machinery, scientific advances and Sputniks" ("Brussels Asks" 27). The Soviets' exhibition of colossal industrial growth was presented as a testament to the triumph of the communist economic revolution. This stood in stark contrast to the mass-produced consumer products at the American pavilion that were intended to represent the success of the American model of corporate capitalism. Where were the corporate giants who had fed the military machinery of the war and were now driving the unprecedented expansion of the American economy?

As noted in previous chapters, the lack of commercial exhibits within the American pavilion is explained by the rules of the Belgian fair planners. Unlike the New York World's Fair of 1939, which is famous for the wonderland of corporate-sponsored utopias that it offered, the Brussels fair planners specified that the fair not be viewed as a trade fair. Therefore, commercial exhibits were not permitted inside the national pavilions. The Belgian officials were in fact distressed by the Soviets' emphasis on heavy industry, since they had asked all nations to show "not what they make, but what they are"

("Where East Meets West: The U.S. At the Fair" 55). That the fair planners thought that national identity could be separated from the kinds of products that nations produced shows a misunderstanding of how the ideological battles of national identity were waged in the 1950s.

With the rapid expansion of mass media in the postwar period, effective visual communication became essential for staging a lasting propaganda offensive. Any visitor who walked into the domestic sphere of the American pavilion immediately recognized the benefits of American capitalism. The Soviets were attacked because the rhetoric of their "hard sell" method seemed less than a benign showcase of cultural, historical or artistic displays. Ironically, the Soviets were doing a lot less "selling" than the Americans. Their showcasing of the sputniks highlighted their remarkable victory over American science and industry, and, in particular, demonstrated a remarkable postwar ascendancy following the utter devastation of World War II. In contrast, the American pavilion's "soft-sell" approach was accepted without complaint. The heavily materialistic and domesticated space of the American pavilion did not represent a threat to the European audiences, who were well acquainted by this time with American products and lifestyles. One interesting feature of the contrast between the soft- and hard-sell strategies of the United States and the Soviets is that as the force of the message — the "hardness" of the hard sell, you might say, is increased by narrowing and concentrating the message on fewer targets or goals. Thus, as the Soviets zeroed in on their industrial might and technological advances, for instance, they offered a concentrated and clearly focused message. In the American pavilion, the message was diffuse and scattered, which lent, in part, the "softness" to the soft-sell strategy. This seems correlated with a higher level of psychological receptivity to the message; on the other hand, the message was not as clear or pronounced. Thus, as noted in previous chapters, in the American pavilion receptivity was generally higher, though the audience seems to have registered a higher level of confusion or lack of clarity regarding the actual message. In the Soviet pavilion, resistance to the message seems more pronounced, but the message is clearer and more defined. This diffusion of signification in the message presented seems to be an implicitly understood feature of American exhibitions; corporate sponsors at the fair, in particular, were well adept at negotiating its parameters with great success.

The only way that a corporation could overtly be part of the American pavilion was through the State Department's good will to put their name in somewhere — either in the official catalogue or in a brief mention in connection with the exhibit they helped sponsor ("Reds Aim" 96). Several hundred companies did provide funding, including Ford Motor Company's sponsorship of Disney's Circarama film. Other U.S. companies that were incorporated in Europe or doing business in these countries decided to exhibit in the Belgian or British sections of the fair. Singer Sewing Machine Company, Coca-Cola, Pan-American World Airways, and Convair Division of General Dynamics each had their own exhibits outside the American pavilion. American dominance in the European marketplace in the postwar period made the fair an ideal setting for a concerted public relations campaign, particularly since, at the time of the fair, America was facing a well-publicized recession that called into question the stability and desirability of the American economic system abroad. Although visitors could touch and experience the consumer products that were the end result of America's exceptional productivity, they were not able to witness how its powerhouse economy functioned. This was a disappointment to Europeans, like Americans, who liked to know that a return to full U.S. prosperity was "closer than 'just around the corner.'" Up to this point the economies of Europe had borne up well in the face of the U.S. recession, but most of them were dependent on the maintenance of a high level of U.S. imports. So, even though the American pavilion was flooded with the consumer products that were material testimonials to the success of the American way, the greatest drop in the U.S. economy was in domestic production, which had dipped sharply in the final quarter of 1957. Imports, though, had held steady at an annual rate of $13.5 billion ("The Missing U.S. Univac").

A total of seven corporations with operations in Belgium erected their own pavilions. Coca-Cola installed a complete bottling operation that produced Cokes to be sold throughout the fair. By the 1950s, Coke was a global symbol of American freedom, and it played a central role in European debates about Americanization following the war. Coca-Cola first entered the European market by way of American GIs, and later became one of the foremost companies involved in establishing a dominant position in the European market (see Wagnleiter). As a result of the war, two-thirds of veterans drank Coke, and 64 bottling plants had been brought overseas mostly at government expense. Robert Woodruff, the company's long-time president, once remarked that within every bottle was "the essence of capitalism" (Kuisel 98). The symbolic power of Coca-Cola was not lost on one visitor to the Brussels World's Fair. He noted that "with its model sputnik on show, its jet aircraft, and its sheer impressive size, the Russian pavilion has made a hit with visitors from all over the world. But as one emerges, gasping for breath, one wonders at the tenacity of this particular culture. For standing at the door is a man selling Coca-Cola" ("Crystal Palaces" 610).

The incentive for American corporations to participate in international events was not dissimilar to the national concerns of the Eisenhower administration. Their desire to invest in public exhibitions was to help wage a persuasive public relations campaign that would create a positive association and image for both the product and the nation, thus permitting the international expansion of American markets along with the American way of life. The challenge for the planners and designers of the corporate pavilions was to choose an appropriate visual model that would signify the corporation and embody the values their products represent. The continual growth and dominance of the Coca-Cola Corporation in the beverage market required a branded identity that could cross over national and political boundaries, particularly since the expansion of Coca-Cola into postwar Europe was met with widespread and vocal opposition leading to charges from many leftist and communist politicians of the Coca-colonialization of Europe. In Belgium alone lawsuits were filed alleging the drink contained an unhealthy level of caffeine.

The political and military hegemony of the U.S. government in Western Europe was obvious, and by 1950, there was significant anxiety over the expansion of American private investment and the arrival of American popular culture. The creation of a miniature Coca-Cola bottling plant at the fair served the dual purpose of countering charges of American economic imperialism in European markets while selling the image of the product the company had cultivated. The Coca-Cola Corporation used the space of the fair as a place to appease fears of Americanization by literally putting the means of production in the hands of European bottlers, while also offering the values of a product that for many was seen as "the most American thing in America."

Like Coca-Cola, most major American corporations were regular participants at world's fairs. Before the advent of television advertising, world's fairs were one of the major public spaces in which corporations could sell themselves to a national and even international audience. Another regular world's fair participant, who had a sizeable presence at the Brussels World's Fair, was International Business Machines (IBM). The IBM pavilion, designed by Eliot Noyes, illustrated the modernistic design aesthetic that the corporation had actively begun to cultivate throughout the 1950s. At the time of the fair, IBM was not experiencing the recession that had hit the rest of the United States. In the first half of 1958 it had recorded the highest sales and earnings for any six-month period in the company's history ("IBM New High" 20:5). Although IBM's domestic growth was up, the decrease in business activities in the United States had affected the company. In order to counterbalance the stagnation in the U.S. market, it focused on building up the international wing of the company, the IBM World Trade Corporation. As *Fortune* reported, "Nothing in U.S. business is quite so engrossing as the spectacle of corporate managers lusting after those foreign markets, particularly the markets of Western Europe, where industrial output will grow by about ten percent this year, as compared with a growth of under four percent in the U.S. And the lust has led to action" (Sheehan 166). IBM's involvement in the European market was far from new. It had been assiduously cultivating foreign markets since the close of World War I. Thomas J. Watson, the president of IBM from 1924 to 1952, espoused the well-known and well-publicized motto, "World Peace through world trade," which became the slogan of IBM and the International Chamber of Commerce (ICC).

In 1937, Thomas Watson met with Hitler and his entourage during the Congress of the International Chamber of Commerce. During these business negotiations, he advocated for the loosening of U.S. credits to German business. He notably failed to do so, but was elected president of the ICC, and the Nazi Government awarded him the two-month-old decoration of the Merit Cross of the German Eagle with Star ("Camera Overseas" 66). Following his meetings in Berlin, Watson traveled to Paris for the opening of the U.S. Pavilion at the Paris Exposition of 1937. For this very political world's fair, falling on the cusp of war in Europe, Watson was appointed the U.S. Commissioner General to the Paris Exposition. *Life* explained his incentive in participating in the fair: "The reason for Mr. Watson's activities in Berlin and Paris is that his company sells U.S. business machines in 78 countries: manufactures in Germany, France and England. And he feels, as most Americans abroad, that backward, politically tortured Europe sadly needs American business machines and methods" ("Camera Overseas" 67). In order to assure his control of the European market, Watson did not hesitate to cross political bridges to guarantee his market share. Edwin Black has documented, as well, the development at this time of a custom punch-card system devised by IBM that would eventually track prisoners in Nazi concentration camps. IBM machines were also used by the Soviets to manage the vast quantity of statistics for Stalin's first Five Year Plan.

During the creation of the Marshall plan, when European recovery was still a distant hope, Watson had the foresight in 1950 to detach IBM's foreign operation from its divisional status and set it up as a wholly owned, but independently administered, subsidiary known as the IBM World Trade Corporation. Watson made sure that IBM was one of the first corporations that returned to Germany following the war. During the war, the business had been devastated. As soon as hostilities ended, the senior Watson arranged to send food to its employees, as well as tools, and used equipment to recondition for rental. As a result, IBM's subsidiary was among the first German businesses to return to full operation after the war (Pugh 259). By 1970, IBM World

Trade Corporation's net earnings matched those of the domestic company, at about $500 million each.

The Brussels World's Fair was as much an ideological battlefield as the Paris Exposition had been in 1937, but the national foes of the Soviets had shifted from the Nazis to the Americans in the Cold War 1950s. Again, for IBM, the world's fair was an arena in which to assure brand recognition for an international audience. National interests were secondary to plans for continued market dominance in the international marketplace. Unlike the advertising strategy of the Coca-Cola Corporation, whose product necessitated the creation of an image and message that would appeal to the broadest of audiences, IBM's was more targeted. As the company shifted in the 1950s from punch hole card tabulating machines to computers, the majority of their business contracts were with businesses and government entities. Most of the visitors to the fair would not have imagined individually purchasing an IBM machine. Yet, the fair provided IBM the opportunity to present itself as the international leader in the field of modern information technology through its reliance on modern good design as a way to sell the corporation to the average European consumer.

Selling Good Design

As the postwar consumer market boomed in the United States, industrial designers played a significant role in producing product styling that made product choices a crucial aspect of middle-class taste culture. Product design choices became reflective of personal lifestyle and identity. The heavy reliance on domestic products at the Brussels fair was a conscious display strategy meant to illustrate to middle- and upper-class Europeans the variety of products available to the American consumer and eventually to the European market. These products represented a distinctive, modern European style modified and altered by American industrial designers to emphasize convenience, affordability and disposability. Developed under the ethos of "good design," the dividing line between American institutions of art and commercial manufacturing began to collapse during the 1940s. Most of this community of American industrial designers had been trained in European modern architecture and design by interwar European emigrants to the United States, most significantly, Walter Gropius, the founder of the Bauhaus, and his protégé, Marcel Breuer, who were both hired to teach at the Harvard Graduate School of Design, and Eliel Saarinen, the Finnish architect who brought the international style to the Cranbrook Academy of Art in Michigan. These practitioners brought with them the modernist goal of linking art with other areas of human activity, including philosophy, metaphysics, ethics, and the physical sciences. The urge of affecting social change through the unity of art, architecture, and design had culminated in the Bauhaus goal of "creating a classless society ... [by] being able to provide all people with the best of everything" (E. Smith 153). This sensibility would undergo a major alteration when employed by American designers working in the postwar consumer economy for major international corporations.

Modern architecture and design entered into the public discourse through the Museum of Modern Art (MoMA). Its programming promoted modern design as a style and commercial enterprise that could directly improve the lifestyle of average Americans through modern functional objects for their suburban homes. In 1940, Alfred H. Barr, Jr., the founding director of MoMA, contacted the offices of Walter Gropius to find a new director to head its first industrial design department. Influenced by the Bauhaus school of pure design, in 1940 the museum hired Eliot Noyes, who had studied under Gropius and Breuer while completing his Masters of Arts degree at Harvard. Noyes shared the museum's position that "distained the American approach to design and with good reason. The Europeans were much more sophisticated whereas the American approach, largely through [Raymond] Loewy, [Walter Dorwin] Teague and [Norman] Bel Geddes, and to some degree Henry [Drey-fuss] were very commercial and very corporate" (Bruce 55).

Throughout the design discourse at the time, American designers were condemned for their reliance on "Hollywood" techniques of product development that emphasized glamour and fantasy over form and functionality. For example, Noyes, writing in a magazine in the 1950s about the Sears Visimatic washing machine, described the machine as "glamorized," and stated that if the designer tried "to beautify such a device and his treatment beg[an] to interfere with the usefulness, he deserve[d] to be strung up by his big thumbs" (McQuade 137). For these designers, working under the Bauhaus ethos of "good design," "Hollywood" implied deception, excess, and spectacle, while modern design stood for rationality, practicality and integrity in form. Those designers who depended on "Hollywood" design were pandering to the most base of popular tastes. These kind of industrial designers were seen as a "shallower kind of salesman, the kind who helps move the same old goods by slick talk — or, in this case, slick, superficial design — making the product look a little different on the surface without actually improving or reshaping it" (McQuade 135).

This American form of industrial design depended on consumer surveys which allowed the shoppers to dictate their own style preferences. Noyes scoffed at consumer surveys, and was solely concerned with the client's demands. He believed that "the mass market will buy good design when it gets the chance to. He aim[ed] at the customers' intelligence, not their well-probed id, and as a result his designs tend[ed] to characterize the producer rather than match the whims of the market" (McQuade 136). The debate over industrial design at the time centered on the issues of class and taste. American design was equated with trashy, mass-produced fantasies that pandered to the desires of the uncultured, in opposition to Noyes's modern design. For many marketing men, "Designers of Noyes's ilk, who ha[d] the vision of a 'clean' industrialism, appeal[ed] only to snobs. They [were] accused of seeking to impose an academic aesthetic, which simply w[ould] not work — i.e. sell" (McQuade 137). It is the MoMA and the fair designers who would turn to this modern, European-influenced design to counter the destructive images produced through the spread of Hollywood films abroad, not the products that in fact most uncouth Americans were buying off department store shelves.

In 1941, Noyes, at the age of 30, became the first director of a museum industrial design department at the MoMA. One of his first actions was to issue a tentative plan for the museum's Department of Industrial Design that explained the interconnection between the museum, manufacturers, and consumers. According to Noyes' vision, "The Museum must take an active part in promoting and making saleable good design, but it must also be able to look ahead and recognize significant design developments before they reach a commercially possible stage.... This activity must be of a sort to encourage designers to produce better design, manufacturers to develop it, and retailers to have it in their stores. It must also be a force to educate the public and encourage it to use its buying power as a stimulus to good design" (Bruce 63). One of the most significant events staged during Noyes' tenure at the MoMA was the "Organic Design in Home Furnishings" Competition, which resulted from a request by Bloomingdale's to discover the best young designers in America to produce a new line of home furnishings for sale in their showrooms. The competition received 900 entries and was judged by a panel that included Alfred H. Barr, Jr., Marcel Breuer, Edgar Kaufmann, Jr., and Edward Durell Stone, the architect of the MoMA and the American pavilion at the Brussels World's Fair. The most important entry and the overwhelming winner of the show were the molded plywood chairs developed by Charles Eames and Eero Saarinen, who were teaching at the Cranbrook Academy of Art. These chairs would go into production after the war and led to entire product lines that still remain popular today. This was also the start of a long and very productive friendship and collaboration between Noyes and the Eameses.

The catalogue for the exhibition opened with a description of the qualities that distinguished organic design from the majority of manufacture products. "A design may be called organic when there is a harmonious organization of the parts within the whole, according to structure, material, and purpose. Within this definition there can be no vain ornamentation or superfluity, but the part of beauty is none the less great — the ideal choice of material, in visual refinement, and in the rational elegance of things intended for use" (Noyes inside cover). The "Organic Design in Home Furnishings" competition was also George Nelson's introduction to Eames's furniture, and it was Nelson who insisted to D. J. De Pree, CEO of the company, that Herman Miller market and distribute his furniture. Eames officially joined Herman Miller as a design consultant under Nelson's direction in 1947, and in 1949 Herman Miller bought the manufacturing rights for his furniture.

The exhibition of the best of household products within a museum setting continued the MoMA's mission of acculturating its audience, but the museum's audience in the postwar period had become middle class and consumerist. The museum continued throughout the early postwar years with an annual "Good Design" competition headed by Edgar Kaufmann, Jr., whose father owned a successful Pittsburgh department store and also commissioned Frank Lloyd Wright to design and build Fallingwater. Good design was a product of exceptional modern design taste rendered by industrial designers schooled in European modernism who were appreciative of the functionality of form and simplicity of beauty manifested in everyday objects. The first "Good Design" exhibit was a joint venture between the Museum of Modern Art and the Chicago Merchandise Mart, which opened in Chicago and was designed by Charles Eames. Because the most important visitors to the Good Design show were wholesale buyers who must spend the working day looking at furniture and housewares, Eames turned it into a gala occasion (Gueft 87). Eames's design exhibit involved "showmanship combined with a sense of humor" and combined manufactured products with Kandinsky paintings, other "art objects" on loan from the Art Institute of Chicago, potted plants and a tumbleweed. With this exhibit, Eames capitalized on the design aesthetic of "showing furniture in settings that suggested rather than recreated domestic interiors," which had gained popularity in the United States in the late 1940s. Eames's and the MOMA's Good Design campaigns along with the promotions by department stores and manufacturers "played an important part in persuading the American public of the desirability of contemporary design" (Kirkham 277).

Good design was meant to mobilize the general population into literally transforming their daily lives through purchasing properly designed and culturally sanctioned products. By the start of the 1950s, the role of industrial design in art museum programming escalated, coinciding with a general surge of activity within the American design community. Products purchased with the Good Design label carried with them the cache of the MoMA's institutional position as the leading institution for modern art and culture, and made living a modern life and the values that good design entailed accessible through individual purchasing decisions.

Postwar modern architect's and designer's interest in working collaboratively with manufacturers in the production of the objects of daily living was part of a larger attempt to transform the tastes of the average consumer and consequently the world they inhabited. Many of these designers and architects possessed a sincere belief in the good of technology, and a faith that good design could solve many of society's problems. Faith in the unity and equality of the fine and applied arts, design, and architecture was widespread among leading American modern museums, educational institutions, and artists during this period. Esther McCoy described this slice of modern culture as "America's last moral era, a time when people stood together, or shared a common belief in the correctness of their actions" (B. Goldstein 8).

Noyes took leave from his position at the MoMA in May 1942 in order to enter active duty as a test pilot in the army–air force glider research program. Noyes's office was adjacent to a pilot who flew B-25s, Thomas Watson, Jr. Their meeting was, as Watson Jr. later described, "the beginning of one of the most precious and fruitful relationships I ever had in my life" (Bruce 78). After the war, Noyes returned to New York and the MoMA, and also took a partnership in the offices of the aging Norman Bel Geddes. Watson returned to IBM as an executive vice president, and through their friendship Noyes won a series of commissions from IBM for the Geddes office. After the closure of the Geddes office, Noyes opened his own architectural and industrial design office. In 1950 Noyes received his first architectural project for IBM, redesigning Watson's office on the 16th floor of IBM World Headquarters in New York.

Thomas Watson, Jr., took over the presidency of IBM in 1952 and implemented a series of radical changes that would have a lasting impact on the future of the company. Unlike his father, who had considered computers a matter of prestige rather than profit for the company, Watson Jr. determined that IBM should by the end of the 1950s corner the entire computer market. This would allow the company to win the newly emerging contracts from the U.S. military and also dominate the lucrative market for computers in the corporate business world.

Watson Jr. also concluded that IBM required a new look to match the radical reorganization of the company. Watson had by chance encountered the sleek, modern design of Olivetti's Manhattan showroom. He compared the overall corporate image of Olivetti, including its advertisements, sales literature and the architecture of their headquarters, plants, sales offices, and employee housing, and advertisements, with IBM's. Watson quickly concluded that the "Olivetti material was filled with color and excitement and fit together like a beautiful picture puzzle. Ours looked like directions on how to make bicarbonate of soda" (Watson 258). Watson immediately turned to his war-time friend, Noyes, and hired him to redesign the IBM lobby and showroom in its corporate headquarters in Manhattan. Watson decided to "put his stamp on IBM through modern design." Since the computers they were building were the "very epitome of modern technology — on the inside. But on the outside they were as exciting as a collection of filing cabinets." Watson Jr. turned to modern design and architecture as the way to "make IBM's products, offices, buildings, brochures, and everything the public saw of our company exciting and modern" (Watson 258).

Noyes declined a full-time position at IBM in order to maintain his own design office, but agreed to become the company's consultant director of design with direct access to top management for design decisions. Eventually, 50 percent of his office's work would be for IBM. One of Noyes' first action in his new role was to secure a letter from Watson to all IBM management that began, "I think you will agree that good design is good business." Noyes systematically began meeting with IBM's designers in order to stimulate advanced design in products, architecture, graphics, interiors, and in displays. In order to combat the threat of obsolescence, Noyes discouraged attempting to create a single, uniform corporate image. Instead, Noyes convinced Watson that IBM should focus on the "best in modern design." As Watson recalled, "Whenever he needed something built or decorated, we would commission the best architects, designers, and artists, and give them a relatively free hand to explore new ideas in their own styles" (Watson 260–61).

Watson utilized modern design to make a clear break from the old IBM of his father and to create a new image for IBM as a global information provider. IBM was not the only major American corporation to turn to modern design to advance their company's commercial aims. The years following the war were, as Michael Bierut describes, "giddy ones not only for American designers, but for the corporations that employed them.... What is striking about these postwar design patrons is ... their seeming conviction that design could do more than simply move product, it could make the world a better place" (Bierut 109). Since American corporations had fueled the arsenals of a war that successfully defeated the axis powers, corporations in the postwar period enjoyed exceptionally strong and widespread public support. The investment by these corporations to develop a comprehensive and saleable corporate image for the general public is evidence that they recognized that their success depended on good public relations. As consumer surveys became standard procedure for evaluating public perception, corporations turned to designers to assist in successfully selling their products. Noyes, though, claimed to shrug off consumer surveys as "just a form of reassurance, something a corporate executive leans to because he is scared not to" (McQuade 135). Noyes' main concern was with the client's preferences because he reasoned that the mass market "will buy good design when it gets the chance to."

At IBM, Noyes assembled an entire design team to oversee the complete overhaul of IBM's corporate image. The team included close professional friends and colleagues including the Eameses and Edgar Kaufmann, Jr., who had worked with Noyes at the MoMA on the Good Design exhibits, the graphic designer Paul Rand, and the designer and critic George Nelson. The Eameses were hired to help with exhibitions and films and would continue to work with Noyes at IBM for the next 20 years. They shared a common understanding of what constituted good modern design, a vision of a future

The IBM pavilion at the Brussels World's Fair, designed by Eliot Noyes (International Lighting Review, n. 3–4, 1958).

world shaped by modern design, and also a trust in corporations and the government to be beneficent agents for social change.

Designers worked for corporations and, therefore, had an intimate knowledge of the production and marketing processes. The community of designers in the 1950s who worked for major American corporations was small and had close ties to the government. Like the mobilization of culture as part of America's foreign affairs policy, design was also seen as a necessary emblem of American taste and ideology. "Just as the public relations counselor is concerned with the corporation's psychological warfare, the industrial designer is concerned with the logistics of taste" (Lynes 302). Their taste was to be a model for the public's taste through the means of mass marketing. "In our industrial society," Arthur A. Houghton, Jr., of Corning Glass said at the *Herald Tribune* Forum of 1953, "it is the professional designer who increasingly is determining the appearance of our physical environment. The individual is less and less able to participate in this determination" (Lynes 303).

Taste became a serious issue in the 1950s, particularly in terms of America's relationship with Europe, with the popular perception on both sides that Americans lacked an authentic and established taste culture. The concept of good taste had become familiar to the public through the considerable efforts of "advertisers, packagers, and manufacturers bent on making design a commodity that consumers would pay for, and would pay for as often as the design changed" (Allen 271). During the 1950s, as Americans became more concerned with social acceptance and prestige, good taste became an emblem of status among Americans (Allen 271). Good taste gained institutional recognition with the inauguration of the Museum of Modern Art's annual "Good Design" exhibit, which was devoted to exemplary contemporary products and graphics. With their connections to the corporate, cultural, and governmental realms of American society, the industrial designer occupied a unique position in 1950s culture as the "new intellectual class" or the "power elite." As C. Wright Mills explained at the time, "The American Designer is at once a central figure which I am going to call the cultural apparatus and an important adjunct of a very peculiar kind of economy. His art is a business, but his business is art and curious things have been happening both to the art and to the business—and so to him" (Mills 374).

In order to assure the dominance of the American way in all spheres of society, panels of experts—these power elites—were assembled across the nation into governmental and corporate think tanks as spokespersons for the free enterprise system. Similar to the panels assembled for the world's fair, these experts came from America's most prestigious institutions and were united in their conviction that all forces, including art and culture, must be mobilized against the threat of Communism, which would destroy the booming American economy and way of life. One of these expert meetings, driven by such an ideological imperative, was the International Design Conference. The idea for the design conference originated with Egbert Jacobsen, the design director of the Container Corporation of America (CCA), and Herbert Bayer, the Bauhaus artist and graphic designer who had been a consultant to CCA since 1946. They sold their idea to Walter Paepcke, the progressive chief executive of the Container Corporation of America. The first conference in 1951 included many of the designers who would in the future be hired by the federal government for its international exhibitions, including the Brussels World's Fair. They would play a central part in the dissemination of modern design at home and abroad during the postwar period. This list included Rene d'Harnoncourt, Edgar Kaufmann, Jr., Louis Kahn, Leo Lionni, Josef Albers, Stanley Marcus, Charles Eames and George Nelson. D'Harnoncourt, who became director of the Museum of Modern Art in 1949, held the fundamental belief that "'modern art in its infinite variety and ceaseless exploration' was the 'foremost symbol' of democracy," and he openly lobbied Congress during the 1950s to finance a cultural campaign against Communism. D'Harnoncourt had clear ties to the U.S. intelligence agencies, consulted with the National Security Council's Operations Coordinating Board, and reported regularly to the State Department (Saunders 262).

The interrelationship between American corporations and the government during the 1950s was a by-product of the popular view that the American way of life was defined by capitalism and in particular the free enterprise system. It was American corporations with their ingenuity and largess who were able to win the war and make the United States into the most powerful and richest nation in the world. This sentiment was expressed by Charles E. Wilson, the president of General Motors who became Secretary of Defense in 1952, when he opined that "what's good for General Motors is good for the country and vice versa" (Allen 230).

At the beginning of the second meeting of the International Design Conference, Paepcke pointed out that the goal of the conference was "to gain a primacy for America in culture equal to that held in military might" (Allen 273). In order to gain this dominance, the most important participants at the Aspen Conference were not the designers, but the businessmen. From the start, it was agreed that "without the attendance of important businessmen there would be no point in the conference," and so the objective of the first meeting, "Design — A Function of Management," was to establish "once and far all the relation of design to business" (Allen 270). Eames, in his presentation at the first Conference, underscored for the assembled corporate leaders the "importance of practical objectives in all types of design — such as those for a chair: maximum space, low upkeep and low cost" (Allen 272).

Good Design and the American Way

The MoMA, under the leadership of Nelson Rockefeller and d'Harnoncourt, was directly responsible for making modern design a key tool of U.S. cultural diplomacy. Rockefeller played a central role in the development and implementation of Eisenhower's psychological warfare program. He headed the Advisory Committee of Government Organization, established in January 19, 1953, that recommended a new foreign information agency that would absorb programs dispersed throughout the federal government. The committee's recommendation led directly to Eisenhower's creation of the USIA on June 1, 1953. In December 1954, Rockefeller became Eisenhower's psychological warfare adviser. Through a five-year annual grant of $125,000 from the Rockefeller Brothers Fund, Rockefeller orchestrated the establishment of the International Council at MoMA along with d'Harnoncourt, in order to further the role of modern art in contemporary society throughout the United States and abroad. By 1956 the International Program had organized 39 international exhibitions while dramatically increasing loans to American embassies and consulates.

Working in collaboration with a number of U.S. government agencies, including the State Department, the Mutual Security Agency and the USIA, the MoMA prepared and circulated in Europe a series of exhibitions dedicated exclusively to American mass-produced and handmade design items: "Design for Use, USA," "U.S. Selections for Berlin Trade Fair," and "American Design for Home and Decorative Use." These exhibitions were primarily funded by the U.S. government in response to the recognition that the Soviets were using trade fairs for the promotion of Communism (McDonald 398). MoMA's original impetus for bringing a modern design exhibition to Europe directly resulted from the success of the Good Design venture. Edgar Kaufmann, Jr., curated a European version of the exhibition, "Design for Use, USA," with the goal of reaching European consumers by marketing to them the products of contemporary American life. Kaufmann asserted, "A discriminating show of American home furnishings can present the best and most progressive side of our life to the European public in terms which are intentionally understandable and sympathetic" ("Europe to See Good Designs from America" P.1). Both the MoMA and the government hoped to use soft power to counter the poor popular perception of the United States within Europe by the mid–1950s.

The MoMA's heavy investment in the use of the American culture as a political and ideological tool was evident at the First Annual Conference of the newly formed International Council of the MoMA in May 1955. The central feature of the conference was a symposium on "International Exchange in the Arts," during which George F. Kennan, who recently returned from the Soviet Union where he had served as U.S. ambassador from 1952 to 1954, delivered the keynote address. Kennan had authored the famous "X" article in the journal of *Foreign Affairs*, which set forth the thesis that dominated the early years of the Cold War. To counter the Kremlin's commitment to dominating "every nook and cranny available ... in the basin of world power" with its "fanatical ideology," he proposed a policy of "unalterable counter force," and "firm and vigilant containment" (Kennan 575).

Kennan drafted in June 1948 the directive NSC-10/2, which called for the adoption of an "expansive conception of [America's] security requirements to include a world substantially made over in its own image" (Larson 349). Eight years after the issuance of the directive, Kennan used his speech to the MoMA community to blame Hollywood and American mass culture for the failure of American propaganda to successfully transform the world into the image of America. Kennan's speech focused squarely on the challenge of developing an acceptable image of America through appropriate forms of culture that would be effective in transmitting the American system of values and ideology abroad. Even after many years of orchestrated attempts by American covert operations to develop a lasting soft power strategy, by the mid–1950s, Kennan argued, there had become "the greatest and most urgent need to correct a number of impressions that the outside world entertains of us, impressions that are beginning to affect our international position in very important ways" (Kennan 9). The image of Americans held by many abroad was of a "nation of vulgar, materialistic *noveaux riches*, lacking in manners and in sensitivity, interested in making money, contemptuous of every refinement of esthetic feeling" (ibid.). The source of this misperception was the heavy reliance on Hollywood films by many American ambassadors that Kennan had witnessed "in more than one instance [who] exhibit[ed] one silly and inferior film after the other to invited foreign audiences, in the happy confidence that no product of Hollywood could fail to be impressive and enjoyable to the foreign audience" (Kennan 12). The speech was really a call for cultural institutions like the MoMA to step forward and correct the errors made by naïve American operatives lacking cultural awareness and critical judgment. For too long, America's cultural elites have been "content to leave the external projection of our cultural life almost exclusively to the blind workings of commercial interests, with results that ... were absolutely frightening" (Kennan 9).

Kennan's speech embodies the paradoxes of national image building during the 1950s and the heavy rhetorical reliance on American culture to sell capitalism. While Kennan articulates the need for an alternative image of Americans as not materialistic, he actually describes American society as bereft of culture due to the impact of mass media and consumerism. He describes a nation transformed by the standardization and centralization of mass media into a country that is an "indifferent home to its own cultural life, a country which, for example, can spend millions annually on horse racing or on the slot machines but cannot have an opera house in its own national capital" (Kennan 14). The "narcotic effect of the modern commercial cultural product" had become so pervasive that Kennan questioned whether the potential creative resources of Americans "are likely to find anything resembling a normal degree of development and expression today" (Kennan 8). For Kennan, a vibrant and well-supported cultural life had become the essential ingredient to the winning of the Cold War. If Americans could "show the outside world both that we have a cultural life and that we care something about it," Kennan would have "willingly trade[d] the entire remaining inventory of political propaganda for the results that could be achieved by such means alone" (Kennan 11).

As Kennan was presenting to the MoMA community his conviction that it was of the utmost importance for American foreign policy to reveal to the world the rich cultural achievements of America, especially within the high arts, the MoMA was sending abroad part of its International Programs exhibitions that foregrounded the consumer tastes of the average American housewife. In the spring of 1955, the MoMA's "50 Years of American Art" exhibition opened at the National Museum of Modern Art in Paris. The exhibit included artfully displayed kitchen utensils and glassware, including a significant selection of Tupperware. The MoMA's "Good Design" displays had brought the department store showroom into the art museum, and now through its international programming, well-designed appliances for the housewife had become the embodiment of the "machine aesthetic of a technologically determined functional form" (Clarke 36). According to Greta Daniel, the curator, "So well conceived were these American productions of industry that they were the decorative arts of the 20th century" (Daniel 76).

To combat images of Americans as crass, uncultured consumers, the MoMA chose to send as part of an exhibit of 50 years of American art an entire exhibit of kitchen utensils displayed with the soft-lighting display techniques employed by the Eameses in their exhibition designs for the "Good Design" displays at the MoMA. In addition, the exhibition catalogue contained the contact information for each of the 160 objects of industrial design on display. Selling the mass-produced products of American manufacturers and designers had become a key component of constructing an image of America as a nation with a vibrant and exceptional cultural life. As Edgar Kaufmann, Jr., would later explain, "The greatest difficulty in the world of design is an extraordinary blindness to its major raw material — the consumer" (Kaufmann 34); designers forget that "the market is the mistress and always has been" (38).

Along with displays of American industrial design, the "50 Years of American Art" exhibit contained giant photographs, models, and plans of the most significant directions in recent American architecture. Most of the buildings were icons of modernist architecture, including homes designed by Charles Eames, Philip Johnson, and Richard Neutra. By the 1950s, the architecture and furniture of the Eameses had become internationally recognized as emblematic of American modern design and good taste. The Eameses, first through their chairs and then their Eames house designed for the Case Study houses in *Art & Architecture* magazine, were much admired and emulated by a new generation of European architects and designers. According to Reyner Banham, the modernist establishment in Europe viewed the architecture of Eames and the Case Study houses as reinforcing the dogma of such European architects as Mies van der Rohe, Walter Gropius, and Le Corbusier. "The appeal of the Case Study houses lay in the way they reinforced the dogmas of honesty, clarity, and unity, the exposure of structure, the use of certifiably modern materials, and the absence of ornament" (Banham 185). But the Eameses' aesthetic was seen as refreshingly new and distinctly American. Their "open-minded, experimental, hands-on, improvisatory, quirky" approach was seen by many European architects as a "much needed antidote to the cut-and-dry recipes of routine modernism then being taught in the schools" (Banham 186).

The IBM pavilion at the fair was designed by Eliot Noyes and judged an "outstanding pavilion of private business." The building was considered "what may be the ideal exposition architecture of the future, without or with moving sidewalks. Its display beckons, in any event, through high walls entirely of glass, with installations necessarily attractive enough, seen through their transparent surroundings to demand entry" (Frankfurter 34). The steel-and-glass construction of the pavilion signaled the beginning of a global industrial vernacular that would come to define high-technology industries. The close industrial ties of designers to their corporate and national sponsors made them instrumental in creating an image that appeared to be devoid of political significance. As Noyes explained, "Industrial design is a curious profession, with no rules. It depends on sheer instinct, logic and that intangible thing called taste" (McQuade 138). This combination of good taste and high technology proved extremely profitable for IBM in its quest for global dominance in the computer market.

The Eameses at the Brussels World's Fair

The Eameses contribution to the IBM pavilion was a short film, *The Information Machine: Creative Man and the Data Processor*. This was the first film they made for a client's commission; all previous films had been in-house productions or parts of other office projects. The production of the film marked the beginning of the Eameses' long association with IBM; IBM became the Eameses' major client after the Henry Miller Company. Charles's involvement with filmmaking stretched all the way back to his work as a set designer at MGM from 1941 to 1942. While in the studio, he worked on such films as *Johnny Eager, I Married an Angel, Random Harvest* and *Mrs. Miniver*. While at MGM, he began his life-long friendship with Billy Wilder on whose film, *The Spirit of St. Louis* (Warner Brothers, 1957), he worked as the second unit director. Eames' film connections also extended into the experimental film community. Through the film salon of John Entenza, editor of *Arts & Architecture* magazine, the Eameses met people responsible for establishing avant-garde film culture in California immediately after the war, including Oskar Fischinger, the Whitney Brothers, James Broughton, Sidney Peterson, Kenneth Anger, Curtis Harrington and Harry Smith (Kirkham 314). John Whitney joined the Eames office staff in 1957, and they along with Fischinger, Harrington, and Wallace Berman set up a distribution and exhibition service for independent films (Kirkham 314). The Eameses brought their knowledge and familiarity of both Hollywood and experimental film techniques to their own work, but the main aesthetic influence on their work was their training and immersion into the world of modern "good design." Eames would produce 125 short films in 28 years even though he considered "film as a little bit of a cheat; I'm sort of using a tool someone else has developed" (Schrader 2).

While historians of modern architecture and design make frequent mention of the films produced by the Eameses, they have received marginal attention from film historians. The most detailed filmic analysis of their work was Paul Schrader's article "Poetry of Ideas" published in 1970. Even in a recent book about the history of avant-garde film in Los Angeles, David E. James states that "the single-screen films remain anomalous; they did not contribute significantly to the formal language of filmmaking, and the Eameses' disinterest in personal expressivity and their films' unreflexive transparency were quite alien to the spirit of the underground and the conceptual films they in other ways parallel" (James 252). James concludes that their oeuvre of more than 80 single-screen films is "essentially sui generic." The marginalization of the Eameses' films is more broadly reflective of the status of industrial films within the history of American filmmaking. The widespread and critical understanding of these films is that their corporate ties have removed any possibility for artistic expression or aesthetic interest. Films produced within the corporate structure of the Hollywood studios maintained an ideological integrity that was seen as antithetical to anything produced for a corporation. And avant-garde films necessarily maintained their aesthetic purity by receiving institutional support from universities and cultural institutions.

The postwar period was the golden period of sponsored films with unprecedented growth in production and exhibition. By 1959, the American industry spent more than $230 million on sponsored films and released 5,400 films to Hollywood's 223 (Caplan 50). The war years had created a vast demand for non-theatrical films that could be used both as instructional films for the military services and also as morale-boosting, nationalistic films to bolster the home front. With most peacetime production put on hold, the major studios were enlisted in the production of sponsored films. The widespread use of these films during the war convinced many companies of the effectiveness of the medium. The dramatic expansion of domestic manufacturing and corporate growth following the war helped sustain the market for these films. The ready availability of war surplus 16 mm equipment significantly reduced production costs and made filmmaking an attractive and viable option for companies.

The Eameses' films were far from "sui generic," but were in fact part of an exceptionally rich and deep period for production of alternative films produced, distributed and exhibited outside the traditional Hollywood studio system. During the 1950s, more people were watching sponsored films in alternative venues like parking lots, department stores, corporate showrooms, classrooms, and club houses than theatrical releases. Many independent documentary and avant-garde film filmmakers moved easily between independent production and commercial work, creating a distinctive genre of films with their own formal conventions. Sponsored films proliferated across postwar America, pulling screens outside of darkened theaters and into public spaces, where they would be viewed as part of the stream of daily life. Television stations also made frequent use of films that were "well made and not overly commercial" (Spielvogel F9). These films were sponsored as a means of corporate branding that included creating for its audience an image of the corporation as an active and responsible social citizen. The best of these films were neither didactically instructional or hard sales pitches; rather filmmakers often drew on their professional and aesthetic abilities to create imaginative films that created lasting and positive associations for the corporation. For corporations like IBM, sponsored films were part of an entire design program and style to inspire in the average citizen faith in and support for the goals and activities of the corporation. Sponsored films were indeed a form of soft power meant to persuade audiences that they shared in the values of the company and that what was good for the corporation was good for the individual.

Sponsored films were recognized as "not just a business phenomenon" but also "an aspect of design, with many of the problems industrial designers tend[ed] to think of as peculiar to their profession" (Caplan 50). Many sponsored films created by industrial designers, including those produced by the Eameses, were recognized by their contemporaries as exceptional. As Ralph Caplan described, "Charles Eames, whose contribution to the process of visual communication [wa]s rivaled only by his contribution to the process of sitting down in style, has designed information films for IBM" (Caplan 50). Because of the revenues generated by the production and sale of their chairs, the Eameses were able to fund their own films or chose to work on corporate and governmental projects that were challenging or consistent with their own aesthetic goals; they never depended on films for their livelihood, and yet filmmaking was central to the work of the Eames Office.

Charles's journey to filmmaking began through his experimentation with still photography. Charles discovered his father's photography equipment at the age of 12, following his father's death. He taught himself photography by developing his photographs with wet emulsions on glass plates. Charles's first job after moving to Los Angeles in 1941 was in the Art Department at MGM. Charles began pursuing photography in earnest through the 1940s and started using fast slide techniques in his lectures. In 1950, the same year that Charles designed and installed the Good Design show at the MoMA, the Eameses began their production of short films, and Charles became a consultant for the Rockefeller Foundation.

Their earliest films display distinctive formal techniques that would continue throughout their body of work. Both *Blacktop* and *Parade* relied heavily on the close-up to draw the viewer directly to an object (these films focus on blacktop being washed and marching toys) and emphasized each object's distinctive and unique form, structure, and function. Sharp focus shooting and richly saturated colors made inanimate objects seem to come to life. Human activity remained outside the camera frame, though the hand of man remained present to activate the film action. As Beatriz Colomina has observed, "The Eameses saw everything through the camera. This explains the astonishing continuity in their work in so many different scales. If the eye is the eye of a camera, size is not fixed, but continuously shifting. This Eameses used to shoot at everything.... They made decisions on the basis of what they saw through the lens" (Colomina 322).

The films frequently followed the real-time enactment of an object-centered event or an argumentative form and are intentionally not structured according to a three-act linear narrative. Charles viewed the postwar period as the era of communication and film as a tool to be used to communicate complex ideas through the language of vision. As Eames explained to Paul Scrader, "They're not experimental films, they're not really films. They're attempts to get across an idea" (Schrader 2). Charles's particular concern was with using film to bridge the two worlds of science and the arts. Drawing on Gyorgy Kepe's *Language of Vision*, the Eameses viewed the language of vision as a real threat to the discontinuity that they were always fighting against. In a speech before the American Academy of Arts and Sciences, he faulted scientists that "tend[ed] to think of the aesthetic level and the scientific level as discontinuous, whereas both actually involve this quality of appropriateness and exhaustive definition of the problem. They fail[ed] to take pleasure seriously" (C. Eames 18). On the part of filmmakers, he was particularly concerned that "film w[ould] be prematurely contaminated by a virus of self-expression" (C. Eames 14). His filmic position reflected the rhetoric of the "good design" movement and its reliance on the concept of "appropriateness" and "how-it-should-be-ness" in the conveyance of a central idea. Filmmakers in particular needed to move away from "creative idiosyncrasies" of the avant-garde in order to get to the "nuts and bolts of the subject." "One of the best ways of doing this," argued Charles, was to "put it on film because through this medium the central idea can be supported by images which give substance and liveliness to it. This reduction of one idea to its essence, using the support of visual images, is the core of several of the films we made" (C. Eames 20–21).

The Eameses' first film on communications theory was *A Communication Primer*. The film was produced as a result of their, and the world's, first multimedia presentation, the seminal Sample Lesson for a Hypothetical Course. In 1945, George Nelson was asked by Lamar Dodd at the University of Georgia in Athens to develop new ways of teaching the arts. Nelson enlisted the assistance of the Eameses and Alexander Girard. Their sample lesson was presented to a class and included slides, film clips, lectures, and even piped-in scents. The ideas that developed from that project lead in 1953 to the production of *A Communication Primer*, which resulted from a problem Eames realized he had to state before he could solve. As he later explained, "I had the feeling that in the world of architecture they were going to get nowhere unless the process of information was going to come and enter city planning in general.... This was the reason for making the first film, because we looked for information on communications" (Schrader 9).

The film is fairly literal in its explanation of communication theory and draws heavily on Claude Shannon's schematic of the process of communication moving from the transmitter to the communication channel, the receiver, and finally its destination. Shot in live action, a sizable portion of the film provides human examples of how noise interrupts the successful transmission of a signal or message. In typical Eamesian fashion, the film moves from a short segment of New York stock brokers sending a message to buy or sell to their Los Angeles office to the emotional transmission of the message "I Love You" through an image of a heart (a similar image ends *The Information Machine*). Offering a wide variety of quickly rendered examples of information transmission in interpersonal relations and larger social networks, the film concludes with the development of the calculator as the most advanced tool for the handling of complex problems. As the film describes, "The ability of these machines to store information and sort and deliver it is fantastic.... It is understandable that they are popularly understood as brains." The film relies heavily on information overload, providing rapid and frequently close-up glimpses of daily life: a man reading on the train, stock brokers in their office, city crowds, cars driving, power lines and the "huge calculator in action." Rather than providing a single thesis or argument that the film answers, it offers a multiplicity of communication events, so the spectator is left with a fundamental understanding of models of communication and the superior ability of information technology to help manage a vastly complex and growing world. Through a sensory immersion that relies on fast cutting, frequent close-ups, and abrupt sounds, you become immersed within the world of communication. The film was important for the Eameses because of the "implicit notion that the discipline of architecture might have a key role in the way communications systems would develop" (Demetrios 146). It was also their first film to deal with the challenge of presenting a scientific concept through film.

The Eameses sent a copy of *A Communication Primer* to Noyes after he was put in charge of IBM's design program, and as a result they were immediately hired by Watson as key consultants. Though the film never advertises IBM or computers as necessary products for consumption, the film is extremely effective in illustrating computer and information technology as the natural and logical evolutionary tool for an advanced society that has reached a remarkable level of productivity. The use of information overload in the structure of the film creates an image of society that appears to be constantly driven by technology and one in which citizens are striving continually to higher and higher levels of achievement. The computer is the tool for America, for a society that has achieved unprecedented material growth and scientific development.

The Eameses' next major film on communication theory for IBM, *The Information Machine*, was produced for the Brussels World's fair. The film repeats many of the same concepts presented in *A Communication Primer* but makes them more accessible to a mainstream audience through its reliance on animation. *The Information Machine* again depicts the computer as the natural and logical development for an advanced society, but it presents it as the "culmination of centuries of tools and systems man had developed to process information" (Neuhart et al. 233). The film was the first completely animated work undertaken by the office, and the drawing was designed and drawn almost entirely by Dolores Cannata. Cannata, along with the experimental filmmaker John Whitney, who shot the film, worked at United Productions of American (UPA) on *The Boing Boing Show*. Throughout the 1950s, UPA would regularly host open houses and screenings to introduce the broader artistic community to their brand of animated filmmaking. Charles was so impressed by the studio's work after attending one of these events that he purchased stock in UPA and began incorporating more animation into his films. The 1950s saw the emergence of a new form of animation, termed "cartoon modern" by Amid Amidi. Reacting against the realism of Disney animation, "designers discarded the earlier reliance on circle and oval graphic formulas and created cartoon characters with a variety of sophisticated 'modern' elements, including hard-edged Cubist shapes and organic biomorphic forms reminiscent of Miro, Calder, and Noguchi" (Amidi 10). According to UPA designer and director Bill Hurtz, the studio's success was a result of the artists' belief that style stemmed from the film's subject matter. "That sort of followed the precepts of modern architecture at the time, 'form follows function,'" Hurtz said (Amidi 112). UPA would be honored with its own exhibition at the MoMA in 1955.

Much of UPA's work was in television animation and was used by Madison Avenue advertisers in an effort to "break away from the antiquated hard sell advertising technique and instead woo viewers with light-hearted wit and whimsy" (Amidi 12). Unlike *Communications Primer*, which used live-action examples to explain Claude Shannon's theory of communication, *The Infor-*

mation Machine utilizes humorous cartoons to make the concept of data processing accessible to the general public. The animation is primarily still drawn images with limited movement and creates the illusion of action through frequent camera movements, and especially zooms. The narrative, written by Charles and read by Vic Perrin, follows a teleological structure that charts the evolution of data processing. The film opens with a domestic dispute in which a caveman accidentally breaks his wife's ceramic pots since he cannot accurately calculate where the tree he is felling will fall. It argues that unique individuals, described as "artists who were seldom bored with anything," were responsible for "building up stores of information in an active memory bank" in their minds. These were the artists and geniuses who were capable of providing the theories that were an enormous help to "creative thinking." The film depicts a technologically driven society where man, through his ingenuity and inquisitiveness, has continued to build the tools necessary for managing a continually advancing society. Information machines (or computers) are a natural outgrowth of human advancement, technological genius, and man's need to process greater and greater quantities of data in order to control the world around him. "In the last century," Eames's narration states, "the complications in our society are compounding themselves ... and the electronic computer has become a tool upon which many of our daily activities depend." The film switches to live action as its shows IBM machines processing vast numbers of punch hole cards. "This is information that's proper use can bring dignity to mankind." The film then moves back to more whimsical animated sequences to illustrate how computers are used for "control or balance," "as a function of design," and "a model of life." The last portion of the film rapidly portrays a highly tuned, well-run capitalist society, using as visual images public utility offices, payroll offices, chemical plants, and railroad systems being managed by computers.

A major goal of the film is to appease the average person's concerns about the power of computers to control mankind. IBM was extremely conscious of the public's reservations about the power of computers, and IBM executives preferred the term "calculators" to describe even the most advanced machines, fearing that "computer" would imply the replacement of humans altogether. These reservations can be heard in Watson's speech for the dedication of the Saarinen-designed Rochester facility in September 1958. "People think we build electronic brains.... Nobody, of course, can build a brain. We build tools to lighten the burden on men's brains and enable them to do greater things with their brains, and we would like to disavow any connection to the brain maker" (Reinhold 153). The Eameses' film, through its use of simply drawn, whimsical animation, continually makes the computer a tool created by man and controlled by man. Mention is made in both *A Communication Primer* and *The Information Machine* that it is the responsibility of mankind to wisely and responsibly use the computer. Eames concludes the film with the statement that "the calculator is helping to define society's most complicated problems. It is a tool for turning inspiration into fruitful predictions. As an information machine it has done much to broaden the base of our growing continent." The film then ends with a sequence of images that move from a drawn rose to a real rose to a drawn heart. The accompanying narration offers that "the real miracle is the promise that there will be room for those smallest details that have been the basis for man's most rewarding wishes." Not only are computers capable of helping manage the functioning of amazingly complicated and dynamic society, but they can also help even in our most intimate and personal interactions. According to the film, "This is a story of technique in the service of mankind."

The Information Machine marked a pivotal point in the Eameses' careers as they turned more and more to the concept of communications theory developed by mathematicians Claude Shannon and Warren Weaver, who worked for Bell Labs. Their enthusiasm for the computer stemmed from their belief that one could take apart everything that had meaning and form and could show it as a simple combination of yes–no binary choices. The Eameses' goal, along with that of IBM, was to popularize the computer for the average person by making the "vernacular of tomorrow" less intimidating and more "user friendly." They attempted to "humanize the modern" by associating these "alien machines" with human feelings. Hand drawings and lettering in the apparently artless style then popular in American graphics were used to lend childlike simplicity to the world of high technology (Kirkham 347). The creative man was the one who would be able to master the computer and dispel the "bogeyman which some [saw] lurking behind every computer" (Kirkham 350). The film was a success not only for IBM. The State Department also gave the Eameses an "In Recognition of Service" award for their production.

The film was so effective in conveying the corporate image of IBM that it remained available for public exhibition many years later. It was also shown at the beginning and end of IBM's own in-house course on communications at their headquarters in Poughkeepsie. The Eameses would continue to work with IBM on a large variety of projects including exhibitions at several other world's fairs including the famous Ovid theater Think presentation at the New York World's Fair of 1964. Eames became IBM's consultant on communications and had a very close working relationship with Thomas Watson, Jr. Charles was one of the few non–IBM employees invited to speak to the Corporate Management Committee, which dispensed millions of dollars of research money within the company over many decades. Watson wanted the Eameses' thinking to be part of the process. Charles also had a "tie-line directly to IBM's offices," which kept him from "not telephoning" (Rogers, "Charles Eames" 52). Annual stockholder meetings for the company were held at the Eameses' house, and Watson called himself one of Charles's "most ardent fans" (ibid.). In an invitation to dinner at his house, Watson spelled out the impact that he felt the Eameses had on his company. "Dear Charlie," he wrote. "In looking back over the years of my association with IBM and the changes that have taken place in the company during the time, I have been struck by the unique contributions that have been made by a few people who are not employees of IBM but who I certainly consider to be members of the IBM family." The dinner was given in order to tell the Eameses how much he "appreciated [their] contributions to my success and the company's success over the years" (R. Eames and C. Eames box 48).

The Eameses' successes at the Brussels World's Fair lead to their involvement in producing the central film at the American Exhibition in Moscow the following year. This time they would be working under the auspices of the USIA and George Nelson, who was hired as the exhibition designer. The Eameses were commissioned to produce a film that showed a day in the life in the United States and would provide the introduction to the exhibition. The roots of the exhibit are clearly drawn from the Disney Circarama film that was screened at Brussels and that would also play a central role at the Moscow exhibit. "Charles and Ray had first envisioned projecting enormous images of landscapes, people, flowers on nine screens in what they dubbed a bagel or circular configuration, surrounding viewers with images.... Nelson however was less enamored of ... the arrangement modeled on Disney's Circarama" (Lipstadt 161). Nelson instead proposed a tic-tac-toe style of a grid of screens that would be ideally suited to "establish credibility for a statement that the products on view were widely purchased by the American people" (Lipstadt 161). The still images chosen by the Eameses were drawn from *Life* and *Look* magazines, similar to the technique employed in "The Family of Man" exhibit that was at Moscow. The images selected for the final film, *Glimpses of America*, were strikingly similar to both Disney's film and the loop films from Brussels.

These works all projected a consistent image of what it meant to be American during the Cold War. The Eameses' film stressed the fruits of abundance and the benefits of consumerism. The image of America that was constructed "defined Americans as white, middle-class members of a nuclear family" (Lipstadt 161). Traditional gender roles were maintained with women preparing all the meals while using the latest in appliances. The most obvious aspect of the American way of life that the film celebrated was commodity capitalism. Of the 2,200 rapidly changing images that were provided in the 12-minute film, there were 70 supermarkets, 70 industrial plants, 42 industrial dams and irrigation systems, and 35 different types of houses of worship. Helene Lipstadt has explained, "The Eameses' Americans lived in nuclear families and relative comfort. The subject of segregation was passed over, poverty hidden, and politics — even the political campaigns and election days that made the U.S.A. a functioning democracy — avoided" (Lipstadt 164). The Eameses had a free hand with the content of the film, and did not preview the film for the USIA staff until its premiere. Arriving in Moscow the night before the opening, the Eameses arrived dressed like Boy and Girl Scouts. Though government officials were anxious about the content of the film, they need not have been. The Eameses were speaking in a language consistent with the goals of Eisenhower's psychological warfare program and framed within the aesthetic goals of the "Good Design" campaigns. The seven-screen film was screened 16 times a day to a total estimated audience of three million Russians. It was ranked the fifth favorite attraction following the cars, color television, Disney's *Circarama*, and "The Family of Man" exhibit.

IBM, the Eameses, and the Military-Industrial Complex

The Eameses were the first to use film to popularize the computer. Noyes and the Eameses applied their aesthetic of Good Design to IBM and the computer in order to sell it to an international audience. Europeans, already familiar with the Eameses' furniture and architecture, would have found in their computer films the belief that a well-designed, functional machine was not only aesthetically beautiful but also capable of improving the world we inhabit. In all his work for IBM, Charles had an ongoing conversation with Watson about the importance of education and understanding in furthering the corporation's goals. "Charles tried to put it in a more hard-nosed context of genuine value for the company over the longer term — not just the notion of a well-educated public would in the long run be a healthier society and a better market for IBM's products, but also that a society with deeper understandings was better one for IBM to operate within" (Demetrios 230). The purpose of IBM's design program was to create a positive, modern image that would immediately create recognition in the average consumer of the business machine. The corporate image, which Boorstin called "the most elaborately and expensively contrived of images of our age," functioned to "exclude undesired and undesirable aspects" (Boorstin 184). When people see the initials

"IBM," the "mechanism is triggered. In a flash the entire corporate image is etched in the mind" (Boorstin 193).

Most of the European visitors to the IBM pavilion were certainly not aware of IBM's ties to the industrial military complex. With the European concerns about the military intentions of the United States, few were aware of the prominent role that IBM played in the national defense system created after the detonation of the first Soviet atomic bomb in 1949. While visitors strolled through the various pavilions at the Brussels World's Fair, the SAGE system became operational at the McGuire Air Force Base in New Jersey. "This extraordinary electronic brain [became] the first of the giant computers to fit into the integrated complex of radar, ships, jet aircraft, communication networks, missiles, and people that [was] rapidly taking shape as the super-sensitive continental air defense system" (Pugh 213). The SAGE computers were directly hooked up to radar installations distributed across the periphery of North America and housed in massive windowless concrete buildings. IBM's military projects were not limited to the creation of a covert international surveillance system. Other classified IBM projects undertaken at the time included the development and construction of a high-speed general-purpose computer for the U.S. Atomic Commission for installation at the Los Alamos Scientific Laboratory, funding for an exploratory study of supercomputer designs to satisfy the requirements of the National Security Agency, and the development of the Ballistic Missile Early Warning System, created in response to the launching of sputnik in October 1957. Like in his projects with IBM, Noyes recognized in his design work for Westinghouse the warlike nature of corporations. He revealed that "Westinghouse is easy to think of as a maker of household appliances. But three-quarters of their business is in a vastly more important and exciting area— the development and distribution of power. What they are doing has implications for the safety of the country, possibly even the survival of the planet" (Kelly 43).

The absence within the American and IBM pavilion of any presentation of technological hardware was striking in comparison to the central role that military hardware played in the Soviet pavilion. The Soviet's exhibit featured "full sized mockups of Sputniks I and II and a large collection of associated rocket equipment, placed in the center of the main hall of the USSR building.... Exhibition models of the latest Russian jet and turboprop transports now entering service with Aeroflot surround[ed] a gigantic statue of Lenin in the place of honor at the rear of the hall" (Anderton 30). With national and corporate interests so closely aligned, the planners of the American pavilions recognized that it was crucial to deflate the widespread European fear of America's involvement in an escalating nuclear buildup. The Europeans were not the only ones left ignorant of the vast SAGE system. Coverage in the mainstream press was minimal. The *New York Times* mentions that the Army Signal Corps awarded a $3,858,970 contract to IBM for "the development of two electronic 'brains' that will be able to add 30,000 ten-digit numbers a second in the heat of battle" ("IBM Contract" 6:6). There is no description of the extensive capabilities of the technology. The actual impact of the system at the time was difficult to imagine since it was the "first time a computer had been used to control a large, geographically distributed system" (Pugh 215). The SAGE system was so effective for the military that it would continue to defend the United States from air attack until January 1984.

IBM's image in Europe was a carefully and expensively produced product of its design program. Any possible connections to the U.S. military establishment were not part of the product it was projecting for its European market. As *Fortune* reported, "No company is more archetypically American, yet none today works the international market in a more sure-footed or sophisticated manner" (Sheehan 167). IBM's World Trade was operated in each country that it had a presence in by a separate national company. World Trade wholly owned these companies, but they were managed and staffed by local citizens. As *Fortune* reported,

> The managers of these companies were to be allowed considerable flexibility in the manner of harmonizing company objectives with national characteristics and customs, especially in advertising, selling, marketing, customer relations, and the like. Watson had no doubts about the eventual triumph of the American way of doing business but when it came to the nuances of business intercourse, he believed in the efficacy of Frenchmen selling Frenchmen, and Germans selling Germans, in their own distinctive way. The distinctions might be summed up by saying that IBM abroad was American in its bones, through the face might be foreign [Sheehan 167].

The employment of a recognizable corporate image sold by knowledgeable locals was extremely effective for IBM, who saw revenues grow four to five times faster than the European gross national product. World Trade's corporate vision went far beyond the European market. By the time of the fair, the New York headquarters was "channeling their thinking and their traveling in the direction of the underdeveloped countries of Africa and Asia, and the unrealized potential of South America." With IBM's ties to the American military, "however remote or exotic some of these countries may be, World Trade has a special entrée: usually the government itself is the first and best customer" (Sheehan 244).

The cultural cold war was marked by the intersection of the disparate worlds of business, government, and academic institutions, who viewed art and culture as crucial weapons against their common enemy: the communists. Many artists were enlisted in this battle without their explicit knowledge, including Charles and Ray Eames. Their names "top the list of American visionaries who transformed decades of American everyday life through design and media" (Villarejo 25). The majority of the critical writing on the Eameses' work makes only passing mention of the political significance of their involvement in many of the dominant institutions of the Cold War. This is particularly significant since, as Peter Smithson claimed, "by the late fifties the Eames way of seeing things had in a sense become everyone's style" (P. Smithson 446). Others conjectured that "one of these days Charles Eames may discover that he's become a cultural hero on the order of Frank Lloyd Wright or Einstein" (McQuade 145). While assuming a position of avant-garde innovation and cutting-edge artistic experimentation, the Eameses maintained extremely close ideological ties with both their corporate and government clients. As Cockcroft states,

> In rejecting the materialistic values of bourgeois society and indulging in the myth that they could exist entirely outside the dominant culture in bohemian enclaves, avant-garde artists generally refused to be recognized or accept their role as producers of a cultural commodity. As a result, especially in the United States, many artists abdicated responsibility both to their economic interests and to the uses of which their artwork was put after in entered the marketplace [Cockcroft 39].

Yet, the Eameses clearly considered the exhibition and marketability of their work of major importance. Their workplace after all was not a studio but was rather called the "Eames Office" because it came out of the world of architectural design. Throughout their careers, they had close working relationships not only with IBM but also with Westinghouse, Boeing, Polaroid, and the Herman Miller Company. Drawing on their own extensive experience as industrial designers, the Eameses had skillfully created their own corporate image, which emphasized play, inventiveness and craft. They projected an image of free, independent Americans who, through skill, intuition and individual initiative, were able to surmount any problem in the pursuit of their own artistic visions. "The common denominator of Eames's occupations [wa]s that he [wa]s, elementally, one thing: a problem solver, with aesthetic and social considerations. He approach[ed] life as a set of problems, each of which must be defined, delineated, abstracted and solved" (Schrader 3).

Charles in particular was the model of the 1950s American male: independent, successful, a "natural Californian Man, using his native resources and know-how — of the filmmaking, the aircraft, and the advertising industries — as others drink water; that is almost without thinking. And it is this combination of expertise, and the availability of the expertise of others, which produces the apparent casualness that is special to the American life-form and its art-form" (P. Smithson 445). The work of the Eames Office, including their house, films, furniture and exhibitions, reflected the playfulness and leisure the new consumer culture celebrated. "Southern California was the chief source of a new American lifestyle ... featuring a relaxed enjoyment of each day in casual indoor-outdoor living, with an accent upon individual gratification, physical health, and pleasant exercise.... The patio, swimming pool and backyard barbeque, furniture and clothing designed for relaxed living, the enjoyment of sunbathing" (Meinig 171). Their aesthetic was not region specific, but compatible with the dominant, national ideology of the time. "Between 1959 and Charles' death in 1978, it is unlikely that the office ever went long without a direct or indirect commission from the government.... The Eameses were treated as representatives of American culture by the federal government, which acted sometimes as an agent and almost always as a fan" (Lipstadt 154). They represented the cultural ethos of the late 1950s with its comfortable consensus and complacent acceptance of America's affluence and dominant position in the world (Allen 247). Through their corporate projects and films they helped support the "European dream of America as a great free place to be in" (A. Smithson 448).

The Eisenhower years are exceptional in the history of the United States for the unique convergence of economic, political and historical forces in the postwar years. At a time of an unprecedented economic boom, an age of peril and anxiety loomed. While the variety of consumer products and opportunities exploded, consensus and conformity defined social structures. As Eisenhower proclaimed his agenda for international peace, he created the largest military industrial complex in the world. And for the first time, the government turned to the arts as an instrumental part of its foreign affairs policies. The convergence of corporate and governmental forces bearing down on the arts was singular and resulted in the production of a distinctly 1950s aesthetic. Though the primary agenda for these artistic forms was the projection of an America that celebrated freedom and democracy through commodity capitalism, the social upheavals occurring within the nation lead to serious discussion and disagreement over what it meant to be American. The film work of the Eameses, along with that of the other filmmakers discussed in the previous chapters, needs to be positioned within the context of the Cold War, and in particular Eisenhower's foreign policies, in order to better understand the impact of ideological imperatives on artistic production. The Brussels World's Fair was an ideal showcase for the American way of life, and it provided a unique and vibrant microcosm of how film functioned as an instrument of ideological warfare for both the government and corporations. But the fair was not simply an example of cultural hegemony. Present at the fair also were the forces of change that would bring about the cultural revolutions of the 1950s, including both the women's and the civil rights movements. Looking back from the perspective of the collapse of the Soviet Empire and the apparent triumph of the American way, it is interesting to note the pre-science of many of the filmic images that were presented at the fair. The Brussels World's Fair did indeed herald in a new age of international relations. Though the fair, with its ephemeral existence, has faded into some lost and distant past, the cultural battles that were waged there reflect the larger social transformations that occurred during the Cold War. As the *New Yorker* reported, "World's fairs are supposed to do a variety of things — to give a good time, help business, symbolize a lofty dream or two, and leave a mark on history. The Brussels Fair has hopes along all these lines" (Christopher Rand 39).

Bibliography

"All's Fair." *Time*, April 28 1958, p. 29.

Allen, James Sloan. *The Romance of Commerce and Culture: Capitalism, Modernism, and the Chicago-Aspen Crusade for Cultural Reform.* Chicago: University of Chicago Press, 1983.

Alpert, Hollis. "Bug-Eye in South Pacific." *Saturday Review*, April 5 1958, p. 35.

Anderton, David A. "Russians Emphasize Space at Brussels." *Aviation Week*, April 28, 1958 , pp. 30–31.

Auerbach, Michael. "Film Notes: A Collection of Stunning Classics and Originals." *LA Weekly*, April 2–8, 1998, p. 82.

Balogh, Brian. *Chain Reaction: Expert Debate and Public Participation in American Commercial Nuclear Power, 1945–1975.* Cambridge; New York: Cambridge University Press, 1991.

Banham, Reyner. "Klarheit, Ehrlichkeit, Einfachkeit ... And Wit Too!: The Case Study Houses in the World's Eyes." In *Blueprints for Modern Living: History and Legacy of the Case Study Houses*, edited by Elizabeth A. T. Smith and Esther McCoy. Los Angeles: Museum of Contemporary Art; Cambridge: MIT Press, 1989.

Bazin, Andrâe. *Orson Welles: A Critical View.* 1st ed. New York: Harper & Row, 1978.

"Belafonte in Rome Denounces Faubus." *New York Times*, September 30, 1958, p. 19.

Belair, Felix, Jr., "United States Has Secret Sonic Weapon — Jazz." *New York Times*, November 6, 1955, p. 1.

Bennett, Tony. *Formations of Pleasure.* London: Routledge, 1983.

"Benny Goodman Scores New Brussels Triumph." *New York Times*, June 1, 1958, p. 60.

Benton, William. "America — as Others See Us." *Department of State Bulletin* 14, no. 341 (January 1946): 11–16.

_____. "Can America Afford to Be Silent?" *Department of State Bulletin* 14, no. 341 (January 1946): 7–9.

Berg, Gretchen. "Shirley Clarke Interview with Gretchen Berg." *Film Culture* 44 (1967).

Bergreen, Laurence. *Louis Armstrong: An Extravagant Life.* New York: Broadway Books, 1997.

Bernays, Doris Fleishman, and Edward Bernays. *What the British Think of Us; a Study of British Hostility to America and Americans and Its Motivation, with Recommendations for Improving Anglo-American Relations.* New York: Unknown Publisher, 1950.

Bierut, Michael. *Seventy-Nine Short Essays on Design.* New York: Princeton Architectural Press, 2007.

"The Big Show Opens in Brussels." *Business Week*, April 12, 1958.

Bigness, Jon. "Coming to a Theater Near You, More TV-Like Commercial." *Northwestern*, September 5, 1999, pp. D1–D4.

Bogart, Leo, and Agnes Bogart. *Premises for Propaganda: The United States Information Agency's Operating Assumptions in the Cold War*. New York: Free Press, 1976.

Boorstin, Daniel J. *The Image: A Guide to Pseudo-Events in America*. New York: Atheneum, 1971.

Bowie, Beverley. "The Dinosaur Hunter." *Time*, April 6 1959.

_____. "The Past Is Present in Greenfield Village." *National Geographic*. July 1958, pp. 96–126.

Brands, H. W. "The Age of Invulnerability: Eisenhower and the National Insecurity State." *American Historical Review* 94, no. 4 (1989): 963–89.

_____. *Cold Warriors: Eisenhower's Generation and American Foreign Policy*. Contemporary American History Series. New York: Columbia University Press, 1988.

Breitrose, Henry. "Films of Shirley Clarke." *Film Quarterly* 13, no. 4 (1960): 57–58.

Brinkley, David. "Downright Shameful, That Brussels Exhibit." *New Republic*, July 7, 1958, p. 8.

Bruce, Gordon. *Eliot Noyes*. London: Phaidon, 2006.

"Brussels Asks World to Its Fair." *Life*, March 31, 1958, p. 27.

"Brussels Exhibit on Bias Is Decried." *New York Times*, June 23, 1958, p. 17.

"Brussels '58: The United States Speaks to the World Progress Report." *Interiors* 67, no. 2 (1957): 140.

"Business Packs Them in at Brussels Fair." *Business Week*, June 15, 1958.

"The Camera Overseas: Big U.S. Businessman Does His Duty in Berlin and Paris." *Life*, July 26 1937, p. 66.

Caplan, Ralph. "The Messages of Industry on the Screen." *Industrial Design* 7 (1960): 50–65.

Ceplair, Larry, and Steven Englund. *The Inquisition in Hollywood: Politics in the Film Community, 1930–1960*. Berkeley: University of California Press, 1983.

Clarke, Alison J. *Tupperware: The Promise of Plastic in 1950s America*. Washington, D.C.: Smithsonian Institution Press, 1999.

Cockcroft, Eva. "Abstract Expressionism, Weapon of the Cold War." *Artforum* 12, no. 10 (1974).

Coleman, Emily. "Organizational Man Named Belafonte: He Has Built a Corporate Enterprise to Guide the Many Careers — as Singer, Actor, Etc. — That Has Made Him at 32 the Highest Paid Negro Entertainer in History." *New York Times Magazine*, December 13 1959, pp. 35+.

Colomina, Beatriz. "1949." In *Autonomy and Ideology: Positioning an Avant-Garde in America*, edited by R. E. Somol. New York: Monacceli Press, 1997.

Comito, Terry. *Touch of Evil: Orson Welles, Director*. Rutgers Films in Print, volume 3. New Brunswick, NJ: Rutgers University Press, 1985.

Corber, Robert J. *In the Name of National Security: Hitchcock, Homophobia, and the Political Construction of Gender in Postwar America*. Durham, NC: Duke University Press, 1993.

Costigliola, Frank. *France and the United States: The Cold Alliance since World War II*. New York: Twayne Publishers and Maxwell Macmillan International; Toronto: Maxwell Macmillan Canada, 1992.

Cousins, Norman. "The Free Ride." *The Saturday Review of Literature* 33, no. 3 (1950): 24–25.

_____. "The Free Ride, Part II." *The Saturday Review of Literature* 33, no. 4 (1950): 20–21.

"Crystal Palaces at Brussels." *Economist* 188 (1958): 610.

Cull, Nicholas. *The Cold War and the United States Information Agency: American Propaganda and Public Diplomacy, 1945–1989.* Cambridge: Cambridge University Press, 2009.

_____. "Public Diplomacy and the Private Sector." In *The US Government, Citizen Groups, and the Cold War: The State-Private Network*, Edited by Helen Laville and Hugh Wilford. London: Routledge, 2006.

Dalrymple, Jean. *September Child.* New York: Dodd, Mead and Company, 1963.

Daniel, Greta. "Les Arts Appliques." In *50 Ans D'art Aux Etats-Unis: Collections Du Museum of Modern Art De New York*, edited by Musée National d'Art Moderne and the Museum of Modern Art. Paris: Musée National d'Art Moderne, 1955.

Daniell, Raymond. "What the Europeans Think of Us." *New York Times*, November 30, 1947, p. SM7+.

Daugherty, William E. *A Psychological Warfare Casebook.* Baltimore: John Hopkins University Press, 1958.

Davies, Thurston. *Letter to Robert Warner.* Folder EXH/405. Records of Minor Congressional Commissions.

De Wouters D'Oplinter, D. "Notes in Passing." *Arts & Architecture* 75 (1958): 11.

Dean, Vera Micheles. "Foreign Policy Spotlight: The World's Unfinished Business." *Foreign Policy Bulletin* 1, no. 38 (1958): 7–8.

_____. "The World's Unfinished Business." *Foreign Policy Bulletin* 38, no. 1 (1958): 7.

DeFleur, Melvin, and Margaret DeFleur. *Learning to Hate Americans.* Spokane, WA: Marquette Books, 2003.

"Disneyland Circarama Is Wow as Transported to Brussels' Big Expo." *Variety*, April 30, 1958.

Djerejian, Edward. "Changing Minds, Winning Peace." Report of the Advisory Group on Public Diplomacy for the Arab and Muslim World, October 1, 2003. Available online at www.state.gov/documents/organization/24882.pdf (accessed October 7 2010).

Eames, Charles. "Language of Vision: Nuts and Bolts." *Bulletin of the American Academy of Arts and Sciences* 28, no. 1 (1974): 13–25.

Eames, Ray, and Charles Eames. "Papers of Ray and Charles Eames." *Letter from Thomas Watson, Jr.* Washington, D.C.: Library of Congress, 1973. Vol. Box 48.

Easlea, Brian. *Fathering the Unthinkable: Masculinity, Scientists, and the Nuclear Arms Race.* London: Pluto Press, 1983.

Eldridge, David N. "'Dear Owen': The CIA, Luigi Luraschi and Hollywood, 1953." *Historical Journal of Film, Radio and Television* 20, no. 2 (2000): 149–96.

"Enchanting but...." *Newsweek*, March 31, 1958, p. 96.

"Europe to See Good Designs from America." *Times Herald*, September 18, 1950, sec. 1, p. 1.

"Fair Exhibits to Symbolize U.S. Problems." *New York Times*, March 11, 1958, p. 12.

Feis, Herbert. *Between War and Peace: The Potsdam Conference.* Princeton, NJ: Princeton University Press, 1960.

"Film at Brussels." *Business Screen*, 19, no. 4 (1958).

"Film Code Drafted on Trading Abroad." *New York Times*, August 4, 1946.

Firestone, Ross. *Swing, Swing, Swing: The Life and Times of Benny Goodman.* New York: W.W. Norton, 1993.

Ford, Daniel F. *The Cult of the Atom: The Secret Papers of the Atomic Energy Commission.* New York: Simon and Schuster, 1982.

Foster, Patrick. *American Motors: The Last Independent*. Iola, WI: Krause Publications, 1993.

Frakes, Margaret. "One Day at Brussels." *Christian Century* October 1 1958: 1109.

Frankfurter, A. "Brussels Sprouts Art." *Art News* 57 (1958): 32–7+.

Funke, Lewis. "Brussels Bound: A Role Call of American Representation at the City's Fair." *Theater Arts* 42.5 (1958).

Gabler, Neal. *Walt Disney: The Triumph of the American Imagination*. New York: Alfred A. Knopf, 2006.

Gates, Henry Louis , Jr., "Belafonte's Balancing Act." *New Yorker* August 26 and September 2 1996: 133–40.

Gillett, John. "The Best at Brussels." *Sight & Sound* 28.1 (1958/9).

Goldstein, Barbara, ed. *Arts & Architecture: The Entenza Years*. Cambridge: MIT Press, 1990.

Goldstein, Cora Sol. *Capturing the German Eye: American Visual Propaganda in Occupied Germany*. Chicago: University of Chicago Press, 2009.

Gonzales, David. *The Rockefellers at Williamsburg: Backstage with the Founders, Restorers and World-Renowned Guests*. McLean, VA: EPM Publications, 1991.

Guback, Thomas. "Shaping the Film Business in Postwar Germany." *The Hollywood Film Industry*. Ed. Paul Kerr. vols. London: Routledge, 1986.

Gueft, Olga. "Good Design Exhibit." *Interiors* March 1950: 87.

Guimond, James. *American Photography and the American Dream*. Chapel Hill: University of North Carolina, 1991.

Gunning, Tom. "The World as Object Lesson: Cinema Audiences, Visual Culture and the St. Louis World's Fair." *Film History* 6.4 (1994).

Haber, Heinz. *The Walt Disney Story of Our Friend the Atom*. New York,: Dell Publishing Co., 1956.

Hales, Peter "The Atomic Sublime." *American Studies* 32.1 (1991): 12.

Hartung, Philip. "Bigger Than Life and Twice as Natural." *Commonweal* 68 (1958): 50.

Hayward, Susan. "Framing National Cinemas." *Cinema and Nation*. Ed. Mette Hjort and Scott Mackenzie. vols. New York: Routledge, 2000.

Heath, Stephen. "Film and System: Terms of Analysis Part Ii." *Screen* 16.2 (1975).

Helmreich, Jonathon E. "The United States and the Formation of the Euratom." *Diplomatic History* 15.3 (1991): 403.

Hill, Gladwin. "Our Film Program in Germany II: How Far Was It a Failure?" *Hollywood Quarterly* 2 (1947): 131–37.

_____. "Whither Go German Films?" *New York Times*, February 3, 1946, p. X3.

Hixson, Walter. *Parting the Curtain: Propaganda, Culture and the Cold War, 1945–1961*. New York: St. Martin's Press, 1997.

Hogan, J. Michael. "Eisenhower and Open Skies: A Case History in 'Psychological Warfare.'" In *Eisenhower's War of Words: Rhetoric and Leadership*, edited by Martin J. Medhurst. East Lansing: Michigan State University Press, 1994.

Hyland, William. *Richard Rodgers*. New Haven: Yale University Press, 1998.

"IBM Earnings Reach New High." *New York Times*, July 12, 1958, sec. 20, p. 5.

"IBM Gets Contract for a Battle Brain." *New York Times*, October 31, 1958, sec. 6, p. 6.

"The Impact of American Commercial Movies in Western Europe." In *Records of the U.S. Information Agency, Part 3: Cold War Era Research Reports Series A: 1960–1963*. Microfilm edition, frame 0083, R166–62. LexisNexis, 2009 [1962]. Available online at http://library.lexisnexis.com/ksc_assets/catalog/103377.pdf (accessed October 7, 2010).

"Interview with Walt Disney and John Hench." Max Frank Millikan Papers, 1913–1969, MC 188, Box 4, f. 119 (MIT Archives)

James, David E. *The Most Typical Avant-Garde: History and Geography of Minor Cinemas in Los Angeles*. Berkeley: University of California Press, 2005.

Jesman, Czeslaw. "Africa at Brussels: A Focus of Attention." *The Tablet* 211 (1958): 486.

Jessup, Philip C., ed. *Atoms for Power: United States Policy in Atomic Energy Development*. Washington, D.C.: The American Assembly; Library of Congress, 1957.

Johnston, Eric. "Messengers from a Free Country." *The Saturday Review of Literature* 33, no. 9 (1950): 9–12.

Jolly, Margaret. "From Point Venus to Bali Ha'i: Eroticism and Exoticism in Representations of the Pacific." In *Sites of Desire, Economies of Pleasure: Sexualities in Asia and the Pacific*, edited by Lenore Manderson and Margaret Jolly. Chicago: University of Chicago Press, 1997.

Joseph, Robert. "Film Program for Germany." *Arts & Architecture* 62 (1945): 16–44.

_____. "Our Film Program in Germany I: How Far Was It a Success?" *Hollywood Quarterly* 2, no. 2 (1947): 122–30.

Kant, Immanuel. *Critique of Judgment*. Translated by Werner S. Pluhar. Indianapolis: Hackett, 1987.

_____. *Observations on the Feeling of the Beautiful and Sublime*. Translated by John T. Goldthwait. Berkeley: University of California Press, 1960.

Kauffman, Stanley. "Whither Welles." *The New Republic* 138, no. 21 (1958).

Kelly, Scott. "Curator of Corporate Character ... Eliot Noyes and Associates." *Industrial Design* 13, no. 5 (1966): 43.

Kennan, George F. *International Exchange in the Arts*. New York: International Council of the Museum of Modern Art, 1956.

King, Margaret. "The Audience in the Wilderness: The Disney Nature Films." *Journal of Popular Film and Television* 24, no. 2 (1996): 63.

Kirkham, Pat. *Charles and Ray Eames: Designers of the Twentieth Century*. Cambridge: MIT Press, 1995.

Klein, Naomi. "The Spectacular Failure of Brand USA." *LA Times*, March 11, 2002. Available online at www.naomiklein.org/articles/2002/02/spectacular-failure-brand-usa (accessed October 7, 2010).

Knight, Arthur. "Dance in the Movies." *Dance Magazine* 6 (1958): 15

_____. "The Sweet Smell of Success." *Saturday Review* 25 (June 7, 1958): 25.

Knorr, Klaus. "American Foreign Policy and the Peaceful Uses of Atomic Energy." In *Atoms for Power: United States Policy in Atomic Energy Development*, edited by Philip C. Jessup. Washington, D.C.: The American Assembly; Library of Congress, 1957.

Kohnstamm, Max. "Europe and Atoms for Power." In *Atoms for Power: United States Policy in Atomic Energy Development*, edited by Philip C. Jessup. Washington, D.C.: The American Assembly, Library of Congress, 1957.

Koppes, Gregory Black, and Clayton R. Koppes. "What to Show the World: The Office of War Information and Hollywood, 1942–1945." *The Journal of American History* 64, no. 1 (1977): 87–105.

Koval, Francis. "Brussels' Film Festival: Wasn't Helped by Brussels' World's Fair." *Films In Review* 9, no. 7 (1958): 358.

Krenn, Michael. "Unfinished Business: Segregation and U.S. Diplomacy at the 1958 World's Fair." *Diplomatic History* 20, no. 4 (1996): 593.

Kuisel, Richard F. *Seducing the French: The Dilemma of Americanization*. Berkeley: University of California Press, 1993.

Laurence, William L. "Nagasaki was the Climax of the New Mexico Test." *Life,* September 24, 1945, 30ff.

Leaming, Barbara. *Orson Welles: A Biography*. New York: Viking, 1985.

"Letter: USIA Washington, Office of Director." Max Frank Millikan Papers, Cambridge.

Lewis, Jon. *Hollywood vs. Hardcore*. New York: New York University Press, 2000.

Lipstadt, Helene. "Natural Overlap: Charles and Ray Eames and the Federal Government." In *The Work of Ray and Charles Eames: A Legacy of Invention*, edited by Donald Albrecht. New York: Harry N. Abrams, in association with the Library of Congress and the Vitra Design Museum, 1997.

Lipton, Norman C. "Disney's Circarama." *Popular Photography* 37 (1955): 96, 97, 182+.

"Living the Daydream." *Time*, August 23 1948, p. 40.

Lynes, Russell. *The Tastemakers*. New York: Harper, 1954.

MacCann, Richard Dyer. "Film and Foreign Policy: The USIA, 1962–67." *Cinema Journal* 9, no. 1 (1969): 23–42.

_____. *The People's Films: A Political History of U.S. Government Motion Pictures*. New York: Hastings House, 1973.

May, Elaine Tyler. *Homeward Bound: American Families in the Cold War Era*. New York: Basic Books, 1988.

May, Lary. *The Big Tomorrow*. Chicago: University of Chicago Press, 2000.

May, Madeleine. "Overheard at the Fair." *Atlantic Monthly*, August 1958, pp. 69–70.

McBride, Joseph. *Orson Welles*. New York: Viking Press, 1972.

McCarten, John. "Polychromatic Jumble." *New Yorker*, March 29, 1958, p. 99.

McDonald, Gay. "Selling the American Dream: MoMA, Industrial Design and Post-War France." *Journal of Design History* 17, no. 4 (2004): 397–412.

McQuade, Walter. "An Industrial Designer with a Conspicuous Conscience." *Fortune*, August 1963.

Mechling, Elizabeth Walker, and Jay Mechling. "The Atom According to Disney." *Quarterly Journal of Speech* 81 (1995): 436.

Medhurst, Martin. "Atoms for Peace and Nuclear Hegemony: The Rhetorical Structure of a Cold War Campaign." *Armed Forces and Society* 23, no. 4 (1997).

Meinig, Donald W. *The Interpretation of Ordinary Landscapes: Geographical Essays*. New York: Oxford University Press, 1979.

Metz, Walter. "Keep the Coffee Hot, Hugo: Nuclear Trauma in Lang's the Big Heat." *Film Criticism* 21 (Spring 1997).

Mills, C. Wright. *Power, Politics, and People: The Collected Essays of C. Wright Mills*. New York: Oxford University Press, 1963.

"The Missing U.S. Univac." *Fortune*, April 1958.

Mooney, Richard. "President Hears Favorable Report on Fair." *New York Times*, June 25, 1958, pp. 89–90.

Mordden, Ethan. *Rodgers & Hammerstein*. New York: H.N. Abrams, 1992.

"More Than Modern." *Time*, March 31, 1958.

Munby, Jonathan. *Public Enemies, Public Heroes: Screening the Gangster from Little Caesar to Touch of Evil*. Chicago: University of Chicago Press, 1999.

Naremore, James. *The Magic World of Orson Welles.* New York: Oxford University Press, 1978.

Neuhart, John, et al. *Eames Design: The Work of the Office of Charles and Ray Eames.* New York: H.N. Abrams, 1989.

"The New Pictures." *Time,* March 31, 1958, pp. 85–86.

Norman, Albert. *Our German Policy: Propaganda and Culture.* New York: Vantage Press, 1951.

Nye, David E. *American Technological Sublime.* Cambridge: MIT Press, 1994.

Oakes, Guy. *The Imaginary War: Civil Defense and American Cold War Culture.* New York: Oxford University Press, 1994.

Osgood, Kenneth. "Form before Substance: Eisenhower's Commitment to Psychological Warfare and Negotiations with the Enemy." *Diplomatic History* 24, no. 3 (2000): 431.

"Overseas Information Programs of the United States: Report on the Committee on Foreign Relations." 82nd Cong., 2d sess. Washington, D.C.: U.S. Government Printing Office, 1953–1954

Palmer, Allen, and Edward Carter. "The Smith-Mundt Act's Ban on Domestic Propaganda." *Communication Law and Policy* (2006): 33–67.

Parry-Giles, Shawn J. "Camouflaged Propaganda: The Truman and Eisenhower Administrations' Covert Manipulation of the News." *Western Journal of Communication* 60, no. 2 (1996).

_____. *The Rhetorical Presidency, Propaganda, and the Cold War, 1945–1955.* Westport, CT: Praeger, 2001.

Pells, Richard. *Not Like Us: How Europeans Have Loved, Hated and Transformed American Culture since World War II.* New York: Basic Books, 1997.

"Plans Are Set up to Sell U.S. Abroad." *New York Times,* December 29, 1945, p. 9.

Plaut, James. *Letter to Cullman.* Folder EXH/405. Records of Minor Congressional Commissions.

Poiger, Uta. *Jazz, Rock and Rebels: Cold War Politics and American Culture in a Divided Germany.* Berkeley: University of California Press, 2000.

"Progress Report on the U.S. Exhibition at the Brussels Fair." September 16, 1957, National Archives, RG 43, Box 14, f. PA-20.

Pryor, Thomas M. "Film Studios Get British Warning." *New York Times,* April 29, 1955, p. 28.

_____. "Films Aid 'Truth Campaign.'" *New York Times,* March 25, 1951, p. 81.

_____. "German Outlines Film Censorship." *New York Times,* October 26, 1956.

_____. "Johnston Expects New Movie Gains." *New York Times,* October 8, 1954, p. 27.

Pugh, Emerson W. *Building IBM: Shaping an Industry and Its Technology.* Cambridge: MIT Press, 1995.

Rabinovitz, Lauren. *Points of Resistance: Women, Power, and Politics in the New York Avant Garde Cinema, 1943–1971.* Urbana: University of Indiana, 1991.

_____. "Transcript of Shirley Clarke Interview with Lauren Rabinovitz, (Shirley Clarke Papers, Wisconsin Historical Society, Box 3, folder 6.

Rand, Christopher. "Letter from Brussels." *The New Yorker,* March 29, 1958, p. 58.

_____. *Letter to Davies.* Folder EXH/405. Records of Minor Congressional Committees.

"Reds Aim to Steal Brussels Show." *Business Week,* January 11, 1958, p. 96.

Reinhold, Martin. "Computer Architectures: Saarinen's Patterns, IBM's Brains." In *Anx-*

ious Modernisms: Experimentation in Postwar Architectural Culture, edited by Sarah Williams Goldhagen and Réjean Legault et al. Cambridge: MIT Press, 2000.

Reisz, Karel. "The Festivals: Experiment at Brussels." *Sight and Sound* 27, no. 5 (1958).

Roesch, Roberta. *World's Fairs: Yesterday, Today, Tomorrow.* New York: John Day, 1967.

Rogers, Susan. "Charles Eames: The Designer Is a Poet." *The New York Post*, May 6, 1970.

Rosen, Marjorie. "Shirley Clarke: Videoscape Explorer." *Ms.*, April 1975.

Rydell, Robert W. *World of Fairs: The Century-of-Progress Expositions.* Chicago: University of Chicago Press, 1993.

Sandeen, Eric J. *Picturing an Exhibition: The Family of Man and 1950s America.* Albuquerque: University of New Mexico Press, 1995.

Saunders, Frances Stonor. *Who Paid the Piper?: The CIA and the Cultural Cold War.* London: Granta Books, 1999.

Schmidt, Dana Adams. "Our Movies Leave Germans Hostile." *New York Times*, July 23, 1946, p. 33.

Schrader, Paul. "Poetry of Ideas: The Films of Charles Eames." *Film Quarterly* 23, no. 3 (1970).

Schulberg, Stuart. "Of All People." *Hollywood Quarterly* 4, no. 2 (1949): 206–8.

Schumach, Murray. *The Face on the Cutting Room Floor: The Story of Movie and Television Censorship.* New York: William Morrow, 1964.

Seeley, Sylvia. "The World's Fair at Brussels." *Canadian Geographical Journal* 57, no. 4 (1958).

Segrave, Kerry. *American Films Abroad: Hollywood's Domination of the World's Movie Screens from the 1890s to the Present.* Jefferson, NC: McFarland, 1997.

Shaw, Tony. "Ambassadors of the Screen: Film and the State-Private Network in Cold War America." In *The US Government, Citizen Groups, and the Cold War: The State-Private Network*, edited by Helen Laville and Hugh Wilford. New York: Routledge, 2006.

Sheehan, Robert. "Q. What Grows Faster Than IBM? A. IBM Abroad." *Fortune*, November 1960.

Simons, Howard. "Brussels Fair and Science." *Science News Letter* 73, no. 2 (1958).

Skouras, Thana. *The Tale of Rodgers and Hammerstein's South Pacific.* New York: Lehmann, 1958.

Smith, Elizabeth A. T. "Arts & Architecture and the Los Angeles Vanguard." In *Blueprints for Modern Living: History and Legacy of the Case Study Houses*, edited by Elizabeth A. T. Smith. Cambridge: MIT Press, 1989.

Smith, Michael. "Advertising the Atom." In *Government and Environmental Politics: Essays on Historical Developments since World War Two*, edited by Michael J. Lacey. Washington, D.C.: The Woodrow Wilson Center Press, 1991.

"Smith Mundt Act." The USC Center on Public Diplomacy at the Annenberg School. Available online at http://publicdiplomacy.wikia.com/wiki/Smith_Mundt_Act (accessed October 7, 2010).

Smith, Robert Freeman. "The Good Neighbor Policy: The Liberal Paradox in United States Relations with Latin America." In *Watershed of Empire: Essays on New Deal Foreign Policy*, edited by Leonard P. Liggio and James J. Martin. Colorado Springs: Ralph Myles, 1976.

Smithson, Alison. "And Now Dharmas Are Dying out in Japan." *Architectural Design* (1966).

Smithson, Peter. "Just a Few Chairs and a House: An Essay on the Eames-Aesthetic." *Architectural Design* (1966): 446.

Smoodin, Eric. *Animating Culture: Hollywood Cartoons from the Sound Era.* New Brunswick, NJ: Rutgers University Press, 1993.

"So Short at the Fair." *The Economist*, March 15, 1958, p. 941.

Spielvogel, Carl. "Advertising: The Company Motion Picture." *New York Times*, February 9, 1958, sec. F, p. 9.

Steichen, Edward. *The Family of Man.* New York: The Museum of Modern Art, 1955.

Sutton, Horace. "Positively the Last Word on the Fair." *Saturday Review*, August 16, 1958, p. 30.

Swann, Paul. "The Little State Department: Washington and Hollywood's Rhetoric of the Postwar Audience." In *Hollywood in Europe: Experiences of a Cultural Hegemony*, edited by David Ellwood and Rob Kroes. Amsterdam: VU University Press, 1994.

Taubman, Howard. "Belafonte Sings at Brussels Fair." *New York Times*, September 6, 1958, p. 9.

_____. "Cold War on the Cultural Front." *New York Times*, April 13, 1958, p. SM12.

_____. "Le Jazz Arrives at Brussels Fair: Sidney Bechet Sextet Saves the Day for U.S. In Poorly Organized Concert." *New York Times*, July 30, 1958, p. 19.

"Techniques at Disney's Tomorrowland." *Business Screen* 16, no. 4 (1955): 38–39.

"Theme Development Staff Discussions." Max Frank Millikan Papers, Cambridge.

"They Cross Iron Curtain to Hear American Jazz." *U.S. News & World Report*, December 2, 1955, p. 54.

Thompson, Howard. "Big Country in Loops." *New York Times*, April 20, 1958.

_____. "Screen: 'Touch of Evil.'" *New York Times*, May 22, 1958, sec. 25, p. 2.

United States Information Agency. "The Overseas Film Program." United States Information Agency, 1959.

"U.S. Lists Movies It Limits Abroad." *New York Times*, May 24, 1959, p. 46.

Villarejo, Amy. "A Complex Legacy: The Works of Charles and Ray Eames." *Afterimage* 27, no. 3 (1999).

Waggoner, Walter. "Goodman's Music Makes Hit at Fair." *New York Times*, May 26, 1958, p. 31.

Wagnleiter, Reinhold. "American Cultural Diplomacy: The Cinema, and the Cold War in Central Europe." In *Hollywood in Europe: Experiences of a Cultural Hegemony*, edited by David Ellwood and Rob Kroes. Amsterdam: VU University Press, 1994.

_____. *Coca-Colonization and the Cold War: The Cultural Mission of the United States in Austria after the Second World War.* Chapel Hill: University of North Carolina Press, 1994.

_____. "The Empire of the Fun, or Talkin' Soviet Union Blues: The Sound of Freedom and U.S. Cultural Hegemony in Europe." In *The Ambiguous Legacy: U.S. Foreign Relations in the American Century*, edited by Michael J. Hogan. New York: Cambridge University Press, 1999.

Walt Disney Imagineering: A Behind the Dreams Look at Making the Magic Real. Disney Editions, 1998, p. 62.

Warner, Robert. "Letter to Howard Cullman." Folder EXH/405. Records of Minor Congressional Commissions.

_____. "Letter to Robert Sivard." Folder EXH/405. Records of Minor Congressional Commissions.

_____. "Letter to Turner Shelton." Folder EXH/405. Records of Minor Congressional Commissions.

Waterman, David. *Hollywood's Road to Riches*. Cambridge: Harvard University Press, 2005.

Watson, Thomas J., and Peter Petre. *Father, Son & Co.: My Life at IBM and Beyond*. New York: Bantam Books, 1990.

Watts, Steven, and Walt Disney. *The Magic Kingdom: Walt Disney and the American Way of Life*. Boston: Houghton Mifflin, 1997.

"We Open in Brussels." *Saturday Review*, May 3, 1958.

Weales, Gerald. "Movies: The Twilight of an Aging Prodigy." *The Reporter* 18, no. 13 (1958).

"We'll Live in a Kingdom All Our Own." *Life*, January 22, 1945, inside cover.

Welles, Orson, Peter Bogdanovich, and Jonathan Rosenbaum. *This Is Orson Welles*. New York: HarperCollins, 1992.

Wells, G. Edward. "Motion Pictures — the Film Two Cities." National Archives. Record Group 59. Records of the Department of State. Decimal Files, 1950–1954.

Westbrook, Robert B. "I Want a Girl, Just Like the Girl That Married Harry James: American Women and the Problem of Political Obligation in World War II." *American Quarterly* 42, no. 4 (1990): 592–94.

"Where East Meets West: The U.S. At the Fair." *Newsweek*, April 14, 1958, p. 53.

Whitebait, William, ed. *International Film Annual*, volume 2. New York: Doubleday, 1958.

Wilson, Theodore A. "Selling America Via the Silver Screen?" In *"Here, There, and Everywhere": The Foreign Politics of American Popular Culture*, edited by Reinhold Wagnleitner and Elaine Tyler May. Hanover: University Press of New England, 2000.

Wollen, Peter. "Foreign Relations: Welles and Touch of Evil." *Sight and Sound* 6, no. 10 (1996).

Index

Numbers in **_bold italics_** indicate pages with photographs.

195